Essentials, Links, and Influences

TIMELESS READINGS FROM WORLD CIVILIZATIONS TO 1500

Second Edition

EDITED BY

Jaeyoon Kim

Point Loma Nazarene University

cognella®

SAN DIEGO

Bassim Hamadeh, CEO and Publisher
Carrie Montoya, Manager, Revisions and Author Care
David Miano, Senior Specialist Acquisitions Editor
Kaela Martin, Project Editor
Casey Hands, Production Editor
David Rajec, Editorial Assistant
Jess Estrella, Senior Graphic Designer
Alexa Lucido, Licensing Manager
Natalie Piccotti, Director of Marketing
Kassie Graves, Vice President of Editorial
Jamie Giganti, Director of Academic Publishing

Cover image: Copyright © 2014 Depositphotos/fergregory.

Printed in the United States of America.

3970 Sorrento Valley Blvd., Ste. 500, San Diego, CA 92121

Contents

Chapter 7: Christians and Barbarians, to Eleventh Century A.D.   119

Chapter 8: Islamic Civilizations, to Fourteenth Century A.D.   133

Chapter 9: African Civilizations, to Fifteenth Century A.D.   149

Chapter 10: India and South Asia to the Mongolian Empire   163

Preface

WHY DO WE need to study the history of world civilizations? As a Roman statesman, Marcus Tullius Cicero, emphasizes a "spirit of humanity" through "civilizations," studying the history of civilizations is an integral part of living in this world as a citizen. Especially in this global age of the twenty-first century, understanding of other societies is a prerequisite for becoming a global leader, when international and cultural exchanges are more active than in the past. By gaining insight into the flow of world civilizations, we can learn about the politics, society, economy, and culture of various societies and have clues to solving real-world problems of today. However, there seems to be a problem in American education in the field of the history of world civilizations.

I have been teaching classes in World and East Asian Civilizations since 1998. Yet I have been struck by the fact that most American students in my courses have never taken any non-Western history classes prior to my classes. Indeed, even today, it is difficult to take such courses—courses in "world history" are not offered in many of the high schools in America—the basic, introductory history course for high school students is Western history or American history. For these students, the Eurocentric notion—the sense of the moral as well as cultural superiority of Western society to the rest of world—is deeply rooted in their minds. One of the great examples is the validity of the images of the world, especially the Mercator projection, which focuses on Western Europe and systematically distorts our image of the Southern Hemisphere, whose actual surface is substantially larger than the map indicates. Although Europe has approximately the square mile area of the other two peninsulas of Asia, India, and Southeast Asia, Europe is called a continent, while India is just a subcontinent; Southeast Asia does not even have that status. Each has about the same number of river systems, language groups, etc. The point is not simply that we make Europe big or put it in the upper center. The issue is the peculiar way our perceptions are distorted by the map projection. This confirms our biases. It flatters our egos. A good example is the misjudgment of the true size of Africa. Most people do not know how much this Mercator projection distorts the relative size of Africa. Even though the actual size of Africa is much bigger than the combination of China, India, America, and most of Europe, Africa gets shrunk down unfairly in size, while places further to the north, like Europe, are bigger than they actually should be. The Mercator projection has fostered imperialist attitudes for centuries and created an ethnic bias against non-Western civilizations such as African and Asian civilizations. In response to this Eurocentrism, non-Western people are often emphasizing their own version of ethnocentric views. Let's examine the upside-down map of the classical Mercator projection world map in Figure 1 below.

In this map, Europe appears off at the right-hand edge, whereas Asia, especially China, is located in the center of the map. The temptation to put not only one's own land in the center of the map but also one's own people in the center of history is universal. The most famous case of this is indeed that of the "Middle Kingdom." Yet what we really want is to face the world as it actually is, not as our self-esteem would like to picture it. Therefore, my focus in this book is to resituate the history of the West or East in a global context and, in the process, unhook it from ethnocentric stereotypes. When we look at mankind as a whole, we want our own parts of it to fall into place so we can see ourselves in true proportion.

Why are students these days required to take World History or World Civilizations courses as general education classes at most American universities? It is not because of the change of historical content but because of the change in historical perception of human civilizations that allows us to broaden our view to include not only Western history and Western civilizations but also the histories and cultures of non-Western areas in our vision of history and civilization. Many considerable world events, such as the rise of certain Asian economies—most notably in Japan, South Korea, India, and the People's Republic of China—and the political and economic challenges represented by events in the Middle East, have served to make us more aware of our need to learn more about other cultures. Developing this awareness is a matter not only of survival in a rapidly changing world but also of the simple integrity of fairness. It is time for us to do justice to other cultures, to recognize that the American or Western way is certainly not the only way to do things and, beyond that rather obvious fact, is not even necessarily the best way.

Documents in this book reflect the conviction that World Civilizations courses should be truly global in scope. These documents will help you develop a broader view of human history and civilization and will encourage you to understand the values and ways of different cultures. In order to ensure the global coverage of a true World Civilizations course, the organization of *Essentials, Links, and Influences: Timeless Readings from World Civilizations to 1500* is based on different cultural areas of the world, leaping from continent to continent, from the beginning of human civilization to the fifteenth century A.D. Yet the problem with the history

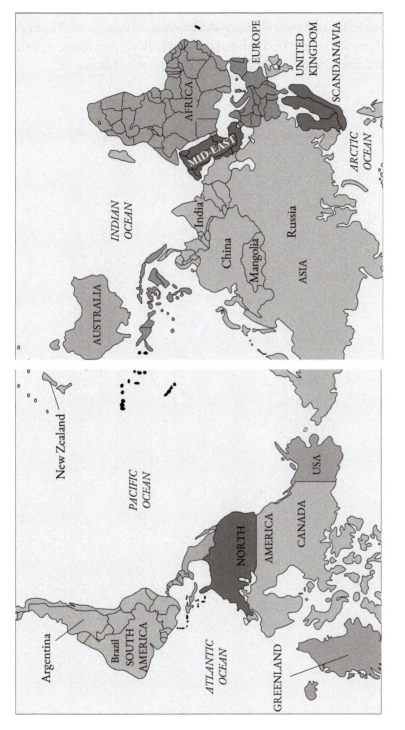

FIGURE 1 World Map.

of the world is that—like the world itself—it is quite vast. Consequently, by its nature, this book cannot follow a relatively neat chronological order and leave out a great deal of many important events in many different parts of the world. Through examination of selected readings from around the world, the student might become more aware of the close connection he or she holds to the rest of humanity.

Image Credits

Fig. 0.1: Source: https://commons.wikimedia.org/wiki/File:Blank-map-world-south-up.png.

Ancient Civilizations in West Asia and Egypt

Introduction

During the period between approximately 5000 B.C. and 1000 B.C., ancient civilizations grew up in the fertile region between the Tigris and Euphrates Rivers, in what is now Iraq—an area known as Mesopotamia (from the Greek for "between the rivers"). The most important and earliest people who settled in this area were the southern Mesopotamians, called the Sumerians.

Their civilization consisted of a series of city-states, including Uruk and Lagash. These had fine buildings and public water supplies and drainage. The Sumerians devised the first known writing system, *cuneiform*; from about 3100 B.C., records were kept on clay tablets, thousands of which have survived. The Sumerians were gradually absorbed by the Semitic people, who founded the great empires of Assyria and Babylonia. The greatest legacy of the Babylonians is the well-known law codes, called the Code of Hammurabi.

The Nile River Valley was one of the most fertile places in the ancient world, with annual floods depositing rich alluvial soil known as *fellahin* ("black earth") along its banks. Unlike Mesopotamia, with its fast-growing cities, Egypt around 3000 B.C. was a land of villages. The Nile served as an artery of communication among those settlements and helped unify the land. The first area to be united under one ruler was Upper Egypt, the land along the Upper Nile. A king named Narmer led forces that conquered Lower Egypt, the Nile Delta area. This unification, around 3000 B.C., ushered in the first of more than 30 dynasties for the next 3,000 years.

The rulers of Egypt, known as *pharaohs*, were more closely identified with the gods than in any other culture. Narmer was the incarnation of Horus and Osiris, the son of the supreme god Ra himself. He was the supreme representative of the religious, as well as political, order. The ruler's relationship to his subjects was thus also a spiritual one.

The following documents from the ancient Egyptians, Mesopotamians, and Hebrews describe the relationship of humans to the rest of nature. Some of these accounts also provide insight into how the people's way of life and their religions, social divisions, and legal and cultural systems arose.

1. CT 1130 and 1031

by Miriam Lichtheim

Beginning in the First Intermediate Period, it became customary to inscribe the coffins of non-royal well-to-do persons with spells designed to protect the dead against the dangers of the netherworld and to bring about an afterlife modeled on that of the divine king. Like the king, the common man (and woman) now desired to rise up to the sky and to join the gods. Along with these grandiose wishes, the texts spell out more ordinary concerns and fears, such as the fear to suffer hunger and thirst, and the wish to be united with one's family.

In inspiration, the Coffin Texts descend directly from the Pyramid Texts, and some of their spells are direct borrowings. But the bulk of the material is new and reflects its non-royal origin. As a corpus, the Coffin Texts are far less coherent than the Pyramid Texts, for they lack a unifying point of view. Inspired by a reliance on magic, they lack the humility of prayer and the restraints of reason. Oscillating between grandiose claims and petty fears, they show the human imagination at its most abstruse. Fear of death and longing for eternal life have been brewed in a sorcerer's cauldron from which they emerge as magic incantations of the most phrenetic sort. The attempt to overcome the fear of death by usurping the royal claims to immortality resulted in delusions of grandeur which accorded so little with the observed facts of life as to appear paranoid.

Now and then a more reasonable attitude prevails, as in the first part of the spell here translated. It consists of a speech of the sun-god Re, in which the god takes credit for four good deeds which he did at the time of creation. In listing the four deeds, the god makes two assertions of prime importance: that he created all men as equals; and that it was not he who taught mankind to do wrong; rather, people do wrong of their own volition. This portion of the text is much above the usual level. The remainder is a typical Coffin Text spell, a grandiose claim that the dead will win entry into heaven and will be the equal of the sun-god.

The spell was used on a number of coffins, and the translation draws on the several versions as found side by side in de Buck's masterly edition.

Publication: de Buck, *Coffin Texts,* VII, 461–471 and 262.

Translation of the first part: J. A. Wilson in *ANET,* pp. 7–8.

Words spoken by Him-whose-names-are-hidden, the All-Lord, as he speaks before those who silence the storm, in the sailing of the court:[1]

Hail in peace! I repeat to you the good deeds which my own heart did for me from within the serpent-coil,[2] in order to silence strife. I did four good deeds within the portal of lightland:

I made the four winds, that every man might breathe in his time. This is one of the deeds.

I made the great inundation, that the humble might benefit by it like the great. This is one of the deeds.

I made every man like his fellow; and I did not command that they do wrong. It is their hearts that disobey what I have said. This is one of the deeds.

I made that their hearts are not disposed to forget the West, in order that sacred offerings be made to the gods of the nomes. This is one of the deeds.

I have created the gods from my sweat, and the people from the tears of my eye.[3]

THE DEAD SPEAKS

I shall shine[4] and be seen every day as a dignitary of the All-Lord, having given satisfaction to the Weary-hearted.[5]

I shall sail rightly in my bark, I am lord of eternity in the crossing of the sky.

I am not afraid in my limbs, for Hu and Hike[6] overthrow for me that evil being.

I shall see lightland, I shall dwell in it. I shall judge the poor and the wealthy.

I shall do the same for the evil-doers; for mine is life, I am its lord, and the scepter will not be taken from me.

I have spent a million years with the Weary-hearted, the son of Geb, dwelling with him in one place; while hills became towns and towns hills, for dwelling destroys dwelling.[7]

I am lord of the flame who lives on truth; lord of eternity maker of joy, against whom that worm shall not rebel.

I am he who is in his shrine, master of action[8] who destroys the storm; who drives off the serpents of many names when he goes from his shrine.

Lord of the winds who announces the northwind, rich in names in the mouth of the Ennead.

Lord of lightland, maker of light, who lights the sky with his beauty.

I am he in his name! Make way for me, that I may see Nun and Amun! For I am that equipped spirit (*akh*) who passes by the [guards].[9] They do not speak for fear of Him-whose-name-is-hidden, who is in my body. I know him, I do not ignore him! I am equipped and effective in opening his portal!

As for any person who knows this spell, he will be like Re in the eastern sky, like Osiris in the netherworld. He will go down to the circle of fire, without the flame touching him ever!

NOTES

1   *Sgrw nšn* might be either the active or the passive participle; Wilson construed it as the passive participle: "those stilled from tumult." In the active sense it would refer to the gods who accompany the sun-god. *Šnwt* are the courtiers, or entourage, of Re.

2   The serpent-dragon Apophis who symbolized the lurking dangers of the world.

3   A wordplay on *rmt*, "people," and *rmyt,* "tears," which occurs a number of times as an allusion to the creation of mankind.

4   Here begins the spell that is put in the mouth of the dead. In four of the versions it is cast in the first person, and in two version in the third person.

5   An epithet of Osiris. The meaning seems to be that the dead must first satisfy Osiris, the ruler of the dead, before he can join the sun-god.

6   The personifications of effective speech and of magic.

7   The claims get successively grander until the dead speaks as if he were the sun-god himself. That this identification is intended is shown by the explanatory remark with which the spell ends.

8   Does *spw* with knife determinative mean "slaughter"?

9   One version has *nhw*, another *hnw*, a third *msw*.

2. The Epic of Gilgamesh

trans. Robert William Rogers

Gilgamesh said to him, to Ut-napishtim, the faraway:

> "I consider thee, O Ut-napishtim,
> Thy appearance is not changed, thou art like me,
> Thou art not different, even as I am, thou art.
> Thy heart is in perfect state, to make combat,
> Thou dost lie down upon thy side, and upon thy back.
> Tell me, how hast thou been exalted, and amid the assembly of the gods hast found life?"

trans. Robert William Rogers, "Tablet XI," *The Epic of Gilgamesh*, 1912.

THE BABYLONIAN FLOOD STORY

Ut-napishtim spoke to him, to Gilgamesh
I will reveal to thee, O Gilgamesh, the hidden word,
And the decision of the gods will I announce to thee.
Shurippak, a city which thou knowest,
Which lies on the bank of the Euphrates,
That city was very old, and the heart of the gods
Within it drove them to send a flood, the great gods;
... their father Anu,
Their counsellor the warrior Ellil,
Their messenger Ninib,
Their prince Ennugi.
The lord of Wisdom, Ea, counselled with them
And repeated their word to the reed hut:

> "O reed hut, reed hut, O, wall, wall,
> O reed hut hearken, O wall attend!
> Oman of Shurippak, son of Ubaratutu,
> Pull down thy house, build a ship,
> Leave thy possessions, take thought for thy life,
> Thy property abandon save thy life,
> Bring living seed of every kind into the ship.
> The ship, that thou shall build
> So shall be the measure of its dimensions.
> Thus shall correspond its breadth and height
> ... the ocean, cover it with a roof.
> I understood it, and spake to Ea, my lord,
> [...] my lord, as thou hast commanded
> I will observe, and I will execute it,
> But what shall I say to the city, the people and the elders?"

Ea opened his mouth and spake.
He said unto me his servant,

> "Thou shalt so say unto them,
> Because Ellil hates me,
> No longer may I dwell in your city, nor remain on Ellil's earth,
> Into the ocean must I fare, with Ea, my lord to dwell.
> Upon you will he then rain fullness.
> [A catch] of birds, a catch of fish
> [... rich] harvest

[A time has Shamash appointed], on an evening the senders of rain
Shall rain upon you a mighty rain-storm.
As soon as the morning glow appeared

[*44–55 broken off*]
The strong one [...] brought what was necessary
On the fifth day I set up its form.

Column II:

In its [plan] 120 cubits high on each of its side-walls.
By 120 cubits it corresponded on each edge of the roof.
I laid down its hull, I enclosed it. I built it in six stories.
I divided it *outside* (?) in seven parts.
Its interior I divided into nine parts.
Water-plugs I fastened within it.
I prepared a rudder, and laid down what was necessary.
Three sars of bitumen I poured over the outside (?)
Three sars of bitumen I poured over the inside,
Three sars of oil the stevedores brought up.
Besides a sar of oil which men use as a libation,
The shipbuilder stowed away two sars of oil.
For the *people* I slaughtered bullocks,
I slew lambs daily.
Of must, beer, oil and wine
I gave the people to drink like water from the river,
A festival [I made], like the days of the feast of Akitu
I opened a box of ointment; I put ointment in my hand.
[At the rising] of the great Shamash the ship was finished.
[...] was hard
[...] above and below
[...] two thirds
With all that I had, I filled it (the ship).
With all that I had of silver, I filled it.
With all that I had of gold I filled it.
With all that I had of living things I filled it.
I brought up into the ship my family and household.
The cattle of the field, the beasts of the field, craftsmen all of them I brought in.
A fixed time had Shamash appointed (saying),

"When the sender of rain sends a heavy rain in the evening,
Then enter into the ship and close thy door."

The appointed time came near,
The senders of the rain in the evening sent heavy rain.
The appearance of the weather I observed,
I feared to behold the weather,
 I entered the ship and closed the door.
To the ship's master, to Puzur-Amurri the sailor,
I entrusted the building with its goods.
When the first flush of dawn appeared,
There came up from the horizon a black cloud.
Adad thundered within it,
While Nebo and Sharru (Marduk) went before.
They go as messengers over mountain and valley.
Nergal tore away the foundations.
Ninib advances, the storm he makes to descend.
The Anunnaki lifted up their torches,
With their brightness they light up the land.
Adad's storm reached unto heaven
All light was turned into darkness
It [flooded] the land like ...
One day the deluge ...

Column III:

Raged high, [the waters covered (?)] the mountains,
Like a besom of destruction they brought it upon men,
No man beheld his fellow,
No more were men recognized in heaven.
The gods feared the deluge,
They drew back, they climbed up to the heaven of Anu.
The gods crouched like a dog, they cowered by the walls.
Ishtar cried like a woman in travail,
Loudly cried the queen of the gods with her beautiful voice,

> "The former time is turned into clay,
> Since I commanded evil, in the assembly of the gods.
> Because I commanded evil in the assembly of the gods
> For the destruction of my people I commanded battle.
> I alone bore my people.
> [And now] like the spawn of fish they fill the sea."

The gods of the Anunnaki wept with her,
The gods sat bowed and weeping,

Covered were their lips [...]
Six days and [six] nights
Blew the wind, the deluge and the tempest overwhelmed the land.
When the seventh day drew nigh, the tempest spent itself in the battle,
Which it had fought like an army.
Then rested the sea, the storm fell asleep, the flood ceased.
I looked upon the sea, there was silence come,
And all mankind was turned to clay.
Like a roof the plain lay level,
I opened the window and the light fell upon my face,
I bowed, I sat down, I wept,
And over my face ran my tears.
I looked in all directions, terrible (?) *was* the sea.
After twelve days, an island arose.
To the land of Nisir the ship made its way,
The mount of Nisir held it fast, that it moved not.
One day, a second day did the mount of Nisir hold it, that it moved not.
A third day, a fourth day did the mount of Xisir hold it, that it moved not.
A fifth day, a sixth day did the mount of Xisir hold it, that it moved not.
When the seventh day approached,
I sent forth a dove and lot her go.
The dove flew away and came back,
For there was no resting place and she returned.
I sent forth a swallow and let her go,
The swallow flew away and came back,
For there was no resting place, and she returned.
I sent forth a raven and let her go,
The raven flew away, she saw the abatement of the waters,
She drew near, she waded, she croaked (?) and came not back.
Then I sent everything forth to the four quarters of heaven, I offered sacrifice,
I made a libation upon the mountain's peak. By sevens I set out the sacrificial vessels,
Beneath them I heaped up reed and cedar wood and myrtle
The gods smelt the savor,
The gods smelt the sweet savor,
The gods gathered like flies over the sacrifices
When at last the Lady of the gods drew near[.]

Column IV:

She raised the great jewel, which Anu according to her wish had made.

"Oh ye gods here—even as I shall not forget the jewels of my neck

Upon these days shall I think, I shall never forget them.
Let the gods come to the offering,
But let Ellil not come to the offering,
For he took not counsel, and sent the deluge
And my people he gave to destruction."

When at last Ellil drew near,
He saw the ship; then was Ellil wroth.
He was filled with anger against the gods the Igigi:

"Who then has escaped with life?
No man must live in the destruction!"

Then Ninib opened his mouth and spake,
He said to the warrior Ellil,

"Who but Ea can plan aught, And Ea knoweth every matter."

Ea opened his mouth, and spake,
He spake to the warrior Ellil,

"Thou wise among the gods, warrior Ellil,
Why couldst thou, without thought, send a flood?
On the sinner lay his sin,
On the slanderer lay his slander,
Forbear, let not [all] be destroyed, have mercy, *that men be not destroyed* (?)
Instead of thy sending a deluge?
Had a lion come and mankind lessened!
Instead of thy sending a deluge?
Had a wolf come and mankind lessened!
Instead of thy sending a deluge?
Had a famine come and the land ...!
Instead of thy sending a deluge?
Had Urra come and mankind [slain]!
I have not divulged the decision of the great gods.
I made Atrakhasis see a dream and so he discovered the secret of the gods.
Now take counsel for him."

Ea went up into the ship.
He took my hand, [and] brought me forth,
He brought forth my wife, and made her kneel at my side,

He turned us toward each other, he stood between us, he blessed us:
"Formerly Ut-napishtim was only a man, but Now let Ut-napishtim and his wife be like the gods even us,
Let Ut-napishtim dwell afar off at the mouth of the rivers."
They took me and afar off, at the mouth of the rivers they made me to dwell.

With these words the long story of the deluge is ended, and Ut-napishtim takes thought for his earthly visitor and says:

> "Who of the gods, will now gather thee to himself
> That thou mayest find the life thou seekest?
> Come, lie not down to sleep six days and seven nights[.]"

The idea is that if he can master sleep, twin brother of death, he might thus learn to master death itself. But the test is too severe and the hero falls asleep. Ut-napishtim mocks his weakness, but his wife, moved with pity for the helpless wanderer, desires her husband to make some provision for getting him back again. Her husband, moved by her appeal, calls to Gilgamesh to secure for himself a certain plant which grew in the bottom of the ocean. Gilgamesh ties heavy stones to his feet and plunges into the sea, from which he brings up the needful plant.

He is overjoyed and thinks that he has possessed himself of the plant of eternal life. So does he boast of it.

Gilgamesh said to him, to Ur-shanabi, the sailor:

> "Ur-shanabi, this plant is a plant of renown,
> Whereby man obtains his longings (?)
> I will carry it to walled Uruk, there will I make to eat of it [...]
> Its name is: 'When old shall man become young again.'
> I myself will eat it, to return to my youth."

Then they made the long journey, and when they had come to land, Gilgamesh went to bathe in a pool of fresh water. While thus employed a serpent stole the precious plant away, and left the hero disconsolate. Overland on foot to Uruk they made their weary way, and the tablet concludes with plans, announced to the sailor by Gilgamesh, for rebuilding the city walls—the very walls which had been the cause of all his troubles in the beginning.

3. Bible: Genesis

King James Version

CHAPTER 1

1. In the beginning God created the heaven and the earth.
2. And the earth was without form, and void; and darkness was upon the face of the deep. And the Spirit of God moved upon the face of the waters.
3. And God said, Let there be light: and there was light.
4. And God saw the light, that it was good: and God divided the light from the darkness.
5. And God called the light Day, and the darkness he called Night. And the evening and the morning were the first day.
6. And God said, Let there be a firmament in the midst of the waters, and let it divide the waters from the waters.
7. And God made the firmament, and divided the waters which were under the firmament from the waters which were above the firmament: and it was so.
8. And God called the firmament Heaven. And the evening and the morning were the second day.
9. And God said, Let the waters under the heaven be gathered together unto one place, and let the dry land appear: and it was so.
10. And God called the dry land Earth; and the gathering together of the waters called he Seas: and God saw that it was good.
11. And God said, Let the earth bring forth grass, the herb yielding seed, and the fruit tree yielding fruit after his kind, whose seed is in itself, upon the earth: and it was so.
12. And the earth brought forth grass, and herb yielding seed after his kind, and the tree yielding fruit, whose seed was in itself, after his kind: and God saw that it was good.
13. And the evening and the morning were the third day.
14. And God said, Let there be lights in the firmament of the heaven to divide the day from the night; and let them be for signs, and for seasons, and for days, and years:
15. And let them be for lights in the firmament of the heaven to give light upon the earth: and it was so.
16. And God made two great lights; the greater light to rule the day, and the lesser light to rule the night: he made the stars also.
17. And God set them in the firmament of the heaven to give light upon the earth,

"Genesis 1 and 2," King James Version, 1611.

18. And to rule over the day and over the night, and to divide the light from the darkness: and God saw that it was good.

19. And the evening and the morning were the fourth day.

20. And God said, Let the waters bring forth abundantly the moving creature that hath life, and fowl that may fly above the earth in the open firmament of heaven.

21. And God created great whales, and every living creature that moveth, which the waters brought forth abundantly, after their kind, and every winged fowl after his kind: and God saw that it was good.

22. And God blessed them, saying, Be fruitful, and multiply, and fill the waters in the seas, and let fowl multiply in the earth.

23. And the evening and the morning were the fifth day.

24. And God said, Let the earth bring forth the living creature after his kind, cattle, and creeping thing, and beast of the earth after his kind: and it was so.

25. And God made the beast of the earth after his kind, and cattle after their kind, and every thing that creepeth upon the earth after his kind: and God saw that it was good.

26. And God said, Let us make man in our image, after our likeness: and let them have dominion over the fish of the sea, and over the fowl of the air, and over the cattle, and over all the earth, and over every creeping thing that creepeth upon the earth.

27. So God created man in his own image, in the image of God created he him; male and female created he them.

28. And God blessed them, and God said unto them, Be fruitful, and multiply, and replenish the earth, and subdue it: and have dominion over the fish of the sea, and over the fowl of the air, and over every living thing that moveth upon the earth.

29. And God said, Behold, I have given you every herb bearing seed, which is upon the face of all the earth, and every tree, in the which is the fruit of a tree yielding seed; to you it shall be for meat.

30. And to every beast of the earth, and to every fowl of the air, and to every thing that creepeth upon the earth, wherein there is life, I have given every green herb for meat: and it was so.

31. And God saw every thing that he had made, and, behold, it was very good. And the evening and the morning were the sixth day.

CHAPTER 2

1. Thus the heavens and the earth were finished, and all the host of them.

2. And on the seventh day God ended his work which he had made; and he rested on the seventh day from all his work which he had made.

3. And God blessed the seventh day, and sanctified it: because that in it he had rested from all his work which God created and made.

4. These are the generations of the heavens and of the earth when they were created, in the day that the LORD God made the earth and the heavens,

5. And every plant of the field before it was in the earth, and every herb of the field before it grew: for the LORD God had not caused it to rain upon the earth, and there was not a man to till the ground.

6. But there went up a mist from the earth, and watered the whole face of the ground.

7. And the LORD God formed man of the dust of the ground, and breathed into his nostrils the breath of life; and man became a living soul.

8. And the LORD God planted a garden eastward in Eden; and there he put the man whom he had formed.

9. And out of the ground made the LORD God to grow every tree that is pleasant to the sight, and good for food; the tree of life also in the midst of the garden, and the tree of knowledge of good and evil.

10. And a river went out of Eden to water the garden; and from thence it was parted, and became into four heads.

11. The name of the first is Pison: that is it which compasseth the whole land of Havilah, where there is gold;

12. And the gold of that land is good: there is bdellium and the onyx stone.

13. And the name of the second river is Gihon: the same is it that compasseth the whole land of Ethiopia.

14. And the name of the third river is Hiddekel: that is it which goeth toward the east of Assyria. And the fourth river is Euphrates.

15. And the LORD God took the man, and put him into the garden of Eden to dress it and to keep it.

16. And the LORD God commanded the man, saying, Of every tree of the garden thou mayest freely eat:

17. But of the tree of the knowledge of good and evil, thou shalt not eat of it: for in the day that thou eatest thereof thou shalt surely die.

18. And the LORD God said, It is not good that the man should be alone; I will make him an help meet for him.

19. And out of the ground the LORD God formed every beast of the field, and every fowl of the air; and brought them unto Adam to see what he would call them: and whatsoever Adam called every living creature, that was the name thereof.

20. And Adam gave names to all cattle, and to the fowl of the air, and to every beast of the field; but for Adam there was not found an help meet for him.

21. And the LORD God caused a deep sleep to fall upon Adam, and he slept: and he took one of his ribs, and closed up the flesh instead thereof;

22. And the rib, which the LORD God had taken from man, made he a woman, and brought her unto the man.

23. And Adam said, This is now bone of my bones, and flesh of my flesh: she shall be called Woman, because she was taken out of Man.

24. Therefore shall a man leave his father and his mother, and shall cleave unto his wife: and they shall be one flesh.
25. And they were both naked, the man and his wife, and were not ashamed.

---

4. Hammurabi's Law Code

trans. C.H.W. Johns

- 1. If a man has accused another of laying a *nertu* [death spell?] upon him, but has not proved it, he shall be put to death.

- 2. If a man has accused another of laying a *kispu* [spell] upon him, but has not proved it, the accused shall go to the sacred river, he shall plunge into the sacred river, and if the river shall conquer him, he that accused him shall take possession of his house. If the sacred river shall show his innocence and he is saved, his accuser shall be put to death. He that plunged into the sacred river shall appropriate the house of him that accused.

- 3. If a man has borne false witness in a trial, or has not established the statement that he has made, if that case be a capital trial, that man shall be put to death.

- 4. If he has borne false witness in a civil law case, he shall pay the damages in that suit.

- 5. If a judge has given a verdict, rendered a decision, granted a written judgment, and afterward has altered his judgment, that judge shall be prosecuted for altering the judgment he gave and shall pay twelvefold the penalty laid down in that judgment. Further, he shall be publicly expelled from his judgment-seat and shall not return nor take his seat with the judges at a trial.

- 6. If a man has stolen goods from a temple, or house, he shall be put to death; and he that has received the stolen property from him shall be put to death.

- 7. If a man has bought or received on deposit from a minor or a slave, either silver, gold, male or female slave, ox, ass, or sheep, or anything else, except by consent of elders, or power of attorney, he shall be put to death for theft.

"Code of Hammurabi," *Babylonian and Assyrian Laws, Contracts and Letters*, trans. C.H.W. Johns, 1904.

- 8. If a patrician has stolen ox, sheep, ass, pig, or ship, whether from a temple, or a house, he shall pay thirtyfold. If he be a plebeian, he shall return tenfold. If the thief cannot pay, he shall be put to death.

- 9. If a man has lost property and some of it be detected in the possession of another, and the holder has said, "A man sold it to me, I bought it in the presence of witnesses"; and if the claimant has said, "I can bring witnesses who know it to be property lost by me"; then the alleged buyer on his part shall produce the man who sold it to him and the witnesses before whom he bought it; the claimant shall on his part produce the witnesses who know it to be his lost property. The judge shall examine their pleas. The witnesses to the sale and the witnesses who identify the lost property shall state on oath what they know. Such a seller is the thief and shall be put to death. The owner of the lost property shall recover his lost property. The buyer shall recoup himself from the seller's estate.

- 10. If the alleged buyer on his part has not produced the seller or the witnesses before whom the sale took place, but the owner of the lost property on his part has produced the witnesses who identify it as his, then the [pretended] buyer is the thief; he shall be put to death. The owner of the lost property shall take his lost property.

- 11. If, on the other hand, the claimant of the lost property has not brought the witnesses that know his lost property, he has been guilty of slander, he has stirred up strife, he shall be put to death.

- 12. If the seller has in the meantime died, the buyer shall take from his estate fivefold the value sued for.

- 13. If a man has not his witnesses at hand, the judge shall set him a fixed time not exceeding six months, and if within six months he has not produced his witnesses, the man has lied; he shall bear the penalty of the suit.

- 14. If a man has stolen a child, he shall be put to death.

- 15. If a man has induced either a male or a female slave from the house of a patrician, or plebeian, to leave the city, he shall be put to death.

- 16. If a man has harbored in his house a male or female slave from a patrician's or plebeian's house, and has not caused the fugitive to leave on the demand of the officer over the slaves condemned to public forced labor, that householder shall be put to death.

- 17. If a man has caught either a male or female runaway slave in the open field and has brought him back to his owner, the owner of the slave shall give him two shekels of silver.

- 18. If such a slave will not name his owner, his captor shall bring him to the palace, where he shall be examined as to his past and returned to his owner.

- 19. If the captor has secreted that slave in his house and afterward that slave has been caught in his possession, he shall be put to death.

- 20. If the slave has fled from the hands of his captor, the latter shall swear to the owner of the slave and he shall be free from blame.

- 21. If a man has broken into a house he shall be killed before the breach and buried there.

- 22. If a man has committed highway robbery and has been caught, that man shall be put to death.

- 23. If the highwayman has not been caught, the man that has been robbed shall state on oath what he has lost and the city or district governor in whose territory or district the robbery took place shall restore to him what he lost.

- 24. If a life [has been lost], the city or district governor shall pay one mina of silver to the deceased's relatives.

- 25. If a fire has broken out in a man's house and one who has come to put it out has coveted the property of the householder and appropriated any of it, that man shall be cast into the self-same fire.

- ... [The creator of this site omits sections 26 through 65 and sections 100 through 127. The intervening sections 66 through 99 appear to be erased and not decipherable on the stone.]

- 128. If a man has taken a wife and has not executed a marriage contract, that woman is not a wife.

- 129. If a man's wife be caught lying with another, they shall be strangled and cast into the water. If the wife's husband would save his wife, the king can save his servant.

- 130. If a man has ravished another's betrothed wife, who is a virgin, while still living in her father's house, and has been caught in the act, that man shall be put to death; the woman shall go free.

- 131. If a man's wife has been accused by her husband, and has not been caught lying with another, she shall swear her innocence, and return to her house.

- 132. If a man's wife has the finger pointed at her on account of another, but has not been caught lying with him, for her husband's sake she shall plunge into the sacred river.

- 133. If a man has been taken captive, and there was maintenance in his house, but his wife has left her house and entered another man's house; because that woman has not preserved her body, and has entered into the house of another, that woman shall be prosecuted and shall be drowned.

- 134. If a man has been taken captive, but there was not maintenance in his house, and his wife has entered into the house of another, that woman has no blame.

- 135. If a man has been taken captive, but there was no maintenance in his house for his wife, and she has entered into the house of another, and has borne him children, if in the future her [first] husband shall return and regain his city, that woman shall return to her first husband, but the children shall follow their own father.

- 136. If a man has left his city and fled, and, after he has gone, his wife has entered into the house of another; if the man return and seize his wife, the wife of the fugitive shall not return to her husband, because he hated his city and fled.

- 137. If a man has determined to divorce a concubine who has borne him children, or a votary who has granted him children, he shall return to that woman her marriage-portion, and shall give her the usufruct of field, garden, and goods, to bring up her children. After her children have grown up, out of whatever is given to her children, they shall give her one son's share, and the husband of her choice shall marry her.

- 138. If a man has divorced his wife, who has not borne him children, he shall pay over to her as much money as was given for her bride-price and the marriage-portion which she brought from her father's house, and so shall divorce her.

- 139. If there was no bride-price, he shall give her one mina of silver, as a price of divorce.

- 140. If he be a plebeian, he shall give her one-third of a mina of silver.

- 141. If a man's wife, living in her husband's house, has persisted in going out, has acted the fool, has wasted her house, has belittled her husband, he shall prosecute her. If her husband has said, "I divorce her," she shall go her way; he shall give her nothing as her price of divorce. If her husband has said, "I will not divorce her," he may take another woman to wife; the wife shall live as a slave in her husband's house.

- 142. If a woman has hated her husband and has said, "You shall not possess me," her past shall be inquired into, as to what she lacks. If she has been discreet, and has no vice, and her husband has gone out, and has greatly belittled her, that woman has no blame, she shall take her marriage-portion and go off to her father's house.

- 143. If she has not been discreet, has gone out, ruined her house, belittled her husband, she shall be drowned.

- 144. If a man has married a votary, and that votary has given a maid to her husband, and so caused him to have children, and, if that man is inclined to marry a concubine, that man shall not be allowed to do so, he shall not marry a concubine.

- 145. If a man has married a votary, and she has not granted him children, and he is determined to marry a concubine, that man shall marry the concubine, and bring her into his house, but the concubine shall not place herself on an equality with the votary.

- 146. If a man has married a votary, and she has given a maid to her husband, and the maid has borne children, and if afterward that maid has placed herself on an equality with her mistress, because she has borne children, her mistress shall not sell her, she shall place a slave-mark upon her, and reckon her with the slave-girls.

- 147. If she has not borne children, her mistress shall sell her.

- 148. If a man has married a wife and a disease has seized her, if he is determined to marry a second wife, he shall marry her. He shall not divorce the wife whom the disease has seized. In the home they made together she shall dwell, and he shall maintain her as long as she lives.

- 149. If that woman was not pleased to stay in her husband's house, he shall pay over to her the marriage-portion which she brought from her father's house, and she shall go away.

- 150. If a man has presented field, garden, house, or goods to his wife, has granted her a deed of gift, her children, after her husband's death, shall not dispute her right; the mother shall leave it after her death to that one of her children whom she loves best. She shall not leave it to her kindred.

- 151. If a woman, who is living in a man's house, has persuaded her husband to bind himself, and grant her a deed to the effect that she shall not be held for debt by a creditor of her husband's; if that man had a debt upon him before he married that woman, his creditor shall not take his wife for it. Also, if that woman had a debt upon her before she entered that man's house, her creditor shall not take her husband for it.

- 152. From the time that the woman entered into the man's house they together shall be liable for all debts subsequently incurred.

- 153. If a man's wife, for the sake of another, has caused her husband to be killed, that woman shall be impaled.

- 154. If a man has committed incest with his daughter, that man shall be banished from the city.

- 155. If a man has betrothed a maiden to his son and his son has known her, and afterward the man has lain in her bosom, and been caught, that man shall be strangled and she shall be cast into the water.

- 156. If a man has betrothed a maiden to his son, and his son has not known her, and that man has lain in her bosom, he shall pay her half a mina of silver, and shall pay over to her whatever she brought from her father's house, and the husband of her choice shall marry her.

- 157. If a man, after his father's death, has lain in the bosom of his mother, they shall both of them be burnt together.

- 158. If a man, after his father's death, be caught in the bosom of his step-mother, who has borne children, that man shall be cut off from his father's house.

- 159. If a man, who has presented a gift to the house of his prospective father-in-law and has given the bride-price, has afterward looked upon another woman and has said to his father-in-law, "I will not marry your daughter"; the father of the girl shall keep whatever he has brought as a present.

- 160. If a man has presented a gift to the house of his prospective father-in-law, and has given the bride-price, but the father of the girl has said, "I will not give you my daughter," the father shall return double all that was presented him.

- 161. If a man has presented a gift to the house of his prospective father-in-law, and has given the bride price, but his comrade has slandered him and his father-in-law has said to the suitor, "You shall not marry my daughter," [the father] shall return double all that was presented him. Further, the comrade shall not marry the girl.

- 162. If a man has married a wife, and she has borne him children, and that woman has gone to her fate, her father shall lay no claim to her marriage-portion. Her marriage-portion is her children's only.

- 163. If a man has married a wife, and she has not borne him children, and that woman has gone to her fate; if his father-in-law has returned to him the bride-price, which that man brought into the house of his father-in-law, her husband shall have no claim on the marriage portion of that woman. Her marriage-portion indeed belongs to her father's house.

- 164. If the father-in-law has not returned the bride-price, the husband shall deduct the amount of her bride-price from her marriage-portion, and shall return her marriage-portion to her father's house.

- 165. If a man has presented field, garden, or house to his son, the first in his eyes, and has written him a deed of gift; after the father has gone to his fate, when the brothers share, he shall keep the present his father gave him, and over and above shall share equally with them in the goods of his father's estate.

- 166. If a man has taken wives for the other sons he had, but has not taken a wife for his young son, after the father has gone to his fate, when the brothers share, they shall set aside from the goods of their father's estate money, as a bride-price, for their young brother, who has not married a wife, over and above his share, and they shall cause him to take a wife.

- 167. If a man has taken a wife, and she has borne him children and that woman has gone to her fate, and he has taken a second wife, and she also has borne children; after the father has gone to his fate, the sons shall not share according to mothers, but each family shall take the marriage-portion of its mother, and all shall share the goods of the father's estate equally.

- 168. If a man has determined to disinherit his son and has declared before the judge, "I cut off my son," the judge shall inquire into the son's past, and, if the son has not committed a grave misdemeanor such as should cut him off from sonship, the father shall [not] disinherit the son.

  [The word "not" as inserted here does not occur in the original C. H. W. Johns text, and is inserted by the creator of this site.]

- 169. If he has committed a grave crime against his father, which cuts off from sonship, for the first offense he shall pardon him. If he has committed a grave crime a second time, the father shall cut off his son from sonship.

- ... [The creator of this site omits sections 170 through 191.]

- 192. If the son of a palace favorite or the son of a vowed woman has said to the father that brought him up, "You are not my father," or to the mother that brought him up, "You are not my mother," his tongue shall be cut out.

- 193. If the son of a palace favorite or the son of a vowed woman has come to know his father's house and has hated his father that brought him up, or his mother that brought him up, and shall go off to his father's house, his eyes shall be torn out.

- 194. If a man has given his son to a wet-nurse to suckle, and that son has died in the hands of the nurse, and the nurse, without consent of the child's father or mother, has nursed another child, they shall prosecute her; because she has nursed another child, without consent of the father or mother, her breasts shall be cut off.

- 195. If a son has struck his father, his hands shall be cut off.

- 196. If a man has knocked out the eye of a patrician, his eye shall be knocked out.

- 197. If he has broken the limb of a patrician, his limb shall be broken.

- 198. If he has knocked out the eye of a plebeian or has broken the limb of a plebeian, he shall pay one mina of silver.

- 199. If he has knocked out the eye of a patrician's servant, or broken the limb of a patrician's servant, he shall pay half his value.

- 200. If a patrician has knocked out the tooth of a man that is his equal, his tooth shall be knocked out.

- 201. If he has knocked out the tooth of a plebeian, he shall pay one-third of a mina of silver.

- 202. If a man has smitten the privates of a man, higher in rank than he, he shall be sourged with sixty blows of an ox-hide scourge, in the assembly.

- 203. If a man has smitten the privates of a patrician of his own rank, he shall pay one mina of silver.

- 204. If a plebeian has smitten the privates of a plebeian, he shall pay ten shekels of silver.

- 205. If a slave of anyone has smitten the privates of a free-born man, his ear shall be cut off.

- 206. If a man has struck another in a quarrel, and caused him a permanent injury, that man shall swear, "I struck him without malice," and shall pay the doctor.

- 207. If he has died of his blows, [the man] shall swear [similarly], and pay one-half a mina of silver; or,

- 208. If [the deceased] was a plebeian, he shall pay one-third of a mina of silver.

- 209. If a man has struck a free woman with child, and has caused her to miscarry, he shall pay ten shekels for her miscarriage.

- 210. If that woman die, his daughter shall be killed.

- 211. If it be the daughter of a plebeian, that has miscarried through his blows, he shall pay five shekels of silver.

- 212. If that woman die, he shall pay half a mina of silver.

- 213. If he has struck a man's maid and caused her to miscarry, he shall pay two shekels of silver.

- 214. If that woman die, he shall pay one-third of a mina of silver.

- 215. If a surgeon has operated with the bronze lancet on a patrician for a serious injury, and has cured him, or has removed with a bronze lancet a cataract for a patrician, and has cured his eye, he shall take ten shekels of silver.

- 216. If it be a plebeian, he shall take five shekels of silver.

- 217. If it be a man's slave, the owner of the slave shall give two shekels of silver to the surgeon.

- 218. If a surgeon has operated with the bronze lancet on a patrician for a serious injury, and has caused his death, or has removed a cataract for a patrician, with the bronze lancet, and has made him lose his eye, his hands shall be cut off.

- 219. If the surgeon has treated a serious injury of a plebeian's slave, with the bronze lancet, and has caused his death, he shall render slave for slave.

- 220. If he has removed a cataract with the bronze lancet, and made the slave lose his eye, he shall pay half his value.

- 221. If a surgeon has cured the limb of a patrician, or has doctored a diseased bowel, the patient shall pay five shekels of silver to the surgeon.

- 222. If he be a plebeian, he shall pay three shekels of silver.

- 223. If he be a man's slave, the owner of the slave shall give two shekels of silver to the doctor.

- 224. If a veterinary surgeon has treated an ox, or an ass, for a severe injury, and cured it, the owner of the ox, or the ass, shall pay the surgeon one-sixth of a shekel of silver, as his fee.

- 225. If he has treated an ox, or an ass, for a severe injury, and caused it to die, he shall pay one-quarter of its value to the owner of the ox, or the ass.

- 226. If a brander has cut out a mark on a slave, without the consent of his owner, that brander shall have his hands cut off.

- 227. If someone has deceived the brander, and induced him to cut out a mark on a slave, that man shall be put to death and buried in his house; the brander shall swear, "I did not mark him knowingly," and shall go free.

- 228. If a builder has built a house for a man, and finished it, he shall pay him a fee of two shekels of silver, for each *SAR* built on.

- 229. If a builder has built a house for a man, and has not made his work sound, and the house he built has fallen, and caused the death of its owner, that builder shall be put to death.

- 230. If it is the owner's son that is killed, the builder's son shall be put to death.

- 231. If it is the slave of the owner that is killed, the builder shall give slave for slave to the owner of the house.

- 232. If he has caused the loss of goods, he shall render back whatever he has destroyed. Moreover, because he did not make sound the house he built, and it fell, at his own cost he shall rebuild the house that fell.

- 233. If a builder has built a house for a man, and has not keyed his work, and the wall has fallen, that builder shall make that wall firm at his own expense.

- 234. If a boatman has built a boat of sixty GUR for a man, he shall pay him a fee of two shekels of silver.

- 235. If a boatman has built a boat for a man, and has not made his work sound, and in that same year that boat is sent on a voyage and suffers damage, the boatman shall rebuild that boat, and, at his own expense, shall make it strong, or shall give a strong boat to the owner.

- 236. If a man has let his boat to a boatman, and the boatman has been careless and the boat has been sunk or lost, the boatman shall restore a boat to the owner.

- 237. If a man has hired a boat and boatman, and loaded it with corn, wool, oil, or dates, or whatever it be, and the boatman has been careless, and sunk the boat, or lost what is in it, the boatman shall restore the boat which he sank, and whatever he lost that was in it.

- 238. If a boatman has sunk a man's boat, and has floated it again, he shall pay half its value in silver.

- 239. If a man has hired a boatman, he shall pay him six GUR of corn yearly.

- 240. If a boat, on its course, has run into a boat at anchor, and sunk it, the owner of the boat that was sunk shall estimate on oath whatsoever was lost in his boat, and the owner of the moving vessel, which sank the boat at anchor, shall make good his boat and what was lost in it.

- ... [The creator of this site omits sections 241 through 277.]

- 278. If a man has bought a male or female slave and the slave has not fulfilled his month, but the *bennu* disease has fallen upon him, he shall return the slave to the seller and the buyer shall take back the money he paid.

- 279. If a man has bought a male or female slave and a claim has been raised, the seller shall answer the claim.

- 280. If a man, in a foreign land, has bought a male, or female, slave of another, and if when he has come home the owner of the male or female slave has recognized his slave, and if the slave be a native of the land, he shall grant him liberty without money.

- 281. If the slave was a native of another country, the buyer shall declare on oath the amount of money he paid, and the owner of the slave shall repay the merchant what he paid and keep his slave.

- 282. If a slave has said to his master, "You are not my master," he shall be brought to account as his slave, and his master shall cut off his ear.

---

5. Bible: Ezra

King James Version

CHAPTER 6

1. Then Darius the king made a decree, and search was made in the house of the rolls, where the treasures were laid up in Babylon.
2. And there was found at Achmetha, in the palace that is in the province of the Medes, a roll, and therein was a record thus written:
3. In the first year of Cyrus the king the same Cyrus the king made a decree concerning the house of God at Jerusalem, Let the house be builded, the place where they offered sacrifices, and let the foundations thereof be strongly laid; the height thereof threescore cubits, and the breadth thereof threescore cubits;

"Ezra 6:1-18," King James Version, 1611.

4. With three rows of great stones, and a row of new timber: and let the expenses be given out of the king's house:

5. And also let the golden and silver vessels of the house of God, which Nebuchadnezzar took forth out of the temple which is at Jerusalem, and brought unto Babylon, be restored, and brought again unto the temple which is at Jerusalem, every one to his place, and place them in the house of God.

6. Now therefore, Tatnai, governor beyond the river, Shetharboznai, and your companions the Apharsachites, which are beyond the river, be ye far from thence:

7. Let the work of this house of God alone; let the governor of the Jews and the elders of the Jews build this house of God in his place.

8. Moreover I make a decree what ye shall do to the elders of these Jews for the building of this house of God: that of the king's goods, even of the tribute beyond the river, forthwith expenses be given unto these men, that they be not hindered.

9. And that which they have need of, both young bullocks, and rams, and lambs, for the burnt offerings of the God of heaven, wheat, salt, wine, and oil, according to the appointment of the priests which are at Jerusalem, let it be given them day by day without fail:

10. That they may offer sacrifices of sweet savours unto the God of heaven, and pray for the life of the king, and of his sons.

11. Also I have made a decree, that whosoever shall alter this word, let timber be pulled down from his house, and being set up, let him be hanged thereon; and let his house be made a dunghill for this.

12. And the God that hath caused his name to dwell there destroy all kings and people, that shall put to their hand to alter and to destroy this house of God which is at Jerusalem. I Darius have made a decree; let it be done with speed.

13. Then Tatnai, governor on this side the river, Shetharboznai, and their companions, according to that which Darius the king had sent, so they did speedily.

14. And the elders of the Jews builded, and they prospered through the prophesying of Haggai the prophet and Zechariah the son of Iddo. And they builded, and finished it, according to the commandment of the God of Israel, and according to the commandment of Cyrus, and Darius, and Artaxerxes king of Persia.

15. And this house was finished on the third day of the month Adar, which was in the sixth year of the reign of Darius the king.

16. And the children of Israel, the priests, and the Levites, and the rest of the children of the captivity, kept the dedication of this house of God with joy.

17. And offered at the dedication of this house of God an hundred bullocks, two hundred rams, four hundred lambs; and for a sin offering for all Israel, twelve he goats, according to the number of the tribes of Israel.

18. And they set the priests in their divisions, and the Levites in their courses, for the service of God, which is at Jerusalem; as it is written in the book of Moses.

Analysis Questions

1. What are the religious outlooks of these documents?
2. What are the similarities and differences between Coffin Text and Genesis?
3. Compare the flood story in Genesis with the one in the *Epic of Gilgamesh*.
4. Compare Hammurabi's law code with modern law code. What are the similarities and differences?
5. Explain the legacy of Darius and Cyrus from the Book of Ezra.

CHAPTER 2

Early Indian Civilization, to Fourth Century A.D.

Introduction

Indian civilization developed first in the Indus River valley of present-day Pakistan and later in the Ganges River valley. Along the Indus River Valley, around 2800 B.C., two of the earliest planned cities—Harappa and Mohenjo Daro—featured water conduits, toilets, straight streets, and standard-size building bricks. This early Indus civilization was not known until 1921, when archaeologists unearthed orderly walled cities and evidence of one of the world's first written languages from a civilization that lasted for more than a thousand years until it was gradually abandoned because of ecological disasters and the breakdown of the interrelationships among the political, social, and economic systems that sustained them.

Around 1500 B.C., the Indus River valley was invaded by Aryans, who entered the region from the northwest. According to the *Vedas* (Hindu hymns), the ritual and philosophical texts of the Aryans showed they were a hard-fighting nomadic people who rode chariots into battle and were organized under tribal chiefs (*rajas*). Aryans imposed a class system that placed them high above those conquered dark-skinned people. Aryan nobility was divided into a priest (*Brahman*) class and a warrior (*Kshatriya*) class. The common class consisted of merchants, artisans, and landowners (*Vaishya*) and peasants/laborers (*Shudra*). Added to this were slaves and the outcastes. The Aryans gradually expanded from the Indus Valley into the Ganges Valley. There were 16 Aryan kingdoms by 700 B.C., and the kingdom of Magadha in the Ganges Valley became the most powerful. In 321 B.C., the Mauryan Empire, the first great empire in India, was eventually founded by Chandragupta, who was a general of Magadha. He united northern India and repelled an attempted invasion by Seleucus Nicator, a general under Alexander the Great. The most famous of the Mauryans was the emperor Ashoka, who expanded his empire by conquering the kingdom of Kalinga in 260 B.C. Ashoka supported Buddhism throughout India by building monasteries and sending missionaries abroad to spread the faith throughout much of Asia.

The outstanding characteristic of early Indian civilization is its emphasis on religion: Hinduism, Jainism, and Buddhism. The Brahmans monopolized sacrificial rituals, worshipping various gods. The commentaries on these rituals, the *Upanishads*, challenged the role of the priests. The Upanishads offered an individual of any rank the hope of attaining holiness and salvation by freeing his soul and allowing him to become one with Brahma. Hinduism grew out of the Upanishads and combined the worship of various gods with the quest for salvation. Jainism, founded by Mahavira, taught that all living things had souls and that those who harmed other souls would not achieve salvation. Buddhism, on the other hand, denied the idea of the individual soul and emphasized the importance of "the middle way," involving good conduct and moderation in all things. The selections below contain the cornerstone doctrines of Brahmanism, Jainism, Buddhism, and Hinduism and explore the mystical aspects of early Indian beliefs, especially the nature of the human soul. Major Indian religious concepts such as *karma, samsara, Brahman,* and *nirvana* are discussed in these documents.

---

6. A Forgotten Empire of Antiquity

by Stuart Piggott

At the time of the first civilizations in Egypt and Mesopotamia a much larger one flourished in western India. It achieved great works, and then curiously did not change for a thousand years

When we think of the birthplace of civilization, we are apt to think only of Babylonia and Egypt. It was in the valleys of the Tigris-Euphrates and of the Nile, the archaeologists say, that agriculture began and mankind built the first villages, the first cities and the first kingdoms—Sumer and Egypt. Few people realize that there was a third great kingdom which rose and flourished side by side with them at the same time. This nameless and forgotten empire of antiquity, occupying the Indus Valley in western India, was far larger and more tightly ruled than Sumer or Egypt. It is nameless, and much less known than the other two, only because its language has not yet been deciphered and the remains of its writings cannot be read. Archaeologists hope that the code may some day be broken, as the hieroglyphics of ancient Egypt were deciphered, by discovery of a bilingual inscription—a Rosetta Stone of the Indus Valley. Until that

HOUSES OF MOHENJO-DARO were made of standardized bricks that had been baked rather than sun-dried. When the city was flooded, it was rebuilt in exactly the same plan.

momentous event, the story of this ancient Indian civilization must remain as incomplete as a silent picture. But the archaeological evidence tells enough to enable us to compare this culture with the more fully documented civilizations of Sumer and Egypt.

The study is a vital and exciting one, for it concerns the history of human ideas. Here in western Asia there rose three parallel but separate civilizations. In all three, technology followed much the same sequence: the invention of writing (that "incidental by-product of a strong sense of private property," as the U. S. archaeologist Ephraim Speiser so pleasantly put it), the development of skill in working bronze and precious metals, the evolution of architecture from mud huts to palaces, the growth of transport and trade and the rise of centralized government. Yet while the technological development of the three empires was nearly identical, their intellectual concepts and forms of society were very different. With respect to the peoples of Sumer and Egypt, we can read their differences of thought in their literature, and in the Indus Valley we can read it in the archaeological record of the people's way of

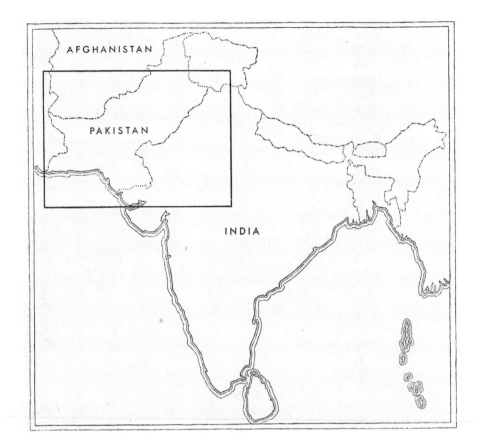

LOCATION of the area in the map on the opposite page is amplified here. The remains of the Harappa Civilization are found principally in the Punjab and Sind regions of Pakistan.

life. For the Indus civilization had a unique individuality of its own, already marked with some of the features of what was to become the characteristic Hindu culture of historic India. The comparative study of these three earliest civilizations shows how varied were the intellectual means whereby mankind found ways to create and maintain a stable society.

Archaeologists have named the Indus kingdom the Harappa Civilization, after a modern village which stands on the site of one of the great ancient towns. The Harappa Civilization had developed from a peasant to an urban culture by about 2500 B.C., and it endured for at least a thousand years before it was destroyed by invaders. It was a nation based on cities, towns and villages, with a Bronze Age technology and a central government strong enough to keep the peace and organize the economy for the common welfare.

Like the other ancient civilizations, it was centered on a river system—that of the Indus and its tributaries. But it was enormously larger, at least seven times bigger in area than the kingdom of Sumer. Two great cities and some 60 to 70 towns, villages and trading posts have already been unearthed, and more are likely to reward diggers in the future. The Harappa empire apparently covered a triangle stretching from a 600-mile seaboard at the base to an apex in the Himalayan foothills nearly 1,000 miles away. Its two cities stood like twin capitals 400 miles apart on the river system; they were at the sites now occupied by Mohenjo-Daro (the Mounds of the Dead) on the Indus and Harappa on the Ravi tributary. The cities were roughly square, and probably each about one square mile in area. We can only guess at their population: probably the cities had some 20,000 inhabitants each and the empire as a whole a population of at least 70,000 to 100,000.

The cities and towns show every evidence of a culture at least as far advanced as that of the neighboring civilizations to the west. Though they had no stone palaces, their buildings were of brick, which, in response to the climate of monsoon rains, was baked hard in the modern manner, instead of being sun-dried as elsewhere in the ancient East. The Harappa people did metalwork in copper and bronze, created jewelry of gold and semiprecious stones, wove cotton cloth, made pottery, used wheeled vehicles and were widely literate.

Even a superficial survey of the material culture of the Harappa Civilization shows that we are not dealing with a loose confederacy of city-states, each with its local customs, but with a highly organized kingdom directed by a strong central government according to a carefully planned scheme. The two major cities are very much alike and appear to have spoken with a single voice. Throughout the area there was a remarkable uniformity of products: pottery was mass-produced and the baked bricks were of standard sizes. Indeed, the weights and measures of the Harappa empire seem to have been regulated to a degree of accuracy unknown elsewhere in the ancient world.

There is little archaeological evidence as to the origins of the Harappa Civilization; we know it only as a fully developed empire. Probably its beginnings stemmed from the region to the northwest some time in the Fourth Millennium B.C. But its development was entirely independent, and even at its height the Harappa kingdom had only sporadic and small-scale trading contacts with Sumer and none at all with the Egyptian empire.

The most remarkable fact about the known history of the Harappa Civilization is its stability and conservatism. For a thousand years, from its arrival at a state of maturity about 2500 B.C., there was almost no significant change, as far as the archaeological record shows. Through all those centuries the culture stood still in an arrested state of development: its script, its pottery, its architecture, its sculpture and seal-engraving, its curiously primitive metal tools—all these remained the same. There are no signs of disturbance by dynastic change or warfare. From time to time the town at Mohenjo-Daro was destroyed by floods, and after each inundation the city was rebuilt exactly as before, even to the same line for the house fronts along the streets. Such immemorial conservatism, such unwavering continuity of tradition, is unparalleled elsewhere in the ancient world, even in Egypt.

When the end did come, it came quickly, and to a people unprepared to defend their long-established civilization against attack from outside. Though the two great cities boasted walled citadels, we find there no sign of weapons such as might equip an army and no evidence of military battles or resistance. Somewhere around 1500 B.C. warrior bands from the west simply overran the kingdom. The urban civilization of the Harappa world ended and was replaced by scattered barbarian farmsteads.

What were the distinctive qualities of this enduring but fragile civilization? For one thing, their writing was unusual for the ancient world. It consisted of a stiff hieroglyphic script with a total of about 400 characters, nearly half of which were variants on a basic 250 or so. This relatively small number of signs in a non-alphabetic language implies an advanced stage in the craft of writing—the earliest writing in Sumer, for instance, had 2,000 signs. The samples of Harappa writing that have been found are mainly engraved stone seals which, as elsewhere in the ancient world, seem to have been used to identify personal property. The Harappa script was pictographic

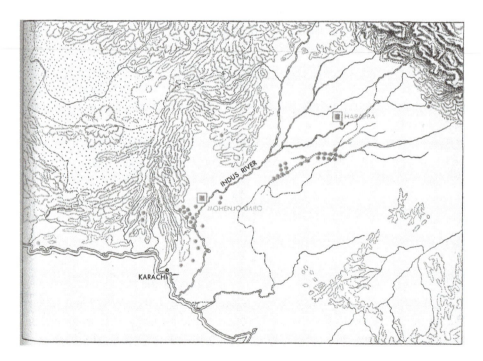

SITES at which the remains of the Harappa Civilization have been found are in red. The twin capitals of the kingdom were near its opposite ends. With Mohenjo-Daro on the Indus and Harappa on its tributary the Ravi, the cities were linked by a 400-mile waterway.

(apparently there was no cursive form), and the longest inscriptions discovered do not exceed 20 characters. Thus even when the Harappa writings are deciphered, they will not give us a lost literature. But to know to what language group they can be assigned will be of great importance.

The Harappa scale of weights was curious and without parallel. The unit was equivalent to 13.64 grams (a little less than half an ounce). But the scale defining multiples of the unit was calculated in a peculiar way: the unit itself was the ratio 16, and at the lower end of the scale the multiples were binary (doubling each time), while the heavier weights were reckoned in decimal multiples. Thus the weights ran in the ratio 1, 2, 8/3, 4, 8, 16, 32, 64, 160, 200, 320, 640 and so on. Fractions of a unit were expressed in thirds. This sequence has been deduced from a number of cubical stone weights found at sites in the Harappa kingdom. Unlike other peoples of antiquity, the Harappans seem

GRAVE at Harappa contained traces of a reed shroud and wooden coffin, customs characteristic of Sumer. There is little evidence, however, of contact between the two civilizations.

to have stuck to their weight system with considerable precision, and the enforcement of the standard over so wide an area suggests careful control and inspection.

The Harappa people also used exact linear measurements. They had two units—a foot of 13.2 inches and a cubit of 20.62 inches. Investigators have found actual Harappa rules, engraved on shell and on bronze, and by check measurements on buildings have ascertained that the units were accurately followed. The Harappa foot and cubit units were the same as those used in other empires of the ancient Orient, which suggests that they came from a common source.

The centralization of authority which the uniformity of weights and measures and of mass-produced products in the Harappa empire bespeaks is even more insistently expressed in the cities themselves. At Mohenjo-Daro enough has been recovered of the town plan to show that it was conceived and laid out as a conscious civic creation from the start; the city was not the rabbit warren typical of the ancient (and much of the modern) Orient. A grid of streets, some of them 30 feet wide, divided the square city into 12 major blocks. Each measured some 1,200 by 800 feet (roughly six times the size of a typical block in New York City). The houses were set closely together, and on the street side they presented blank walls without any architectural embellishment except their doorways. In back they faced interior courtyards and were separated by lanes and alleyways. The dwellings were extremely well built of fired brick, and their walls seem to have been plastered and painted inside and out. They had bathrooms with paved floors, and drains leading to a main sewer system beneath the streets, where manholes covered by large tiles gave access for cleaning. In the walls were rubbish chutes opening into brick bins. The whole system shows a concern for sanitation and cleanliness, and a civic organization to that end, unique in oriental antiquity.

The houses generally did not vary greatly in size, suggesting no more inequalities in wealth than one would expect to find in a middle-class population of shopkeepers, craftsmen and merchants. But in both major cities there were separate blocks of two-room cottages which apparently were the quarters of manual workers—a supposition which is reinforced by the fact that at Harappa this housing stood hard by a group of circular corn-grinding platforms and a great communal granary.

The dominant feature of each city was its citadel, a massive rectangular platform at least 50 feet high. At Mohenjo-Daro this structure appears to have occupied one of the central blocks on the western side of the grid. The citadel at Harappa seems to have been similarly placed, but its position is less certain because the city is much less well preserved than its twin and has been badly plundered for its brick. The citadel platforms were built of mud brick with walls of burnt brick. Terraced ways led up to their gates, and the citadels were topped by rectangular bastions and angle-towers.

PLATFORM of bricks at Harappa is where workers stood while they pounded grain. In the section of earth above the center of the platform are traces of the wooden grain mortar.

At Mohenjo-Daro the granary was within the citadel walls; there are still remnants of the loading platforms built to handle the grain. Of the buildings that stood on the citadel platform the most remarkable was an open bath about 8 feet deep and 40 feet long by 24 feet wide. The bath was surrounded by a veranda and changing-rooms and had steps leading down into it. Near it was a large building with a cloistered court and a pillared hall some 80 feet square. There was also a building, possibly a temple, which unfortunately is now almost obliterated by a Buddhist monastery later built on the site. And there were buildings similar in plan to the dwellings of the town. But none of the structures in the citadel could be interpreted as a palace.

These citadels, with their monumental walls, gateways, approach ramps and special buildings, must have been the seats of the centralized power of the Harappa Civilization. What was the source of the rulers' extraordinary authority? Clearly it was not primarily the force of arms, for no sign of any distinctively military equipment has been found in the kingdom. One can guess that their authority was spiritual. The

WALL is excavated by Indian workers at Harappa. It is the side of a platform 1,200 by 600 feet that rose some 30 feet above the city. On top of the platform was a citadel of public buildings. At Mohenjo-Daro, which has much the same plan, there is a similar structure.

POTTERY from Harappa is red with black designs. Most pottery from Harappa, however, is of a plain, mass-produced variety which did not change during the history of the city.

conservative uniformity of the culture and the peaceful coexistence of the two major cities suggest that the kingdom was ruled by men who were priests before they were kings. The art and architecture of the Harappa Civilization look very much like precursors of the Hindu culture: nothing could be more characteristic of a Hindu sacred site than the great bath or "tank" at Mohenjo-Daro. On an engraved seal found in the same city is a figure which is easily recognizable as the prototype of Siva, one of the Hindu divinities. There are a hundred similar indications. All the archaeological evidence suggests that the Harappa polity was a theocracy ruled by priest-kings from sacred citadels, as Tibet is ruled today from the Potala at Lhasa and from Shigatse.

With ancient Egypt and Babylonia, the Harappa Civilization in India takes its place as the third area where urban civilization was born in the Old World. Like the others, it was based on a common stock of peasant skills acquired in little corn-growing, cattle-breeding communities, such as had grown up during the fifth and fourth millennia B.C. in many regions between the Nile and the Indus. But the Harappa people, like those of Egypt and Sumer, worked out their own distinctive and arresting variant of an urban civilization.

The very qualities that enabled the Harappa Civilization to endure unchanged for a thousand years apparently were responsible for its quick collapse at the end. Its peaceful, delicately adjusted economy could not survive an invasion. The invaders probably were the Indo-European tribes (the originators of the languages which were to become Sanskrit and Iranian) who began to migrate eastward from the western rim

FIGURINES from Harappa are made of clay. Mostly representing women, they were either private deities or toys. No large statues have been found in either Mohenjo-Daro or Harappa.

of Asia soon after 2000 B.C. These horse-driving squires and cattle drovers trampled out the Harappa culture, and a Dark Age of comparative barbarism ensued. But the Harappa Civilization was not completely extinguished, and from the new mixture of peoples and ideas came the traditions which molded historic Hinduism.

7. Buddhism and Jainism

by Eugene F. Gorski

HINDUISM CHALLENGED

In India in the late fifth century BCE, a spiritual vacuum arouse out of a complex matrix of factors that challenged Hinduism and give rise to Buddhism and Jainism. The first factor was that of a spiritual malaise. By this time, the doctrines of *karma* and *samsara*, which had been controversial at the time of Yajnavalkya, were universally accepted by the people.[1] "Bad" karma meant that individuals would be reborn as slaves, animals, or plants. "Good" karma would ensure their rebirth as kings or gods. But this was not a fortunate occurrence: even gods would exhaust this beneficent karma, die, and be reborn in a less exalted state on Earth. As this teaching took hold, the mood of India changed, and many people became depressed with the fear of being doomed to one transient life after another. Not even good karma could save them. As they reflected on their community, they could see only pain and suffering. Wealth and material pleasure were darkened with the grim reality of old age and mortality. As this gloom became more and more intense people sought to find a way out.

People became increasingly unsatisfied with the old Vedic rituals that could not provide a solution to this problem. The very best these rituals could do was provide a rebirth in the domain of the gods, but this could be only a temporary release from the relentless and suffering-producing cycle of samsara. Some even rejected the spirituality of the *Upanishads,* which was not for everyone. It was a full-time task, demanding hours of effort each day, and it was incompatible with the duties of a householder. And at this time the revolution that produced bhakti devotion as the universally accessible means to salvation had not yet taken place. So, because of the prevailing malaise of doom and despair, many people in India were looking for a spiritual solution and longing for a *jina,* a spiritual conqueror or a Buddha, an enlightened one who had woken up to a different dimension of existence.

Social, Political, and Economic Change

In addition to the spiritual malaise of this time, there was a social crisis. The people of northern India were undergoing major political and economic changes. The Vedic system had been the spirituality that supported a highly mobile society, constantly engaged in migration. But the peoples of sixth and fifth centuries were settling down in increasingly larger communities that were focused on agricultural production. There was also political development. The small chiefdoms had been absorbed into the larger units of kingdoms. As a result, the *Kshatriya* kingly warrior class had become more prominent. The new kingdoms stimulated trade in the Ganges basin. This generated more wealth, which the kings could spend on luxury goods, on their armies, and on the new cities that were becoming centers of trade and industry.

This new urbanization was another blow for Vedic spirituality, which was not well suited to urban culture and civilization. The kings began to shrug off control of the priests, and the urban republics tended to ignore the Brahmin class altogether and put a limit on the traditional sacrifices. The lavish sacrifices had been designed to impress the gods and enhance the prestige of the patrons. By the fifth century, the eastern peoples realized that their trade and culture brought much more wealth and status than the Vedic sacrifice rites. Instead of conforming to the old traditional ways, the new cities encouraged personal initiative and innovation; individualism was replacing tribal, communal identity; the lower classes of the Vedic system were acquiring wealth and status that once would have been inconceivable.

These massive social changes brought about by urbanization were unsettling and left many people feeling disoriented and lost. The tensions were especially acute in the East, where urbanization was more advanced and where the next phase of the Indian Axial Age began. Here, life probably was experienced as particularly ephemeral, transient, plagued by disease and anomie, confirming the now well-established belief that life was *dukka,* suffering. The urban class was ambitious and powerful, but the gambling, theater, prostitution, and spirited tavern life of the towns seemed disarming to the people who still trusted in the older values.

Radical Dissent

Life was becoming more and more aggressive than before, in strong contrast to the older ideal of *ahimsa* that had become so crucial in north India. In the kingdoms there was infighting and civil strife. The economy was moved by greed and rugged competition. Life was experienced as even more violent and terrifying than when cattle rustling had been the backbone of the economy. The Vedic religion impressed people as increasingly out of touch with the violence of contemporary public life. People needed a different religious situation.

These ideas of radical dissent, along with the spiritual malaise and social, economic, and political crisis of the time, formed the complex matrix from which Buddhism and Jainism emerged during the Axial Age to vex the course of Hinduism. The founders of these religions, Siddhattha Gotama and Mahavira, provided alternative solutions to what had become the central problem of Indian life: how to find self-transcendence and salvation from the continual cycle of rebirths in the frightening and suffering-producing world. The Buddhists and Jains, of the warrior tribes and the *Kshatriya* caste, were more than ready to contest the Brahmins' claim to cultural control. They did not appreciate either the social or the religious implications of the Brahmins' teaching. Among the ranks of the Buddhists and Jains there were persons of brilliant mind for whom the costly sacrifices prescribed by the priests were not satisfactory. They and others like them had no interest in priestly sacrifices that did not immediately give them solace or fulfill their spiritual needs; they sought near-at-hand practical modes of release from their growing sense of the essential misery of existence. Like the authors of the *Upani-shads,* they considered the world flawed and a cause of suffering. So they rejected the religion controlled by the Brahmins as being ineffectual for souls inwardly pained. Their radicalism was in their rejection of the sacrificial system of the *Bramanas* as well as their refusal to give the Brahmins first place of prescriptive rights in their urgent search for ways to liberation from the plight of suffering and the cycle of rebirths.

BUDDHISM

Buddhism emerged from the complex matrix of radical dissent, spiritual malaise, and the social, economic, and political crisis of the Indian Axial Age. About its founder, the Buddha, historians are confident of a few key facts. He was born into the family of King Shuddhodana and Queen Maya about the year 566 BCE in a region of the Indian subcontinent that now lies in southern Nepal. This date has been questioned recently by a group of historians who place his birth in the fifth century BCE. Most scholars now think that the Buddha in fact lived around 490 to 410. He was a member of the Shakya tribe, his clan name being Gotama, his given name Siddhattha. It is common to refer to him as *Siddhattha Gotama* or, more commonly as *Shakyamuni,* "The Sage of the Shakya Tribe." He was one among the thousands of brave individuals who searched in the northeastern forests of India to end samsara, the transmigration of life, during the Axial Age. Like many others, Gotama had become convinced that conquering the suffering of samsaric existence was the highest aspiration of life. Nothing else was of equal importance. And like others, he willingly gave up everything to attain that goal.

He departed from his princely existence and began his search for salvation as a wandering mendicant. For six years following his departure from palace life, he made serious efforts to attain his spiritual goal. As he engaged in this quest, he came to the conclusion that the philosophy of the Brahmins was unacceptable and their claims unsubstantiated. He also denied the saving efficacy of the *Vedas* and the ritual obser-vances based on them. But he did take up the options available to him for practicing the ascetic and contemplative disciplines. Quickly he mastered the extreme ascetic method for reaching union with Brahman but found it did not bring him what he was looking for. After many years of frustrating searching, he decided to abandon the well-trodden spiritual paths passed on to him by his teachers and to devise his own path. Within a short time after this decision, he went to a nearby river, cleansed himself of the dust that had accumulated on his body for many months, and then ate a bowl of milk rice. According to his new, self-taught approach to the spiritual journey, he would have to care for his body because physical well-being was necessary to pursue liberation from samsara. The traditional harsh forms of self-mortification he had fol-lowed previously had to be abandoned. Shortly later, on the evening of the full moon in the month of Vesakha (which is between April and May) he sat beneath the *bodhi* tree near the village of Bodhgaya in the present Indian state of Bihar. Resting in the shade of that tree released an old memory of sitting under a rose-apple tree as a child during a clan agricultural festival. Gotama recalled that as his father was engaged in a ceremonial plowing action, he became restless and bored. And with nothing else to do, he began to pay close attention to his breath. In those moments, he experienced a heightened sense of awareness and a pervasive serenity that diminished his boredom and restlessness. Remembering that time of his childhood, Siddhattha thought that this gentle practice of awareness meditation might be useful for the spiritual practices he wanted to devise for himself.

This form of meditation was different from the practices of his teachers in that it emphasized the quality of *mindfulness*. While the goal of other meditations was to become absorbed in exceptional states of mind, *his* mindfulness meditation aimed at attaining a heightened awareness of the immediate present moment, so that one became attentive to what was occurring in the mind, the body, and the external environment and observing these processes without judgment. By putting aside goals and releasing preconceptions and judgments, the Buddha believed the mind would become more open to insight into the nature of the world and self. Gotama sat beneath the huge tree, practicing his meditation, and vowed not to leave the spot until he realized the liberating knowledge he had sought for so many years.

In his mindfulness he scrutinized his behavior, carefully noting the ebb and flow of his feelings and sensations as well as the fluctuations of his consciousness. He made himself aware of the constant stream of desires, irritations, and ideas that coursed thorough his mind in the space of a single hour. By this introspection, he was becoming acquainted with the working of his mind and body in order to exploit their capacities and use them to best advantage. Finally, at dawn, he was convinced that he had attained the knowledge that liberates and conquers samsara. At this moment Gotama earned the title, the *Buddha*, which means the "awakened one."

For forty-nine days, the Buddha enjoyed his liberation. He then decided to teach others the knowledge with which he had been enlightened. He found five former disciples and delivered to them a discourse that is sometimes called the "Buddha's First Discourse and Turning the Wheel of Dhamma." This formal talk consisted of a concise formulation of the insights that he had received under the bodhi tree. It contained what the Buddhist tradition calls the "Four Noble Truths," considered by many to be the essence of Buddhism. Most of the Buddha's subsequent teachings might be considered explanations or amplifications of these basic points. As the four truths are discussed here, other teachings in the Pali scriptures will be used to clarify them.

The First Noble Truth: Suffering

The first noble truth is that life is *dukka*—suffering—and that craving for things of the world is responsible for suffering. It was not only the traumas of old age, sickness, and death that made life so unsatisfactory. "Human existence was filled with countless frustrations, disappointments, and its nature was impermanent. Pain, grief and despair are *dukka*," he explained. "Being forced into proximity with what we hate is suffering; being separated from what we love is suffering; not getting what we want is suffering."[2] Suffering includes a whole range of human experiences from the usual events of getting sick, growing old and dying, to not getting what we want and getting what we do not want. Suffering is the fundamental quality of the whole of existence. The very makeup of human existence is entangled in suffering. The whole of human life—not only certain occasions—is suffering. In his mindfulness he also observed how one craving after another took hold of him, how he was ceaselessly yearning to become something else, go somewhere else, and get something he did not have.

We might ask, Why did the Buddha teach that suffering is comprehensive and constant and not simply episodic in human life? Mark W. Muesse suggests the reason the Buddha taught this "is because we do no fully appreciate the extent to which we suffer or feel the unsatisfactoriness of existence."[3] The First Noble Truth is not a statement of a self-evident fact of life; rather, for individuals it is a challenge to discover for themselves the depth and breadth of *dukka* by the means of introspection and observation. The Buddha himself hinted at much when he said, "'This Dhamma that I have attained is profound, hard to see and hard to understand, peaceful and sublime, unattainable by mere reasoning, subtle, to be experienced by the wise.'"[4] Muesse adds, "I would even go so far as to say that one cannot realize the nature and extent of *dukka* until the moment of complete awakening, as the Buddha himself did on the full moon of Vesakha. The true depth of suffering can only be seen from the perspective of the enlightened mind."[5] Recognizing that suffering is manifested not only in particular experiences, but in the whole of existence requires persistent and attentive awareness.

The Second Noble Truth: The Cause of Suffering

In the Second Noble Truth, the Buddha states that the root of suffering is desire, or craving. This aspect of the Buddha's teaching distinguishes it the most from other religious perspectives.

The cause of suffering is *tanha*, desire. Desires are problematic when they are self-centered and become intense craving: that is, when an object of desiring becomes a matter of necessity, as if our lives depended on it. Or when we already possess what we desire and believe that losing it would be devastating to our existence. And such craving can lead to the point where relationships to objects, people, values, beliefs, ideas, power, status, experience, and sensation have the nature of attachments or clinging. The problem is not with the objects of attachment themselves, but with the nature of a person's relationships to them, which can become addictions. Since everything in the world is of constant change, nothing can support a person's attachments;

all things to which we become attached are subject to change, and this causes suffering. To allay this suffering we seek something else to cling to, but the more we try to secure happiness through acquisition the more we suffer. Attachment can also include an aversion to an object or situation, causing a negative relationship that is just as difficult to relinquish as an attachment. Both Hinduism and Buddhism recognize attachments as mechanisms that lead to samsara and suffering. The Buddha's answer to the dual dangers of attachments and aversion is equanimity, the Middle Way between the two extremes.

Now that the effects of *tanha* and attachments have been discussed, we ask in turn about their antecedent causes. What makes us have desires that become attachments? The cause is ignorance: ignorance of the true nature of ourselves and the world. We develop strong desires and attachments when we are ignorant of the fact that the world and self are really impermanent; they are not things, they are only processes. In the mind of the Buddha, change and impermanence are constant, persistent. Even solid objects are in constant flux. The Buddha viewed the cosmos as a complex arrangement of processes rather than a set of things. It is not only that things change, but that change is the only thing there is. Unlike the Vedanta tradition of Hinduism, the Buddha held that the soul or true self of the human person is impermanent.

No-Self Anatta

On his spiritual journey, the Buddha eventually became convinced that the ultimate cause of his suffering and unfulfilled longing was delusion about himself. He failed to see that he was selfless. The human person as "me" or "I" forms a distorting lens through which the world takes on a false character. In that lens the universe is misinterpreted as structured around "me," and the world process is accordingly experienced as a stream of objects of my desires and aversions, hopes, and fears that give rise to grasping. This covetousness expresses itself in egotism, injustice, and cruelty, in a pervasive self-regarding anxiety in face of life's uncertainties, in the inevitability of final decay and death—all of which comprehensively constitute the "suffering of human existence," *dukka*. The salvation Siddhattha searched for was liberation from the suffering caused by the powerful illusion of "me" or "self." It involved the recognition of his having *no* self: his selflessness. Being liberated from the illusory and falsely evaluating "me" was for him to exchange the realm of ego-infected consciousness for the sublime freedom of *nirvana*.

What the Buddha came to perceive and teach his followers about selflessness is called *anatta* in Pali. However, the Sanskrit term, *anatman* ("no-self") makes it evident that the Buddha denies the reality of the *atman*, the Hindu concept of the permanent, immortal, substantial soul or true self. Most interpreters of Buddhism hold that *anatta* was meant to be a doctrine or concept or an ontological statement-theory about the nonexistence of the conscious subject. But it is perhaps more appropriate to hold that it was intended to refer to an *anti-concept* as well as an *axiological or value-oriented, realistic prescription for a certain kind of moral practice.* It is more a denial of what humans ordinarily believe themselves to be. Let us develop this position, first focusing on *anatta* as an anti-concept.

Anatta *as Anti-Concept and Axiological Prescription*

The Buddha held that the concept of the self can promote fruitless speculation and contribute to humankind's suffering. Instead of putting forth another view of self, the Buddha simply indicates that the concept of the self is an inept way of thinking about human beings. While it is permitted to refer to the self reflexively, as in talking about ourselves, the Buddha insisted that we should never consider that it refers to anything substantial or permanent. However, one should not think that the Buddha denies human existence or suggests that human life is unreal or an illusion. *Anatta* means essentially that human beings do not exist in the way they think they do, that is, as separate, substantial selves. To hold this is to hold to an illusion, an unsubstantiated belief in the same way a rainbow is an optical illusion, created by the convergence of various conditions.[6] To the Buddha, atman is an illusion supported by changing conditions. That is why no one is able to identify or pinpoint the soul or essential self. The Buddha taught that the problems of human beings arise when they ascribe reality to this illusion. Belief in a permanent, substantial self is the origin of suffering; it sets into motion a series of thoughts, words, and actions that bring on anguish and disappointment. The so-called self is not a thing; it is no-thing, nothing; it is insubstantial; it lacks permanence and immortality. The Buddha's denial of self states that no concept is able to express the reality of who we are. His intention is merely to attempt to disrupt human beings' old habits about who they are.

Instead of viewing individuals as immortal souls in perishable bodies, the Buddha saw the human person as a complex of interconnected and ever-in-flux energies or forces that he called the "Five Aggregates of Being." These are (1) matter, one's physical makeup; (2) sensation or feeling, the way one judges experiences as pleasant, unpleasant, or neutral (such judgments condition one's tendencies of attachment and aversion); (3) perception and apperception; (4) mental formations, the sources of desire, craving, and intention; mental formations are, in the Buddha's thinking, the sources of karma; therefore as long as there is craving, there will be rebirth; (5) consciousness, the process of awareness. There is nothing about these components that endures. All of them are in flux. Neither is there a permanent agent of subject that underlies these processes.

The Buddha's teaching, then, about *anatta* is an anti-concept. Furthermore, it is appropriate to understand it also as an axiological or value-oriented and practical ethical prescription about how one should direct his or her life in order to attain salvation. A person should live in a way that is selfless, that is, without being attached to the notion of "my self"—and this is truly a way of being that is "authentically myself." It is the distinctive and famous path to axial self-transcendence that Gotama personally chose to follow. It led to the overturning of the delusion of self and discovering nirvana, the Place of Peace, of inner freedom and the extinction of suffering.

The Third Noble Truth: The Cessation of Suffering

The Buddha's good news for humanity can be found in the Third and Fourth Noble Truths. The Third Noble Truth is direct and clear: "Now this, bhikkus, is the noble truth of the cessation of suffering: it is the remainderless fading away and cessation of the same craving, the giving up and relinquishing of it, freedom from it, non-reliance on it."[7] One does not have to suffer. If *tanha*, thirst or craving, is the cause of suffering, then clearly the solution is to cease from craving, and when persons end craving, attachments dissolve, and they are liberated from the cycle of suffering and rebirth. The reason to end craving is *nibbana*, in Pali, or *nirvana* in Sanskrit. *Nirvana* means the eradication of desire, the cessation of thirst, and the destruction of the illusion that one is a separate, substantial self. It is the end of suffering, the point where a person ceases craving for reality to be other than that what it is, radically accepting the way the world and the self truly are. The *method* for quenching thirst is set forth in the Fourth Noble Truth. But before we focus about the way to the goal, let us discuss the goal itself.

Nirvana is experienced at death, but a form of it can be realized in one's historical lifetime. One who achieves this is called an *arahant:* he or she has fully realized the truth of the Buddha's vision and is free from craving, aversion, and ignorance. *Arahants* continue to experience physical pain and other forms of old karma. However, even with physical pain, one does not suffer. Suffering is distinguished from pain; pain is a bodily sensation, while suffering pertains to the mental anguish that comes from resisting pain or merely resisting the way things are. The *arahant* does not generate new karmas but still must experience effects of the old ones. When at death nirvana is experienced, all karmic forces that sustain existence are dissipated, and the *arahant* is released from rebirth. The image that is frequently associated with final nirvana is a candle, the flame of which has gone out because the fuel and the oxygen have been exhausted. In a parallel fashion, without karma to perpetuate rebirth, the flame of the candle belonging to the *arahant* "goes out."

The Buddha's disciples, of course, were strongly interested in what occurs at final nirvana. One of the central issues of the Axial Age, as we have seen, was the matter of an individual's destiny after death. So the disciples were curious: whether an *arahant* exists after death or does not exist after death; or both exists and does not exist after death; or neither exists nor does not exist after death. But the Buddha refused to respond because knowing the answer was not essential to seeing nirvana, and dwelling on such questions was an obstacle to the goal. The Buddha was generally reticent about issues that were not essential to the termination of suffering.

It should be noted that, for the Buddha, freedom from suffering was not received as a grace or gift from God. Like the path of knowledge in Hinduism, the Buddha's Middle

Way required great effort and discipline because human beings are the cause of their own suffering and only they themselves can find freedom from it. The Buddha only shows the way to that freedom.

The Fourth Noble Truth: The Eightfold Path to Enlightenment

In this final truth, the Buddha shows the way to enlightenment with an outline of what the discipline involves. "Now this, bhikkus, is the noble truth of the way leading to the cessation of suffering: It is this Noble Eightfold Path that is right understanding, right intention, right speech, right action, right livelihood, right mindfulness and right concentration."[8] The Noble Eightfold Path the Buddha followed and taught was in the middle between simply giving in to the sensual, vulgar desires of an ordinary foolish person and depriving oneself of even the very necessities of existence. Traditionally, the eight components of the plan of action have been divined into three sections: *conduct,* or developing ethical behavior; *concentration,* or developing the mind by meditation; and *study,* or cultivating the wisdom that enabled persons to see themselves and all things as they truly are. For this reason the Noble Path is sometimes called the "Triple Practice." By following his middle path and thus avoiding the two extremes, Gotama achieved, at Bodhgaya in Bihar, the enlightenment for which he passionately searched.

Right Understanding

The Buddha recognized that to begin engaging in the Eightfold Path requires some initial understanding of his teaching about the Middle Way and the Four Noble Truths, and that this understanding is achieved by study, discussion, and reflection. The result of such study and reflection is, however, only a glimmer of the truth that the practitioner sees that prompts him or her to take the path at the outset.

Right Intention

The interior motive bridges right understanding and the next division of the triple practice, developing moral conduct. Right intention involves the determination to practice specific virtues that neutralize the conditioned tendencies of individuals toward greed, hatred, and harming. The virtues that exert the counteracting effect are nonattachment, goodwill, and harmlessness.

Right Speech-Action-Livelihood

Developing moral conduct, the second part of the triple practice, is the chief part of the Buddha's path. This moral behavior is not commanded either by a god or by the Buddha. It is rooted, the Buddha believed, in the very nature of human beings. He also held that karma is generated only by intentional acts; the source of karma is the aggregate of mental formations, the idea of desire and intention. An appropriate way to discuss the moral dimension of the Buddha's teaching is to start with what he called the "Five Precepts":

1. "I will refrain from harming sentient beings."
2. "I will refrain from taking what is not offered"; that is, one promises not to steal or to covet.
3. "I will refrain from sexual misconduct."
4. "I will refrain from false speech"; not only lying and slandering, but also gossiping, cursing, loud talk, idle chatter.
5. "I will refrain from stupefying drink"; intoxicants.[9]

Right Mindfulness-Concentration

Virtuous moral behavior is central to the holy life, but the Buddha considered it equally important to discipline the mind. As self-absorbed habits hinder the basic compassion of the human heart, so misled habits of the thinking mind obstruct the ability to understand the world and the self as they truly are. For the Buddha, the mind meant the complex of thoughts, sensations, feeling, and consciousness that in each moment arise and fall away. The mind has great power and potential; however, in its unenlightened condition it is out of control, unruly and undisciplined. And to bring it under control requires skill, persistent training, and patience.

Right concentration involves the practice of meditation to strengthen the virtues of attentiveness and nonattachment. The Buddha intended the practice of meditation to heighten consciousness of the world and self by being attentive to the events of ordinary life in the present moment. The fundamental meditative practice, based on the Buddha's own experiences, involved attending to the breath and observing without judgment the coming and going of thoughts, sensations, feeling, and perceptions. As these phenomena come to awareness, the subject notes them and allows them to fall away without dwelling on them. Simply by being observant of the mind, the body, and the surrounding world, the Buddha held it was possible to gain an insight into the true essence of the world and the self, and on the basis of such insight to act and think accordingly. He believed this meditative practice would disclose the illusionary nature of self and the origin of suffering in the mind's tendency to thirst for new pleasures and to avoid unpleasant experiences. He also held that meditation could hold back the mind's inclination to make spontaneous judgments and to become absorbed in thoughts about the future and the past, all of which were considered to be unwholesome habits.

In the development of mindfulness and the practice of contemplation, the Buddha also fostered the skillful states of a lucid, conscious mind, completely alert, filled with compassion and loving welfare for all beings.[10] By performing these mental exercises at sufficient depth, they could, he was convinced, transform the restless and destructive tendencies of his conscious and unconscious mind. At each stage of his journey into the depths of his mind, he intentionally evoked the emotion of love and directed it to the four corners of the Earth without omitting a single plant, animal, friend, or foe from its embrace. This outpouring of loving kindness was a fourfold program. First, he developed an attitude of friendship for everything and for everybody. Next, he culti-vated an empathy with their pain and suffering. In the third stage of his mindfulness, he evoked a "sympathetic joy" that rejoiced in the happiness of others, without envy or a sense of personal diminishment. Finally, he aspired to an attitude of complete equanimity toward others, feeling neither attraction nor antipathy.

This expression of universal love was a difficult challenge because it involved Got-ama's turning away completely from the egotism that always is concerned with how other people and things might benefit or detract from the self. He was learning to surrender his entire being to others, and thus to transcend the ego in compassion and loving kindness for all creatures.[11]

Enlightenment

In the Buddhist tradition there are two levels of understanding. The first is attained by mere reasoning. The second form is the understanding that occurs in enlightenment; it is the content of enlightened experience. Gotama's great experience of enlighten-ment was the first most significant event in the history of Buddhism. His followers who follow his Eightfold Path aspire to achieve that same enlightened experience. When they arrive at this goal, then in light of the eternal reality of being itself—the transcen-dent stream of Universal Being—they see themselves and the world around them, as he himself saw, as passing, unsubstantial expressions of the Absolute. This is seeing reality as it is, unfettered by expectation, belief, or defilement of any kind. In this form of comprehension, one knows for certain the authenticity of the Four Noble Truths without reliance on authorities other than one's own experience. To comprehend the Buddha's teaching at this level means to live one's life in accord with the truth. One no longer seeks for or aspires to nirvana. Nirvana has been seen.

In written accounts of the Buddha's enlightenment, he is described as rapt in ecstatic joy, imbued with a compassionate love of all sentient beings, "as a mother toward the only child," and endowed with the equanimity of a perfectly liberated person. In monastic commentaries, this state of even-mindedness is described as the opposite of three kinds of experience: the pleasure that comes with attachment, the displeasure due to aversion, and an ignorant kind of indifference. What the Buddha experienced was nirvana: It transformed his life.

Nirvana

What was nirvana? It was the extinguishing of the fires of greed, hatred, and delusion, the elimination of the craving, hatred, and ignorance that subjugate humanity. And even though the Buddha was still subject to physical ailments and other vicissitudes, nothing could cause him serious mental pain or diminish his inner peace of complete selflessness. The Buddha would continue to suffer; he would grow old and sick like everybody else; but by following his Noble Eightfold Path, he had found the inner haven that enables a person to live with suffering, take possession of it, affirm it, and experience in its midst a profound serenity.

The Buddha was convinced that nirvana was a transcendent state because it lay beyond the capacities of those who had not achieved the inner awakening of enlightenment. And while no words could adequately describe it, in mundane terms it could be called "Nothing" since it corresponded to no recognizable reality. But those who had been able to find this sacred peace realized that they lived a limitlessly richer life.[12] Later monotheists would speak about God in similar terms, claiming that God was "nothing" because "he" was not another being; and that it was more precise to state that he did not exist because human notions of existence were too limited to apply to the divine reality.[13] They would also state that a selfless, compassionate life would bring people into God's presence.

But, like other Indian sages and mystics, the Buddha found the idea of a personalized deity too limiting. He always denied the existence of a supreme being because such a deity would become another block to enlightenment. The Buddhist Pali texts never mention Brahman. Gotama's rejection of God was a calm and measured posture. He simply put the notion serenely out of his mind.

When Gotama made an effort to give his disciples a hint of what nirvana was like, he used both negative and positive terms. Nirvana was the "extinction of greed, hatred and delusion"; it was "taintless," "unweakening," "undisintegrating," "inviolable," "non-distress," "unhostility," and "deathless." Nirvana was "the Truth," "the Subtle," "the Other Shore," "Peace," "the Everlasting," "the Supreme Goal," "Purity, Freedom, Independence, the Island, the Shelter, the Harbor, the Refuge, the Beyond."[14] It was the supreme goal of humans and gods, an incomprehensible serenity, an utterly safe refuge. Many of these images are suggestive of words later used by monotheists to describe their experiences of the ineffable God.

The Buddha as Teacher

After the important event of his enlightenment, for nearly a half-century the Buddha traveled the Gangetic basin teaching his doctrine and building a community of followers. After his initial enlightenment at Bodhgaya, the second most significant occurrence in the history of Buddhism is Gotama's first sermon, which was given at Sarnath. In this presentation to his first five followers, he began to expound the Middle Path and the Four Noble Truths as the kernel of his awakening experience. The principle conception of his teaching was the doctrine of *anatta*, "No Self," and the invitation to his listeners to a way of life that leads to the Axial ideals of self-transcendence and salvation from the suffering and dissatisfaction that is part and parcel of human existence.

At the age of eighty, the Buddha peacefully died and passed into final nirvana. After his death, the Sangha or Buddhist community continued his teaching, and with grand success. They gathered together to consider how to preserve the Buddha's teaching. Early Buddhist councils led to the creation of authoritative texts and to the discussion of important doctrinal issues. This ultimately divided the community into several sects. Of the eighteen different varieties of Buddhist schools, only the Theravada school remains, making it the oldest extant Buddhist tradition. It probably represents the form closest to the way Buddhism was practiced around the time of the Buddha.

Around the first century CE the Mahayana form of Buddhism began to take shape in northwestern India; it added a substantially different dimension and new views about the Buddha and his role in making salvation accessible to humanity. New narratives were created that ascribed to the Buddha divine, godlike status. Mahayana developed the idea of the *bodhisattva,* an enlightened being who remained in the samsaric circle or in the heavenly domain in order to help others attain enlightenment and salvation. Mahayana was carried to China, Korea, and Japan. It eventually became the most popular form of Buddhism but has also fragmented over time into new schools. Out of the Mahayana emerged the third major form of Buddhism, the Vajrayana, practiced for centuries in Tibet and Mongolia.

Gotama's doctrine of "No Self" is at the heart of both the Theravada and the Mahayana schools of Buddhism. In Theravada there is a psychological realization of *anatta* which is the loss of "conceit of I am." This constitutes the attainment of the state of enlightenment, the state of be an *arahant.* In Mahayana the same concept of liberation from self applies, but here the aim is not to become an *arahant* but a *bodhisattva,* an enlightened person whose openness to the Transcendent is expressed in unlimited compassion for all sentient beings. For to live as a "self' is to seek happiness for oneself. But transcending the ego, becoming a manifestation of the universal Buddha nature, is to seek the happiness of all.

Today there are a total of approximately 329 million Buddhists in many areas of the world, including Sri Lanka, Burma, Thailand, Cambodia, Laos, China, Korea, Japan, Tibet, Mongolia, Europe, and the United States. One hundred twenty-four million Buddhists are of the Theravada branch; 20 million are of the Vajrayana; 185 million are of the Mahayana.[15]

JAINISM

Almost all estimates indicate that there are 350 million Buddhists in the world today and fewer than 5 million Jains, almost all of them in India, mostly in Mumbai and other large urban centers.[16] While they account for less than 5 percent of the Indian population, their influence on the religious, social, political, and economic life of India has been, and is, quite out of proportion to their numbers. In Europe, largely in the United Kingdom, there are presently estimated to be 25,000 Jains. Some estimates suggest a similar number may be found in North America. There is a vast disparity in the number of Buddhists and Jains, but the two traditions share similar histories, beliefs, and practices. Both reject the authority of the *Vedas,* and both accept rebirth and karma and aspire to release from samsara.

Modern history specifies the origins of Jainism in the same cultural environment that gave rise to Hinduism and Buddhism. Jainism grew from the struggle for enlightenment of its main figure, Vardhamana Jnatrputra (c. 497–425 BCE), called the *Jina* ("Conqueror") or *Mahavira* ("Great Hero"). Sometimes he is referred to by outsiders as the founder of Jainism, but Jains themselves see their religion as a tradition going back dozens of generations before Mahavira. Devout adherents of Jainism insist that their religious tradition is eternal, based on truths that have no beginning in time. At certain moments in the universal life cycle, these truths have been forgotten and lost, but then rediscovered and reintroduced to humanity. When an Axial Age sage named Vardhamana Mahavira began to teach the doctrines of Jainism, he was only communicating a religion that had been taught many times before by others. Each of these former teachers was a *Tirkanthara,* a word that means "bridge builder" ("those who find a ford over the river of suffering"). The *Tirthankaras* were exceptional individuals who showed the way to salvation by their words and example. In the last turn of the universal cycle, there have been twenty-four *Tirthankaras.* The most recent was Vardhamana, portrayed mythically as being of supernatural birth and the twenty-third and last in a long line of *Tirthankaras.* He is not considered to be the founder of Jainism, only its reformer and reviver. It should be noted that there is no historical evidence to support the existence of the first twenty-two *Tirthankaras.*

Modern scholarship locates the origins of Jainism in the person of Vardhamana Mahavira of the Axial Age, who according to tradition was born into the *Kshatriya* in 599 BCE. Both Buddhist and Jain texts indicate that the Buddha and Mahavira were contemporaries living in the same region of northeastern India, in Bihar state. The texts indicate that they knew of each other but never actually met. However, if the Buddha in fact lived around 490 to 410, as most scholars now think, then the traditional dates of Mahavira would be inaccurate.

After the death of his parents, at the age of thirty Mahavira gave up his princely life and became a wondering monk in search of liberation from death and rebirth, following a harsh lifestyle as a *samana,* a renouncer of wealth and life in society. For the next twelve years, he practiced intense asceticism, including fasting for long periods of time, mortification of the flesh, meditation, and the practice of silence. He scrupulously avoided harming other living beings, including animals and plants. By dedication to these austere practices he merited a title given to him by his admirers, the *Mahavira,* meaning the "Great Hero." At the age of forty-two, after twelve years of uncompromising dedication to self-discipline, he believed he was simply the latest in a long line of *jinas* who achieved complete victory over his body and the desires that bound him to the world of matter and sin; he had crossed the river of *dukka* (suffering) to find access to liberation and enlightenment. In his enlightened state he attained a transcendent knowledge that gave him a unique perspective of the world. He was able to perceive all levels of reality simultaneously, in every dimension of time and space, as though he were a god. In fact, for Mahavira, God was simply a creature who had accomplished supreme knowledge by perceiving and respecting the single divine transcendent soul that existed in every single creature. This state of mind could not be described, because it entirely transcended ordinary consciousness. It was a state of absolute friendliness with all creatures, however lowly. He had crossed the river of *dukka* to find access to liberation and enlightenment.

For the next thirty years he roamed around the Ganges region teaching others his principles and practices for achieving liberation from samsara, for which he used both the terms *moksha* and *nirvana*. Like the Buddha, he drew men and women and children from all social strata. His followers were called "Jainas," or now, according to a more modern pronunciation, "Jains," because they were disciples of the *jina*. Some legends indicate that at one point Mahavira had gathered more than 400,000 disciples. He organized his followers into an order of monks, nuns, and laypersons. To attain liberation, one had to become a monk because of the austere discipline required to achieve it. Laypersons expected to strive for *moksha* in a future life-time when circumstances were more favorable for such a pursuit. His teaching became the basis of the *Agam Sutras,* one of the most important scriptures in Jainism. According to tradition, Mahavira died and attained final nirvana at the age of seventy-two, after thirty years of successful teaching and organizing. He is now, according to all Jain sects, at the top of the universe, where all perfect ones go, enjoying complete self-transcendent bliss in a state no longer subject to rebirth. After his death, the Jains would develop an elaborate prehistory, claiming that in previous eras there had been twenty-four of these ford makers who had discovered the bridge to salvation.

Mahavira taught his followers in conformity with this vision. Like Buddhists and Hindus, he appropriated many of the basic assumptions and beliefs circulating in the Ganges basin in the early Indian Axial Age, but he reinterpreted them to fit his partic-ular enlightened view of the world. We now explore how Mahavira understood these concepts, including his idea of time, the structure of the world, the nature of the soul, karma, and the path to salvation.

Time

Mahavira was of the belief that the world was never created and will never be destroyed. Cosmic time, therefore, is infinite, but it does conform to a cyclical pattern. Each cycle has two half-segments, a period of decline and a period of ascendancy. Each segment is further divided into six unequal parts. The half-cycles are incalculably long. One half-cycle is a time of decline. During the first part of this period, people are very tall and live lives that are very long. They are exceed-ingly happy, wise, and virtuous, with no need of religion or ethics. All of their needs are provided by wish-granting trees. As the cycle proceeds, conditions become progressively worse. The world and life are gradually tainted with corruption and deterioration; ethics and religion are then introduced; writing is invented, since peoples' memories begin to fail. During these times the *Tirthankaras* appear. When the lowest point of the cycle of decline is reached, people will be only about three feet tall and live twenty years. Like animals, they will live in caves and pursue all sorts of immoral activity.

But as time reaches its lowest point, it begins to ascend, and the world becomes increasingly better. People then start to live longer, healthier lives, to conduct themselves in more compassionate ways, and to experience greater happiness. When this cycle reaches its apex, time begins again its downward motion. The pattern is repeated over and over again, forever. According to Jain belief, we are presently in the fifth stage of the cycle of descent, a period when things are bad and will become even worse. The current era began a little over 2,500 years ago and will continue for a total of 21,000 years. When this period ends, Jainism will be lost and will be reintroduced by the next *Tirthankaras* after the half-cycle of ascent commences again.

Structure of the World

According to the teaching of Mahavira, the physical world is made up of three levels: the underworld; the surface of the world, or the middle realm; and the heavens. In the underworld are a series of seven or eight hell realms, and each of these is colder than the next. The hell realms are for the punishment of the wicked as a means of purifying negative karma. The Jain hells are more like a purgatory than a location of ultimate condemnation. When souls have suffered sufficiently for their sins, they may be reborn in another realm. The middle level is the place of life; it is known by the name of *Jambudvipa,* or the island of the rose-apple tree. It is a name used also by Buddhists and Hindus. The upper level of the world is the realm of the gods. It has sixteen heavens and fourteen celestial abodes. And then, above the ceiling of the universe is a crescent-shaped structure where the *Tirthankaras* and the completely liberated souls dwell. This is the ultimate goal and destination of those who attain *moksha.*

Nature of the Soul

Mahavira, like the sages who wrote the *Upanishads,* believed that the soul was real, not illusionary as the Buddha thought. Mahavira considered the soul to be a living, luminous, and intelligent entity within the material body; it was unchanging in essence, but its characteristics were subject to change. It was also his conviction that there were an infinite number of souls, each an actual, separate individual. Therefore, Mahavira would not have accepted the Vedantic idea that soul and ultimate reality are consubstantial, since that view denies individuality. Furthermore, all souls are of equal value; one is no better than another. Souls may be embodied in gods and in humans, as well as in animals and plants, and even, according to some, stones, minerals, bodies of water, fire, and the winds. By the karmas of former lives they had been brought to their present existence. Therefore, all beings share the same nature and must be treated with equal respect and care that persons would want to receive themselves.[17]

Karma

In its pure state, the soul enjoys perception, knowledge, happiness, power, all of which are perfect. However, at the present time, all souls, with the exception of the completely liberated ones, are defiled because they are embodied and tainted with karma. The Jain understanding of karma is of a fine, material substance that clings to and stains the soul. Karmas are invisible particles, floating throughout the world. When a soul commits a karmic act, it attracts these fine articles, which adhere to the soul and weigh it down. These karmas accumulate and, in due course, color the soul. We cannot see a soul because of our defiled state; but if we could, we could with ease detect a soul's moral and spiritual quality. The souls that are worse are stained black, and the purest are white. And in between, from bad to good, the soul may be blue, gray, red, lotus-pink, or yellow. Like in Buddhism and Hinduism, karma determines persons' future births and keeps them bound to the material, samsaric world.

Since they are imprisoned in matter, souls do not enjoy omniscience as they do in their pure state. Karmic stains cause our perceptions to be distorted and our knowledge of the world limited. These distortions urge the soul to seek pleasure in material possessions and fleeting enjoyments, which further lead to self-absorbed thoughts and anger, hatred, greed, and other states of the mind. These, in turn, bring about the further accumulation of karma. Consequently, the cycle is a vicious one.

The limitations that result from karmic defilement also mean that we are unable to understand the great richness and complexity of reality. The Jains propose that reality is many sided; this means that the world is made up of an infinite number of material and spiritual substances, each with an infinite number of qualities and manifestations. Since the universe is complex and our knowledge is limited, all claims of truth must be tentative. The Jains refer to the principle as "non-absolutism," which means making no categorical or unconditional statements.

Path to Liberation

In Mahavira's teaching, liberation meant the release of one's true self from the constraints of body and thus the achievement of salvation, inner control, and transcendent peace of mind, enlightenment, all being the great values of the Axial Age. The path to liberation is simple. At first, preventing the flow of new karma and then, second, eliminating the old karmas that have already accumulated and weigh the soul down.

To attain the first goal, Mahavira urged his followers to fulfill five Great Vows. The first and foremost of these vows is *ahimsa*, to avoid harming any living beings. The Jains take this rule further than the Buddhists, who drew the line at sentient life, not at life itself. The Jains are convinced that even unintentionally injuring another creature causes negative karma. In line with these beliefs, Jains are vegetarians and refuse to use leather or other animal products. Most avoid agriculture, because the plow might inadvertently damage a worm, and other kinds of occupations that might cause harm to other forms of life. Some, especially the monks, use a cloth to cover a glass when they drink so as to strain out insects that may have fallen into the liquid; and they sweep the pathways before them to avoid stepping on bugs. *Ahimsa*, however, means more than avoiding physical injury to life. It also involves what the Jains call *ahimsa* of the mind and *ahimsa* of speech. The former is the practice of right thought. Evil thoughts are held to generate negative karma. The latter is speaking in a nonhurtful way, using kind, compassionate language.

Achieving salvation is centered on not harming one's fellow creatures. Until persons had acquired this empathetic view of the world, they could not attain salvation. Consequently, nonviolence was a strict religious duty. All other ethical and religious practices were useless without *ahimsa*, and this could not be achieved until the Jain had acquired a state of empathy, an attitude of positive benevolence, with every single creature. All living creatures should be of support and assistance to one another. They should relate to every single human being, animal, plant, insect, or pebble with friendship, goodwill, patience, and gentleness.

The other four vows are connected to *ahimsa* and the cessation of karmic accumulation. They are always to speak the truth; not to steal or take what is not given; chastity, which is understood as celibacy for the monks, and faithfulness in marriage for the laypeople; and last, nonattachment to people and material things.

Preventing new karmas from staining the soul is the first step to liberation; purification of the stains of old karmas is the next. Good deeds and asceticism are the principle means of eliminating the accumulation of karmas. Those who desired to attain perfect enlightenment must, like Mahavira, practice fasting, engage in certain types of meditation, penance, yoga, study, and recitation of the scriptures. These acts purge the soul of its karmic deposit. They lead to transcendence over one's own physical state and to a trance state marked by complete disassociation from the outer world. This trance state is believed to be like the one Mahavira entered into in the thirteenth year of his seeking and assured him of his final liberation.

The ultimate ascetic observance, assumed by many throughout history, is fasting to death. The fast is the symbol and producer of absolute renunciation. Before this point, the ascetic has abstained from all but food and water. And then in a profound meditative state, food and water are given up, ending for good all attachments to samsara. This fast is not considered an act of violence, but a gesture of compassion, because there is no anger or pain associated with it.

The purging of all karmas restores the soul to its pure, undefiled state. It then has perfect knowledge, perfect perception and power. It is no longer weighed down by the burden of its karma, so it ascends to the very ceiling of the universe, where it enjoys the bliss of nirvana in the company of other liberated beings.

Similar to the Buddha and the Upanishadic sages, Mahavira taught a path of self-salvation. Since each individual soul is responsible for its own karmas, only the individual person is able to reverse the karmic accumulations. The purpose of the monastic community was to provide a supportive context for the pursuit of nirvana. Because the Jain search for nirvana required a more austere asceticism than the Buddha's Middle Way, taking on the life of a monk or nun was more vital to the realization of nirvana in Jainism than in Buddhism. The monks were also responsible for safeguarding the Mahavira's teaching, first in oral tradition and then in writing.

Although there are in Jainism differences of doctrine and practice, they should not be overemphasized. According to the contemporary Jains scholar, Nathmal Tatia, all Jains agree on the central message of Jainism, which is nonviolence, non-absolutism, and nonattachment.[18] These basic observances are the elements in the Jain quest for personal liberation from samsara and the communitarian goal of peace throughout the world.

Conclusion
With this we conclude our study of Jainism and the Indian Axial Age.

NOTES
1   Thomas J. Hopkins, *The Hindu Religious Tradition* (Encino, CA, and Belmont, CA: Dickenson, 1971), 50–51.

2   *Vinaya: Mahavagga* 16. This text is part of the *Vinaya Pitaka*, the *Book of Monastic Discipline*, which codifies the rule of the Buddhist order. Cited in Karen Armstrong, *The Great Transformation: The Beginning of Our Religious Traditions* (New York/Toronto: Knopf, 2006), 278.

3   Mark W. Muesse, *Religions of the Axial Age: An Approach to the World's Religions* (Chantilly, VA: Teaching Company, 2007), part 1, 175.

4   Ibid.

5   Ibid.

6   Ibid., part 2, 16.

7   Cited in Ibid., part 2, 23.

8   Ibid., 26.

9   Ibid., 28–29.

10 *Majjhima Nikaya* (MN) 38. Cited in Armstrong, *The Great Transformation*, 278. The Pali scriptures include four collections of the Buddha's sermons (*Majjhima Nikaya, Digha Nikaya, Anguttara Nikaya,* and *Samyutta Nikaya*) and an anthology of minor works, which include *Udana,* a collection of the Buddha's maxims, and the *Jataka,* stories about the past lives of the Buddha and his companions.

11 Hermann Oldenberg, *Buddha: His Life, His Doctrine, His Order* (London and Edinburgh: Williams & Norgate, 1882), 299–302.

12 Muesse, *Religions of the Axial Age,* part I, 97–98.

13 Karen Armstrong, *A History of God: The 4000-Year Quest of Judaism, Christianity and Islam* (New York: Knopf, 1993).

14 *Sutta-Nipata* 43:1–43; cited in Armstrong, *Great Transformation,* 282. The *Sutta-Nipata* is an anthology of early Buddhist poetry.

15 Major Religions of the World Ranked by Number of Adherents. Available at: http://www.adherents.com/adh_branches.html.

16 Ibid.

17 Muesse, *Religions of the Axial Age,* part 2, 59–62.

18 *That Which Is: Tattvartha Sutra,* trans. Nathmal Tatia (San Francisco: HarperCollins, 1994).

Analysis Questions

1. What are the main characteristics of the early Indus civilization?
2. Discuss the concepts of Brahman, karma, and nirvana. Are there similar concepts in the other religions?

CHAPTER 3

China's Classical Age, to Third Century B.C.

Introduction

Knowledge of ancient China has been revolutionized by ongoing archaeological discoveries. The major site of the Shang Dynasty (c. 2200 B.C.-1046 B.C.) was found at Anyang in the Yellow River Valley (in modern-day Henan Province). Exactly when a kingdom first arose in China remains uncertain, but by 1750 B.C., Shang rulers had asserted control over much of the Yellow River Valley. The Shang developed a form of script, which has been found inscribed on thousands of pieces of bone and tortoise shell used for divination (oracle bones).

The Shang Dynasty was replaced in 1046 B.C. by the Zhou Dynasty. This lasted effectively until 771 B.C. and in attenuated form until 256 B.C. During the Spring and Autumn period (771–453 B.C.), there was still an overall cultural community, but China was divided up into de facto independent states in competition with each other. The Zhou kings remained theoretical overlords, but actual power was divided among hegemons tied to the Zhou by lineage but, in fact, independent. Smaller states were often swallowed up by larger, more powerful states, which became increasingly centralized. During this period of political flux and frequent warfare, Chinese philosophy originated. The followers of Confucius (551–479 B.C.) specialized in advice on the traditional norms and rituals (*li*) based on the moral concept of humanity (*ren*). Mencius (379–304 B.C.) was the most famous Confucian scholar. He embraced the idea of the "Mandate of Heaven" and talked about the innate goodness of human nature. Shang Yang (~338 B.C.), a chief minister of the state of Qin, introduced a new realistic way of thinking, emphasizing the written laws of the ruler. On the other hand, Laozi and Zhuangzi (~286 B.C.) proposed a return to primitive simplicity, withdrawal from the world, and spontaneity (*wuwei*).

8. The *Analects*, Excerpts

by Confucius (c. 500 A.D.); trans. James Legge

Themes in Confucian Teaching
- *Jen (Ren)—Humaneness*
- *Chun-tzu (Junzi)—the Superior Man, or Gentleman, or Scholar*
- *Li—Rites*
- *Yüeh (Yue)—Music*
- Learning and Teaching
- Government
- Rectifying The Names

JEN (HUMANENESS)[1]

XII.22: Fan-ch'ih asked about jen. The Master said, "It is to love all men." He asked about knowledge. "It is to know all men." Fan ch'ih did not immediately understand these answers. The Master said, "Employ the upright and put aside all the crooked; in this way, the crooked can be made to be upright."

VII.29: The Master said, "Is humaneness a thing remote? I wish to be humane, and behold! humaneness is at hand."

VI.28: Tzu-kung said, "Suppose I put the case of a man who extensively confers benefits on the people, and is able to assist everyone, what would you say about him? Might he be called perfectly humane?" The Master said, "Why speak only of humaneness in connection with him? Must he not have the qualities of a sage? ... Now the man of perfect humaneness, wishing to be established himself, seeks also to establish others; wishing to be enlarged himself, he seeks also to enlarge others. To be able to judge of others by what is nearby in ourselves, that is what we might call the art of humaneness."

XV.23: Tzu-kung asked, saying, "Is there one world which may serve as a rule of practice for all one's life?" The Master said, "Is not reciprocity such a word? What you do not want done to yourself, do not do to others."

XIV.36: Someone said, "What do you say concerning the principle that injury should be recompensed with kindness?" The Master said, "With what then will you recompense kindness? Recompense injury with justice, and recompense kindness with kindness."

Confucius, *The Analects*, trans. James Legge, 1893.

VII.15: The Master said, "With coarse rice to eat, with water to drink, and my bended arm for a pillow; I still have joy in the midst of these things. Riches and honors acquired by inhumanity are to me as a floating cloud."

IV.25: The Master said, "Virtue is not left to stand alone. He who practices it will have neighbors."

XV.8: The Master said, "The determined scholar and the man of virtue will not seek to live at the expense of humanity. They will even sacrifice their lives to preserve their humanity."

VII.6: The Master said, "Let the will be set on the path of duty. Let every attainment in what is good be firmly grasped. Let perfect virtue be accorded with. Let relaxation and enjoyment be found in the polite arts."

The Superior Man (*chün-tzu*)[2]

XX.3: The Master said, "Without recognizing the ordinances of Heaven, it is impossible to be a superior man (*chün tzu*)."

XV.17: The Master said, "The superior man in everything considers righteousness to be essential. He performs it according to the rules of propriety (*li*). He brings it forth in humility. He completes it with sincerity. This is indeed a superior man."

XV.31: The Master said, "The object of the superior man is truth, not food. ... The superior man is anxious lest he should not get truth; he is not anxious lest poverty should come upon him."

IV.16: The Master said, "The mind of the superior man is conversant with virtue; the mind of the base man is conversant with gain."

IV.5: The Master said, "Riches and honors are what men desire. If they cannot be obtained in the proper way, they should not be held. Poverty and baseness are what men dislike. If they cannot be avoided in the proper way, they should not be avoided. ... The superior man does not, even for the space of a single meal, act contrary to virtue. In moments of haste, he cleaves to it. In seasons of danger, he cleaves to it."

XV.20: The Master said, "What the superior man seeks, is in himself. What the mean man seeks, is in others."

XII.4: Ssu-ma Niu asked about the superior man. The Master said, "The superior man has neither anxiety nor fear." "Being without anxiety or fear!" said Ssu-ma, "does this constitute what we call the superior man?" The Master said, "When internal examination discovers nothing wrong, what is there to be anxious about, what is there to fear?"

XIV.24: The Master said, "The progress of the superior man is upwards; the progress of the mean man is downwards."

XVI.8: Confucius said, "There are three things of which the superior man stand in awe. He stands in awe of the ordinances of Heaven. He stands in awe of great men. He stands in awe of the words of the sages. The mean man does not know the ordinances of Heaven, and consequently does not stand in awe of them. He is disrespectful to great men. He makes sport of the words of the sages."

XIV.29: The Master said, "The superior man is modest in his speech, but exceeds in his actions."

XV.18: The Master said, "The superior man is distressed by his want of ability. He is not distressed by men not knowing of him."

XV.21: The Master said, "The superior man is dignified, but does not wrangle. He is sociable, but not partisan."

XVII.24: Tzu-kung asked, "Has the superior man his hatreds also?" The Master said, "He has his hatreds. He hates those who proclaim the evil of others. He hates the man who, being in a low station, slanders his superiors. He hates those who have valor merely, and are unobservant of propriety (*li*). He hates those who are forward and determined, and, at the same time, of contracted understanding."

XVI.10: Confucius said, "The superior man has nine things which are subjects with him of thoughtful consideration. In regard to the use of his eyes, he is anxious to see clearly. In regard to the use of his ears, he is anxious to hear distinctly. In regard to his countenance, he is anxious that it should be benign. In regard to his speech, he is anxious that it should be sincere. In regard to his doing of business, he is anxious that it should be reverently careful. In regard to what he doubts about, he is anxious to question others. When he is angry, he thinks of the difficulties his anger may involve him in. When he sees gain to be got, he thinks of righteousness."

XIX.9: Tzu-hsia[3] said, "The superior man undergoes three changes. Looked at from a distance, he appears stern; when approached, he is mild; when he is heard to speak, his language is firm and decided."

XV.36: The superior man is correctly firm, and not merely firm.

LI (RITES)[4]

III.3: The Master said, "If a man be without the virtues proper to humanity,[5] what has he to do with the rites of propriety?[6] If a man be without the virtues of humanity, what has he to do with music?"

VIII.2: The Master said, "Respectfulness, without the rules of propriety,[7] becomes laborious bustle; carefulness, without the rules of propriety, becomes timidity; boldness, without the rules of propriety, becomes insubordination; straightforwardness, without the rules of propriety, becomes rudeness."

III.4: Lin Fang asked what was the first thing to be attended to in ceremonies. The Master said, "A great question, indeed! In festive ceremonies, it is better to be sparing than extravagant. In the ceremonies of mourning, it is better that there be deep sorrow than a minute attention to the observances."

III.26: The Master said, "High station filled without indulgent generosity; ceremonies performed without reverence; mourning conducted without sorrow wherewith should I contemplate such ways?"

XI.1: The Master said, "The men of former times, in the matters of ceremonies and music,[8] were rustics, it is said, while the men of these latter times, in ceremonies and music, are accomplished gentlemen. If I have occasion to use those things, I follow the men of former times."

III.17: Tzu Kung wished to do away with the offering of a sheep connected with the inauguration of the first day of each month. The Master said, "Tzu Kung, you love the sheep; I love the ceremony."

Yüeh (Music)

III.23: The Master instructing the Grand music master of Lu said, "How to play music may be known. At the commencement of the piece, all the parts should sound together. As it proceeds, they should be in harmony, severally distinct and flowing without a break, and thus on to the conclusion."

IX.14: The Master said, "I returned from Wei to Lu, and then the music was reformed, and the pieces in the Imperial songs and Praise songs found all their proper place."

Learning and Teaching

IX.4: There were four things from which the Master was entirely free. He had no foregone conclusions, no arbitrary predeterminations, no obstinacy, and no egotism.

XVII.2: The Master said, "By nature, men are nearly alike; by practice, they get to be wide apart."

XVI.9: Confucius said, "Those who are born with the possession of knowledge are the highest class of men. Those who learn, and so readily get possession of knowledge, are the next. Those who are dull and stupid, and yet compass the learning are another class next to these. As to those who are dull and stupid and yet do not learn—they are the lowest of the people."

VII.8: The Master said, "I do not open up the truth to one who is not eager to get knowledge, nor help out any one who is not anxious to explain himself. When I have presented one corner of a subject to any one, and he cannot from it learn the other three, I do not repeat my lesson."

IV.9: The Master said, "A scholar, whose mind is set on truth, and who is ashamed of bad clothes and bad food, is not fit to be discoursed with."

VIII.12: The Master said, "It is not easy to find a man who has learned for three years without coming to be good."

XII.15: The Master said, "By extensively studying all learning, and keeping himself under the restraint of the rules of propriety, one may thus likewise not err from what is right."

IX.18: The Master said, "The course of learning may be compared to what may happen in raising a mound. If there want but one basket of earth to complete the work, and I stop, the stopping is my own work. It may be compared to throwing down the earth on the level ground. Though but one basketful is thrown at a time, the advancing with it is my own going forward."

XIV.47: A youth of the village of Ch'üeh was employed by Kung to carry the messages between him and his visitors. Someone asked about him, saying, "I suppose he has made great progress." The Master said, "I observe that he is fond of occupying the seat of a full-grown man; I observe that he walks shoulder to shoulder with his elders. He is not one who is seeking to make progress in learning. He wishes quickly to become a man."

XIV.25: The Master said, "In ancient times, men learned with a view to their own improvement. Nowadays, men learn with a view to the approbation of others."

XV.29: The Master said, "To have faults and not to reform them—this, indeed, should be pronounced having faults."

IX.28: The Master said, "The wise are free from perplexities; the virtuous from anxiety; and the bold from fear."

Government

XII.7: Tzu-kung asked about government. The Master said, "The requisites of government are that there be sufficiency of food, sufficiency of military equipment, and the confidence of the people in their ruler." Tzu Kung said, "If it cannot be helped, and one of these must be dispensed with, which of the three should be foregone first?" "The military equipment," said the Master. Tzu Kung again asked, "If it cannot be helped and one of the remaining two must be dispensed with, which of them should be foregone?" The Master answered, "Part with the food. From of old, death has been the lot of humanity; but if the people have no faith in their rulers, there is no standing for the state."

XII.14: Tzu-chang asked about government. The Master said, "The art of governing is to keep its affairs before the mind without weariness, and to practice these affairs with undeviating consistency."

XII.19: Chi K'ang-tzu asked Confucius about government, saying, "What do you say to killing unprincipled people for the sake of principled people?" Confucius replied, "Sir, in carrying on your government, why should you use killing at all? Let your evinced desires be for what is good, and the people will be good. The relation between superiors (*chün-tzu*) and inferiors is like that between the wind and the grass. The grass must bend, when the wind blows across it."

XIII.6: The Master said, "When a prince's personal conduct is correct, his government is effective without the issuing of orders. If his personal conduct is not correct, he may issue orders, but they will not be followed."

VII.10: The Master said to Yen Yuen, "When called to office, undertake its duties; when not so called, then lie retired ... Tzu-lu said, "If you had the conduct of the armies of a great state, whom would you have to act with you?" The Master said, "I would not have him to act with me, who will unarmed attack a tiger, or cross a river without a boat, dying without any regret. My associate must be the man who proceeds to action full of caution, who is fond of adjusting his plans, and then carries them into execution."

XIV.23: Tzu-lu asked how a sovereign should be served. The Master said, "Do not impose on him, and, moreover, withstand him to his face."

III.18: The Master said, "The full observance of the rules of propriety[9] in serving one's prince is accounted by people to be flattery."

XI.23: "What is called a great minister,[10] is one who serves his prince according to what is right, and when he finds he cannot do so, retires."

XIV.1: Hsien asked what was shameful. The Master said, "When good government prevails in a state, to be thinking only of one's salary. When bad government prevails, to be thinking, in the same way, only of one's salary. That is what is shameful."

IX.13: "When a country is well governed, poverty and mean condition are things to be ashamed of. When a country is poorly governed, riches and honor are things to be ashamed of."

XIV.20: The Master was speaking about the unprincipled actions of the duke Ling of Wei, when K'ang Tzu said, "Since he is of such a character, how is it he does not lose his throne?" Kung Fu-Tzu said, "Chung-shu Yu has the superintendence of his guests and strangers; the litanist, T'uo, has the management of his ancestral temple; and Wang-sun Chia has the direction of the army and forces: with such officers as these, how should he lose his throne?"

Rectifying the Names

XII.17: Chi Kang-tzu asked Confucius about government. Confucius replied, "To govern (*cheng*) means to rectify (*cheng*).[11] If you lead on the people with correctness, who will dare not to be correct?"

XIII.3: Tzu-lu said, "The prince of Wei has been waiting for you, in order that you administer (cheng) the government. What will you consider the first thing to be done?" The Master replied, "What is necessary is to rectify (cheng) names." "So, indeed!" said Tzu-lu. "You are wide of the mark. Why must their be such rectification?" The Master said, "How uncultivated you are, Yu! A superior man, in regard to what he does not know, shows a cautious reserve. If names be not correct, language is not in accordance with the truth of things. If language be not in accordance with the truth of things, affairs cannot be carried on to success. When affairs cannot be carried on to success, proprieties (*li*) and music (yüeh) will not flourish. When proprieties and music do not flourish, punishments will not be properly awarded. When punishments are not properly awarded, the people do not know how to move hand or foot. Therefore a superior man considers it necessary that the names he uses may be spoken appropriately, and also that what he speaks may be carried out appropriately. What the superior man requires, is just that in his words there may be nothing incorrect."

NOTES

1   See the introduction above for the meaning of this word. From this point on, I will use "humaneness" or "humanity" or "virtue" to translate this word rather than Legge's "benevolence."

2   Or the "gentleman."

3   This is Pu Shang, a disciple of Confucius and the man primarily responsible for the transmission of the Confucian Classics. He figures prominently in *Analects* XIX.

4   *Li* refers to more than just "rites," but also means something like "decorum," "propriety," or "manners," that is, all those traditional, stable and ritualized forms of behavior which govern our day to day conduct. The word does, however, sometimes refer specifically to religious or political rituals.

5   "The virtues proper to humanity" is another way of translating *jen*.

6   "Rites of propriety" is a translation of *li*.

7   The "rules of propriety" is another way of translating *li*.

8   *Li* and *Yüeh*.

9   *Li*

10 That is, a minister or servant to a prince.

11 Or "correct." The meaning of this sentence derives, of course, from the similarities between the word "to govern" and "to correct."

---

9. The *Shu Jing* (Classic of History)— The Mandate of Heaven

trans. James Legge

In the twelfth month of the first year ... Yi Yin sacrificed to the former king, and presented the heir-king reverently before the shrine of his grandfather. All the princes from the domain of the nobles and the royal domain were present; all the officers also, each continuing to discharge his particular duties, were there to receive the orders of the chief minister. Yi Yin then clearly described the complete virtue of the Meritorious Ancestor for the instruction of the young king.

He said, "Oh! of old the former kings of Xia cultivated earnestly their virtue, and then there were no calamities from Heaven. The spirits of the hills and rivers alike were all in tranquility; and the birds and beasts, the fishes and tortoises, all enjoyed their existence according to their nature. But their descendant did not follow their example, and great Heaven sent down calamities, employing the agency of our ruler- who was in possession of its favoring appointment. The attack on Xia may be traced to the orgies in Ming Tiao ... Our king of Shang brilliantly displayed his sagely prowess; for oppression he substituted his generous gentleness; and the millions of the people gave him their hearts. Now your Majesty is entering on the inheritance of his virtue;—all depends on how you commence your reign. To set up love, it is For you to love your relations; to

"Shu Jing (The Classic of History)," *The Sacred Books of the East*, vol. 28, trans. James Legge, 1899.

set up respect, it is for you to respect your elders. The commencement is in the family and the state. ...

"Oh! the former king began with careful attention to the bonds thar hold men together. He listened to expostulation, and did not seek to resist it; he conformed to the wisdom of the ancients; occupying the highest position, he displayed intelligence; occupying an inferior position, he displayed his loyalty; he allowed the good qualities of the men whom he employed and did not seek that they should have every talent. ...

"He extensively sought out wise men, who should be helpful to you, his descendant and heir. He laid down the punishments for officers, and warned those who were in authority, saying, 'If you dare to have constant dancing in your palaces, and drunken singing in your chambers,—that is called the fashion of sorcerers; if you dare to see your hearts on wealth and women, and abandon yourselves to wandering about or to the chase,—thar is called the fashion of extravagance; if you dare to despise sage words, to resist the loyal and upright, to put far from you the aged and virtuous, and to seek the company of ... youths,—that is called the fashion of disorder. Now if a high noble or officer be addicted to one of these three fashions with their ten evil ways, his family will surely come to ruin; if the prince of a country be so addicted, his state will surely come to ruin. The minister who does not try to correct such vices in the sovereign shall be punished with branding.' ...

"Oh! do you, who now succeed to the throne, revere these warnings in your person. Think of them!—sacred counsels of vast importance, admirable words forcibly set forth! The ways of Heaven are not invariable:—on the good-doer it sends down all blessings, and on the evil-doer it sends down all miseries. Do you but be virtuous, be it in small things or in large, and the myriad regions will have cause for rejoicing. If you not be virtuous, be it in large things or in small, it will bring the ruin of your ancestral temple."

---

10. The Sayings of Lao-Tzu (Laozi)

trans. Lionel Giles

TAO (DAO) IN ITS TRANSCENDENTAL ASPECT, AND IN ITS PHYSICAL MANIFESTATION

THE Tao which can be expressed in words is not the eternal Tao; the name which can be uttered is not its eternal name. Without a name, it is the Beginning of Heaven

"Tao in its Transcendental Aspect, And In Its Physical Manifestation," *The Sayings of Lao-Tzu*, trans. Lionel Giles, 1905.

and Earth; with a name, it is the Mother of all things. Only one who is eternally free from earthly passions can apprehend its spiritual essence; he who is ever clogged by passions can see no more than its outer form. These two things, the spiritual and the material, though we call them by different names, in their origin are one and the same. This sameness is a mystery,—the mystery of mysteries. It is the gate of all spirituality.

How unfathomable is Tao! It seems to be the ancestral progenitor of all things. How pure and clear is Tao! It would seem to be everlasting. I know not of whom it is the offspring. It appears to have been anterior to any Sovereign Power.[1]

Tao eludes the sense of sight, and is therefore called colourless. It eludes the sense of hearing, and is therefore called soundless. It eludes the sense of touch, and is therefore called incorporeal. These three qualities cannot be apprehended, and hence they may be blended into unity.

Its upper part is not bright, and its lower part is not obscure. Ceaseless in action, it cannot be named, but returns again to nothingness. We may call it the form of the formless, the image of the imageless, the fleeting and the indeterminable. Would you go before it, you cannot see its face; would you go behind it, you cannot see its back.

The mightiest manifestations of active force flow solely from Tao.

Tao in itself is vague, impalpable,—how impalpable, how vague! Yet within it there is Form. How vague, how impalpable! Yet within it there is Substance. How profound, how obscure! Yet within it there is a Vital Principle. This principle is the Quintessence of Reality, and out of it comes Truth.

From of old until now, its name has never passed away. It watches over the beginning of all things. How do I know this about the beginning of things? Through Tao.

There is something, chaotic yet complete, which existed before Heaven and Earth. Oh, how still it is, and formless, standing alone without changing, reaching everywhere without suffering harm! It must be regarded as the Mother of the Universe. Its name I know not. To designate it, I call it Tao. Endeavouring to describe it, I call it Great. Being great, it passes on; passing on, it becomes remote; having become remote, it returns.

Therefore Tao is great; Heaven is great; Earth is great; and the Sovereign also is great. In the Universe there are four powers, of which the Sovereign is one. Man takes his law from the Earth; the Earth takes its law from Heaven; Heaven takes its law from Tao; but the law of Tao is its own spontaneity.

Tao in its unchanging aspect has no name. Small though it be in its primordial simplicity, mankind dare not claim its service. Could princes and kings hold and keep it, all creation would spontaneously pay homage. Heaven and Earth would unite in sending down sweet dew, and the people would be righteous unbidden and of their own accord.

---

1   This sentence is admittedly obscure, and it may be an interpolation. Lao Tzǔ's system of cosmogony has no place for any Divine Being independent of Tao. On the other hand, to translate *ti* by "Emperor," as some have done, necessarily involves us in an absurd anti-climax.

As soon as Tao creates order, it becomes nameable. When it once has a name, men will know how to rest in it. Knowing how to rest in it, they will run no risk of harm.

Tao as it exists in the world is like the great rivers and seas which receive the streams from the valleys.

All-pervading is the Great Tao. It can be at once on the right hand and on the left. All things depend on it for life, and it rejects them not. Its task accomplished, it takes no credit. It loves and nourishes all things, but does not act as master. It is ever free from desire. We may call it small. All things return to it, yet it does not act as master. We may call it great.

The whole world will flock to him who holds the mighty form of Tao. They will come and receive no hurt, but find rest, peace, and tranquillity.

With music and dainties we may detain the passing guest. But if we open our mouths to speak of Tao, he finds it tasteless and insipid.

Not visible to the sight, not audible to the ear, in its use it is inexhaustible.

Retrogression is the movement of Tao. Weakness is the character of Tao.

All things under Heaven derive their being from Tao in the form of Existence; Tao in the form of Existence sprang from Tao in the form of Non-Existence.

Tao is a great square with no angles, a great vessel which takes long to complete, a great sound which cannot be heard, a great image with no form.

Tao lies hid and cannot be named, yet it has the power of transmuting and perfecting all things.

Tao produced Unity; Unity produced Duality; Duality produced Trinity; and Trinity produced all existing objects. These myriad objects leave darkness behind them and embrace the light, being harmonised by the breath of Vacancy.

Tao produces all things; its Virtue nourishes them; its Nature gives them form; its Force perfects them.

Hence there is not a single thing but pays homage to Tao and extols its Virtue. This homage paid to Tao, this extolling of its Virtue, is due to no command, but is always spontaneous.

Thus it is that Tao, engendering all things, nourishes them, develops them, and fosters them; perfects them, ripens them, tends them, and protects them.

Production without possession, action without self-assertion, development without domination this is its mysterious operation.

The World has a First Cause, which may be regarded as the Mother of the World. When one has the Mother, one can know the Child. He who knows the Child and still keeps the Mother, though his body perish, shall run no risk of harm.

It is the Way of Heaven not to strive, and yet it knows how to overcome; not to speak, and yet it knows how to obtain a response; it calls not, and things come of themselves; it is slow to move, but excellent in its designs.

Heaven's net is vast; though its meshes are wide, it lets nothing slip through.

The Way of Heaven is like the drawing of a bow: it brings down what is high and raises what is low. It is the Way of Heaven to take from those who have too much, and give to those who have too little. But the way of man is not so. He takes away from those who have too little, to add to his own superabundance. What man is there that can take of his own superabundance and give it to mankind? Only he who possesses Tao.

The Tao of Heaven has no favourites. It gives to all good men without distinction.

Things wax strong and then decay. This is the contrary of Tao. What is contrary to Tao soon perishes.

Analysis Questions

1. What are the key virtues of Confucianism?
2. What is the Mandate of Heaven? How does it relate to Confucianism?
3. What is *Tao* ("the Way") and its political idea?

CHAPTER 4

Ancient Greek Experience

Introduction

All of present-day Western civilization owes its origins to the classical civilizations of Greece and Rome. In contrast to the Chinese, the Greeks were seafarers, splitting up into tiny communities on land. When the Greeks emerged from nomadic tribalism, they settled in territorial groups called *poleis* (city-states). In Homer's epics, we find people already organized in territorial units called *poleis* (singular *polis*), consisting of a warlord, his family and followers, and others. These were face-to-face communities, small enough for all citizens to meet together in one place (the *agora*, both marketplace and assembly). In this environment, the Athenians developed not only the concept of government by the people but also the basis of modern science and philosophy. The chief cities included Sparta, Thebes, Athens, Olympia, Corinth, and Argos. Ancient Greece gradually declined in power, torn apart by rivalries among its warring cities, especially Athens and Sparta, and the leadership of Greece shifted to Macedonia.

Alexander the Great was responsible for creating a new era of Greek civilization—the Hellenistic Age, lasting from about 323 to 30 B.C. Alexander invaded and conquered many lands and created Greek-style colonies in Greece, Persia, northern Africa, and India. Chief among these was Alexandria in Egypt, which became a cosmopolitan learning center that endured for centuries. The Hellenistic Age eventually laid the groundwork for the triumph of Roman imperialism. The following selections describe various aspects of ancient Greece, including the nature of Athenian politics and the elements of Greek and local culture.

11. The *Iliad* by Homer

by Homer; trans. S.O. Andrew and M. J. Oakley

Then bright-plum'd Hector spake in answer to her:
'Lady mother, bring me no wine that sweetens the heart,
Lest, crippled by thee, I forget my strength and my might.
With hands unwashen to pour libation to Zeus
Of sparkling wine, is shame to me; nor may a man
In any wise pray to Cronion, lord of the storm-cloud,
When defil'd with blood and with filth. But go thou to the shrine
Of Athena, driver of spoil; take offerings with thee,
Assembling the aged wives, and the robe thou accountest
Most graceful and large of those in thy hall, and the dearest
To thine own self; on the knees of fair-hair'd Athena
Lay it, and vow thou wilt offer her there in her shrine
Twelve yearling kine that have toil'd not, if she will but pity
Troy town and the Trojan wives and their little children;
If from holy Troy she may ward that furious spearman,
The son of Tydeus, a mighty deviser of fear.
Go then to the shrine of Athena, the driver of spoil;
To Paris will I go, to call him, if he will but hear me.
Would that the earth might gape at once to receive him!
For the lord of Olympus has rear'd him, a grievous bane
To the Trojans, to great-hearted Priam and all of his sons.
Him if I might behold descending to Hades,
I well might deem my heart had forgotten its woe.'
So spake he; she, calling her maids, went into the hall,
And they gather'd the aged wives from about the city;
But she herself went down to the sweet-smelling closet
Where her broider'd robes were, the work of women of Sidon,
Brought thither once by the godlike Paris himself
As he sail'd the stretching ocean upon that journey
Whereon the high-born Helen he brought to his home.
One of these did Hecuba choose as a gift for Athena,
The fairest embroider'd and largest; it gleam'd like a star
And under the rest it lay. Then forth she did hie.
And after her hasten'd many an aged wife.

When they came to Athena's shrine on the city's height,
It was fair-cheek'd Theáno who open'd the doors for them,
Horse-taming Antenor's wife and daughter of Cisseus;
For the Trojans had made her priestess of the Goddess Athena.
Then with wailing cries all lifted their hands to Athena;
Then took the fair-cheek'd Theano the broider'd robe
And upon the knees of the fair-hair'd Athena she laid it,
And with prayer besought the daughter of mighty Zeus:
'O Lady Athena, who keepest guard on our city,
Fairest of Goddesses, break now this Diomed's spear;
Make him headlong to fall in front of the Scaean gates;
That we twelve yearling kine that never have toil'd
May sacrifice in thy shrine, if thou wilt but pity
Troy town and the Trojan wives and their little children.'
Away to the wall she made haste, as if out of her mind;
And along with her is the nursemaid, holding the child.'
   So the housekeeper spake, and Hector sped back from the house
The way he had come by, over the well-builded streets.
Now when, as he cross'd the great city, he came to the gate,
The Scaean gate, for he meant to go back to the plain,
His wife, many-gifted Andromache, ran to his side;
The daughter she was of Eetion, noble of heart,
A man who had made under forested Placus his home,
In Thebe-by-Placus, and rul'd the Cilician men.
His daughter it was that Hector, the bronze-clad, had wed.
She now came to meet him; a handmaid walk'd at her side
Holding a child to her breast, his own little son,
The darling of Hector's heart, like a beautiful star.
Scamandrius, Hector call'd him; but all of the rest
Astyanax, seeing that Hector alone was the guard
Of Ilios town. And Hector, beholding the child,
Was silent and smil'd; but Andromache came to his side
And held him close, and the tears stream'd forth from her eyes;
And she clasp'd his hand in her own and spake to him thus:
'Dear heart, this valour of thine will be thy undoing,
No pity thou hast for thy little one here, nor for me,
Poor wretch that I am, and that soon thy widow shall be;
For soon shall the Argives all set upon thee in a band
And put thee to death; and better it were for me,
If I should lose thee, to go to my grave, for no more
Shall I have comfort, when thou hast gone to thy doom,

But grief only. Nor father nor mother have I;
My father was slain by the goodly Achilles, who laid
Utterly waste the Cilicians' well-peopled town,
High-gated Thebe. Eetion slew he in truth,
Yet did he not despoil him, for awe held him back;
But he burn'd him clad as he was in his rich-graven armour,
And over him heap'd up a barrow, where nymphs of the hills,
Daughters of shield-bearing Zeus, set elm-trees about.
As for the seven brothers I had in our halls,
All in a single day to the underworld went;
For the goodly Achilles, the swift-footed, slaughter'd them all
Amidst their slow-footed kine and their white-coated sheep.
And my mother, that under forested Placus was queen,
He brought to this place along with the rest of the spoil.
But freed her thereafter for ransom innumerable;
Yet Artemis put her to death in her father's halls.
Hector, thou art my father, my mother art thou
And my brother too and my husband stalwart in might.
Come now, have pity on me and abide on the wall,
And make not thy child an orphan, a widow thy wife.
By the wild fig-tree halt thou the host, where the town
Is most easy to scale, and the wall invites an assault.
Thrice there have the best of them tried to break in,
With the Ajaxes both and Idomeneus brave in the fight
And the sons of Atreus and Tydeus' valiant son;
Perhaps one skill'd in soothsaying gave them a hint,
Or haply their own spirit has driven them there.'
 Then Hector the great, the bright-plum'd, spake to her thus:
'That is my concern, dear wife; I were strangely asham'd
The Trojans to meet, and their wives in their trailing robes,
If here like a coward I skulk'd aloof from the fray.
My own heart will not let me; for aye have I learn'd
To be brave, and amid the foremost Trojans to fight,
In quest of my father's great glory and eke of mine own.
For this do I know for sure in my heart and my soul:
There shall be a day when holy Ilios falls
And with Priam the people of Priam with good ashen spear.
Yet not so much does the grief of the Trojans hereafter
Move me, nor Hecuba's, even, nor Priam the King's,
Nor my brothers' grief, who, many and brave though they be,
Shall fall in the dust, laid low by the foemen's hands,

As thine own grief, when one of the bronze-coated Argives
Shall lead thee weeping away, thy liberty lost.
For some other woman in Argos thou'lt work at the loom,
From Messeis carry water, or else Hypereia,
Hating thy task, and strong necessity bind thee.
And someone shall say of thee then, beholding thy tears:
"That is the wife of Hector, unmatch'd in the fray
Of all horse-taming Trojans that fought about Ilios town."
So shall he say; and for thee fresh grief there shall be
To want for a man like me to keep thee from bondage.
But let me be dead, let the heap'd earth cover me up
Ere ever I hear thy cries as they drag thee away.'
    So saying, the glorious Hector stretch'd out his arms
To the child; but back to the breast of his fair-girdled nurse
He shrank with a cry, for his dear father's look made him fear;
Affrighted he was by the bronze and the horse-hair plume
As he mark'd how grimly it waved from the top of the helm.
Then laugh'd his dear father and lady mother aloud;
And glorious Hector took the helm from his head
And set it upon the ground, where brightly it gleam'd.
But he kiss'd his dear son and fondled him in his arms
Then in prayer to Zeus and the rest of the Gods did he speak:
'O Zeus and ye other Gods, grant that this boy of mine here
May be even as I am, surpassing all others in Troy,
As brave and as strong, and firmly o'er Ilios rule.
And let him be call'd, as back he shall come from the war,
A better man than his father; and let him bring back
The spoils of the foe he has slain, and gladden his mother.'
So saying, within the arms of the wife that he lov'd
He plac'd his child, and she took him with smiling and tears,
To her sweet-smelling bosom. Her husband, pitying, mark'd it
And, stroking her with his hand, he address'd her and said:
'Dear wife, grieve not for me too much in thy heart;
No man shall send me below if it be not my time;
Yet from doom, methinks, no man has ever escap'd,
Whether coward or brave, when once he has come to this life.
But do thou go home and busy thyself with thy tasks,
Thy loom and thy distaff, and bid the women about thee
Attend to their work; but war is the business of men,
Everyman's business in Ilios, mine most of all.'
So glorious Hector spake, and took up his helm

With its horse-hair crest; but homeward his dear wife went,
With many a backward glance and many a tear.
And soon thereafter she came to the well-builded house
Of manslaying Hector, and there her handmaids she found
In many a band, and she made them all to lament;
In his own house they lamented for Hector alive,
For they deem'd that he from the dreadful fray would return
Never again, nor escape the hands of the Argives.
Not long Alexander delay'd in his high-built house,
But, donning his glorious armour, figur'd with bronze,
He sped through the city, trusting his fleetness of foot.
Like a stall'd horse that, fed to the full at his manger,
Breaks loose from his halter, stampeding over the plain,
Glad at heart, for his wont is to bathe in the fair-flowing river;
High does he hold up his head, and about him his mane
On his shoulders streams out; in his glory he trusts; and his knees
Bear him fleetly away to the haunts and pastures of mares:
So Priam's son Paris down from high Pergamus came
Resplendent in armour, like to the light of the sun,
And laughing aloud as his swift feet carried him on.
Soon he met Hector, his brother, who then was about
To turn back from the place where late he commun'd with his wife.
And the first to speak was godlike Paris, and said:
'Thou wouldst speed on ahead, brother; I, with my lingering gait,
Delay thee, not coming in time, as thou gavest command.'
Then in answer to him spake bright-plum'd Hector, and said:
'No-one, brother, who thinks what is proper and right,
Would despise what thou dost in the fray, for valiant thou art;
Yet thou purposely slackest and hast no care; and for that
Is the heart in me griev'd whenever I hear thee revil'd
By Trojans who suffer for thy sake labour full great.
But let us be gone; hereafter for this we'll atone,
If Zeus shall grant us to set in our halls for the Gods
That for ever are in the skies, a deliverance-bowl
When from Troyland we shall have driven the well-greav'd Achaeans.'

12. The Persian Wars: The Battle of Marathon

by Herodotus; trans. George Rawlinson

The barbarians were conducted to Marathon by Hippias, the son of Pisistratus, who the night before had seen a strange vision in his sleep. He dreamt of lying in his mother's arms, and conjectured the dream to mean that he would be restored to Athens, recover the power which he had lost, and afterwards live to a good old age in his native country. Such was the sense in which he interpreted the vision. He now proceeded to act as guide to the Persians, and, in the first place, he landed the prisoners taken from Eretria upon the island that is called Aegileia, a tract belonging to the Styreans, after which he brought the fleet to anchor off Marathon and marshalled the bands of the barbarians as they disembarked. As he was thus employed, it chanced that he sneezed and at the same time coughed with more violence than was his wont. Now, as he was a man advanced in years, and the greater number of his teeth were loose, it so happened that one of them was driven out with the force of the cough, and fell down into the sand. Hippias took all the pains he could to find it, but the tooth was nowhere to be seen, whereupon he fetched a deep sigh, and said to the bystanders,[1] "After all, the land is not ours, and we shall never be able to bring it under. All my share in it is the portion of which my tooth has possession."

So Hippias believed that in this way his dream was fulfilled.

The Athenians were drawn up in order of battle in a sacred close belonging to Hercules when they were joined by the Plataeans, who came in full force to their aid. Some time before, the Plataeans had put themselves under the rule of the Athenians, and these last had already undertaken many labours on their behalf. The occasion of the surrender was the following. The Plataeans suffered grievous things at the hands of the men of Thebes; so, as it chanced that Cleomenes, the son of Anaxandridas, and the Lacedaemonians were in their neighbourhood, they first of all offered to surrender themselves to them. But the Lacedaemonians refused to receive them, and said, "We dwell too far off from you, and ours would be but chill succour. Ye might oftentimes be carried into slavery before one of us heard of it. We counsel you rather to give yourselves up to the Athenians, who are your next neighbours, and well able to shelter you."

This they said, not so much out of good will towards the Plataeans as because they wished to involve the Athenians in trouble by engaging them in wars with the Boeotians. The Plataeans, however, when the Lacedaemonians gave them this counsel, complied at once, and when the sacrifice to the Twelve Gods was being offered at Athens, they came and sat as suppliants about the altar and gave themselves up to the Athenians. The Thebans no sooner learnt what the Plataeans had done than instantly they marched out against them, while the Athenians sent troops to their aid. As the

Herodotus, "The Battle of Marathon," *The History of Herodotus*, trans. George Rawlinson, 1860.

two armies were about to join battle, the Corinthians, who chanced to be at hand, would not allow them to engage; both sides consented to take them for arbitrators, whereupon they made up the quarrel, and fixed the boundary-line between the two states upon this condition: to wit, that if any of the Boeotians wished no longer to belong to Boeotia, the Thebans should allow them to follow their own inclinations. The Corinthians, when they had thus decreed, forthwith departed to their homes. The Athenians likewise set off on their return; but the Boeotians fell upon them during the march, and a battle was fought wherein they were worsted by the Athenians. Hereupon these last would not be bound by the line which the Corinthians had fixed, but advanced beyond those limits and made the Asopus the boundary-line between the country of the Thebans and that of the Plataeans and Hysians. Under such circumstances did the Plataeans give themselves up to Athens, and now they were come to Marathon to bear the Athenians aid.

The Athenian generals were divided in their opinions, and some advised not to risk a battle, because they were too few to engage such a host as that of the Medes, while others were for fighting at once, and among these last was Miltiades. He therefore, seeing that opinions were thus divided, and that the less worthy counsel appeared likely to prevail, resolved to go to the Polemarch, and have a conference with him. For the man on whom the lot fell to be Polemarch at Athens was entitled to give his vote with the ten generals, since anciently the Athenians allowed him an equal right of voting with them. The Polemarch at this juncture was Callimachus of Aphidnae; to him therefore Miltiades went, and said:

"With thee it rests Callimachus, either to bring Athens to slavery, or, by securing her freedom, to leave behind thee to all future generations a memory beyond even Harmodius and Aristogeiton. For never since the time that the Athenians became a people were they in so great a danger as now. If they bow their necks beneath the yoke of the Medes, the woes which they will have to suffer when given into the power of Hippias are already determined on. If, on the other hand, they fight and overcome, Athens may rise to be the very first city in Greece. How it comes to pass that these things are likely to happen, and how the determining of them in some sort rests with thee, I will now proceed to make clear. We generals are ten in number, and our votes are divided; half of us wish to engage, half to avoid a combat. Now, if we do not fight, I look to see a great disturbance at Athens which will shake men's resolutions, and then I fear they will submit themselves, but if we fight the battle before any unsoundness show itself among our citizens, let the gods but give us fair play, and we are well able to overcome the enemy. On thee therefore we depend in this matter, which lies wholly in thine own power. Thou hast only to add thy vote to my side and thy country will be free, and not free only, but the first state in Greece. Or, if thou preferrest to give thy vote to them who would decline the combat, then the reverse will follow."

Miltiades by these words gained Callimachus; and the addition of the Polemarch's vote caused the decision to be in favor of fighting. Hereupon all those generals who had been desirous of hazarding a battle, when their turn came to command the army, gave up their right to Miltiades. He however, though he accepted their offers, nevertheless waited, and would not fight until his own day of command arrived in due course. Then at length, when his own turn was come, the Athenian battle was set in array, and this was the order of it. Callimachus the Polemarch led the right wing, for it was at that time a rule with the Athenians to give the right wing to the Polemarch. After this followed the tribes, according as they were numbered, in an unbroken line; while last of all came the Plataeans, forming the left wing. And ever since that day it has been a custom with the Athenians, in the sacrifices and assemblies held each fifth year at Athens, for the Athenian herald to implore the blessing of the gods on the Plataeans conjointly with the Athenians. Now, as they marshalled the host upon the field of Marathon, in order that the Athenian front might he of equal length with the Median, the ranks of the centre were diminished, and it became the weakest part of the line, while the wings were both made strong with a depth of many ranks.

So when the battle was set in array, and the victims showed themselves favourable, instantly the Athenians, so soon as they were let go, charged the barbarians at a . Now the distance between the two armies was little short of eight furlongs. The Persians, therefore, when they saw the Greeks coming on at speed, made ready to receive them, although it seemed to them that the Athenians were bereft of their senses, and bent upon their own destruction; for they saw a mere handful of men coming on at a run without either horsemen or archers. Such was the opinion of the barbarians, but the Athenians in close array fell upon them, and fought in a manner worthy of being recorded. They were the first of the Greeks, so far as I know, who introduced the custom of charging the enemy at a run, and they were likewise the first who dared to look upon the Median garb and to face men clad in that fashion. Until this time the very name of the Medes had been a terror to the Greeks to hear.

The two armies fought together on the plain of Marathon for a length of time, and in the mid battle, where the Persians themselves and the Sacae had their place, the barbarians were victorious and broke and pursued the Greeks into the inner country, but on the two wings the Athenians and the Plataeans defeated the enemy. Having so done, they suffered the routed barbarians to fly at their ease, and joining the two wings in one, fell upon those who had broken their own centre, and fought and conquered them. These likewise fled, and now the Athenians hung upon the runaways and cut them down, chasing them all the way to the shore, on reaching which they laid hold of the ships and called aloud for fire.

It was in the struggle here that Callimachus the Polemarch, after greatly distinguishing himself, lost his life; Stesilaus too, the son of Thrasilaus, one of the generals, was slain; and Cynaegirus, the son of Euphorion, having seized on a vessel of the enemy's by the ornament at the stern, had his hand cut off by the blow of an axe, and so perished; as likewise did many other Athenians of note and name.

Nevertheless, the Athenians secured in this way seven of the vessels; while with the remainder the barbarians pushed off, and taking aboard their Eretrian prisoners from the island where they had left them, doubled Cape Sunium, hoping to reach Athens before the return of the Athenians. The Alcmaeonidae were accused by their countrymen of suggesting this course to them; they had, it was said, an understanding with the Persians, and made a signal to them, by raising a shield, after they were embarked in their ships. The Persians accordingly sailed round Sunium. But the Athenians with all possible speed marched away to the defence of their city, and succeeded in reaching Athens before the appearance of the barbarians, and as their camp at Marathon had been pitched in a precinct of Hercules, so now they encamped in another precinct of the same god at Cynosarges. The barbarian fleet arrived, and lay to off Phalerum, which was at that time the haven of Athens; but after resting awhile upon their oars, they departed and sailed away to Asia.

There fell in this battle of Marathon, on the side of the barbarians, about six thousand and four hundred men; on that of the Athenians, one hundred and ninety-two. Such was the number of the slain on the one side and the other. A strange prodigy likewise happened at this fight. Epizelus, the son of Cuphagoras, an Athenian, was in the thick of the fray, and behaving himself as a brave man should, when suddenly he was stricken with blindness, without blow of sword or dart; and this blindness continued thenceforth during the whole of his after life. The following is the account which he himself, as I have heard, gave of the matter: he said that a gigantic warrior, with a huge beard, which shaded all his shield, stood over against him, but the ghostly semblance passed him by, and slew the man at his side. Such, as I understand, was the tale which Epizelus told.

---

13. Life of Alexander

by Plutarch; ed. and trans. John Langhorne and William Langhorne

Plutarch, a Roman historian who lived during the first century AD (ca. 46–119), wrote his Lives of the Noble Grecians and Romans intending to draw parallels between great figures of Greek antiquity and Romans of his own time. He chose to compare Alexander the Great with Julius Caesar. In his Life of Alexander, Plutarch tells some of the most famous stories related about Alexander.

When Philonieus, the Thessalian, offered the horse named Bucephalus in sale to Philip [Alexander's father], at the price of thirteen talents, the king, with the prince and many others, went into the field to see some trial made of him. The horse

Plutarch, "The Life of Alexander," *Plutarch's Lives*, ed. and trans. John Langhorne and William Langhorne, pp. 434-439, 1874.

appeared extremely vicious and unmanageable, and was so far from suffering himself to be mounted, that he would not bear to be spoken to, but turned fiercely on all the grooms. Philip was displeased at their bringing him so wild and ungovernable a horse, and bade them take him away. But Alexander, who had observed him well, said, "What a horse they are losing, for want of skill and spirit to manage him!" Philip at first took no notice of this, but, upon the prince's often repeating the same expression, and showing great uneasiness, said, "Young man, you find fault with your elders, as if you knew more than they, or could manage the horse better." "And I certainly could," answered the prince. "If you should not be able to ride him, what forfeiture will you submit to for your rashness?" "I will pay the price of the horse."

Upon this all the company laughed, but the king and prince agreeing as to the forfeiture, Alexander ran to the horse, and laying hold on the bridle, turned him to the sun; for he had observed, it seems, that the shadow which fell before the horse, and continually moved as he moved, greatly disturbed him. While his fierceness and fury abated, he kept speaking to him softly and stroking him; after which he gently let fall his mantle, leaped lightly upon his back, and got his seat very safe. Then, without pulling the reins too hard, or using either whip or spur, he set him a-going. As soon as he perceived his uneasiness abated, and that he wanted only to run, he put him in a full gallop, and pushed him on both with the voice and spur.

Philip and all his court were in great distress for him at first, and a profound silence took place. But when the prince had turned him and brought him straight back, they all received him with loud acclamations, except his father, who wept for joy, and kissing him, said, "Seek another kingdom, my son, that may be worthy of thy abilities; for Macedonia is too small for thee …"

[Philip] sent for Aristotle, the most celebrated and learned of all the philosophers; and the reward he gave him for forming his son Alexander was not only honorable, but remarkable for its propriety. He had formerly dismantled the city of Stagira, where that philosopher was born, and now he re-built it, and reestablished the inhabitants, who had either fled or been reduced to slavery … Aristotle was the man Alexander admired in his younger years, and, as he said himself, he had no less affection for him than for his own father …

[Alexander] was only twenty years old when he succeeded to the crown, and he found the kingdom torn into pieces by dangerous parties and implacable animosities. The barbarous nations, even those that bordered upon Macedonia, could not brook subjection, and they longed for their natural kings … Alexander was of opinion, that the only way to security, and a thorough establishment of his affairs, was to proceed with spirit and magnanimity. For he was persuaded, that if he appeared to abate of his dignity in the least article, he would be universally insulted. He therefore quieted the commotions, and put a stop to the rising wars among the barbarians, by marching with the utmost expediency as far as the Danube, where he fought a great battle …

The barbarians, we are told, lost in this battle twenty thousand foot and two thousand five hundred horse, whereas Alexander had no more than thirty-four men killed, nine of which were the infantry. To do honor to their memory, he erected a statue to each of them in brass, the workmanship of Lysippus. And that the Greeks might have their share in the glory of the day, he sent them presents out of the spoil: to the Athenians in particular he sent three hundred bucklers. Upon the rest of the spoils he put this pompous inscription, WON BY ALEXANDER THE SON OF PHILIP, AND THE GREEKS (EXCEPTING THE LACEDAEMONIANS), OF THE BARBARIANS IN ASIA. The greatest part of the plate, the purple furniture, and other things of that kind which he took from the Persians, he sent to his mother.

Analysis Questions

1. What is the *Iliad's* description of the relationships among early *poleis*?
2. How does Herodotus describe the battle of Marathon? Do you consider his writing an objective historical writing or not? Explain!
3. What are the characteristics of Alexander?

CHAPTER 5

The Rise of Roman Power

Introduction

Around 2,000 years ago, the Roman Empire was the greatest power in the Western world, with a population of 50 million, embracing the territory of 25 modern countries. Despite war and strife, an advanced culture evolved that continues to influence modern society.

The Romans were a harder-headed and more practical people than the Greeks. Rome, founded as a city-state in 753 B.C., adopted the concept of a *republic* for its government. In other words, Rome was governed by the Senate and the people of Rome. But in reality, after 31 B.C., Rome was controlled by a single ruler. It became one of the greatest empires the world has ever seen, an empire of unified government, good communications, and strong defense.

In 264 B.C., Rome successfully challenged Carthage for control of Sicily. Hannibal, the Carthaginian general, sought revenge in 218 B.C., marching over the Alps into Italy. Despite some spectacular victories, he was forced back into Africa and was defeated by Scipio at Zama in 202 B.C.

In the first century B.C., a widening gulf between rich and poor led to civil war. Julius Caesar, Marcus Crassus, and Gnaeus Pompeius united as the First Triumvirate in 60 B.C. to restore order. But it wasn't long before Caesar seized sole power and ruled as dictator until he was assassinated in 44 B.C. Caesar's death was followed by a civil war between his heir, Octavian, and his aide, Mark Antony. After victory at the Battle of Actium in 31 B.C., Octavian took the title *Augustus*, meaning "revered," and became the first Roman emperor, launching a golden age for Rome. The following descriptions show not only the accomplishments of Roman leaders but also the diffusion of other cultures in the Roman Empire.

14. The Foundation of the Roman Republic

by David Mulroy

SOURCE: LIVY, *HISTORY OF ROME*, 1.49–60 (ROMAN)

After Romulus, Rome was ruled by other kings, his successors, for over 200 years. The seventh and last king of Rome, Lucius Tarquinius Superbus (the Proud) gained the throne in violent coup d'état. His predecessor, Servius Tullius, was Tarquinius's own father-in-law, and Tarquinius had him assassinated with the help of his wife, the king's wicked daughter, Tullia. It is said that when Tullia was returning to her house from the forum on the day of the assassination, she encountered her father's dead body in the road and drove her carriage over it. Thereafter, the roadway in which this occurred was called the *Vicus Sceleratus*, Street of Crime.

Tarquinius ruled by terror, condemning citizens to death if he suspected them of treason—or simply disliked them or desired their wealth. He forced the common people to labor at public works, especially Rome's great sewer.

Once, a giant snake appeared in his palace. Considering this to be a terrible portent, Tarquinius sent an embassy to the oracle of Delphi to interpret it. The ambassadors were two of his sons and his nephew, Lucius Junius Brutus.[1] Brutus secretly longed for freedom and justice in Rome, but he was afraid of drawing attention to himself. Hence, he pretended to be stupid and indolent, even accepting the nickname Brutus, which means stupid. When he went to Delphi, he dedicated a hollow wooden staff that was filled with gold as a gift to Apollo. This was a symbol of his character.

The oracle of Delphi predicted the next one of the ambassadors to kiss his mother would rule in Rome. Tarquinius's two sons decided to conceal the oracle from their brother, Sextus, who was not present, and to cast lots to decide who would kiss their mother first. Brutus, however, interpreted the oracle differently. As he left the temple, he deliberately stumbled, fell to the ground, and secretly kissed mother earth.

Later, Tarquinius declared war on the town of Ardea, simply because he envied its wealth. After an attempt to storm its walls failed, the Roman army laid siege to it. The men conducting the siege, especially the officers, had many idle hours. By chance, Sextus Tarquinius, the king's son, was drinking with a group of other officers, when the subject of wives came up. Each man boasted that his own wife was the best. One of the officers, Collatinus, was especially proud of his wife, Lucretia. He suggested that

---

1   The ancestor of the later L. Junius Brutus involved in the assassination of Julius Caesar in 44 B.C.

they ride back to Rome and see how their wives were acting when their husbands came home unexpectedly. All agreed.

The other wives were discovered wasting time with their friends in banquets and other luxurious activities. Though it was late at night, Lucretia was working at her loom and supervising the work of her maids. She received her husband and his friends graciously.

Lucretia won the contest. Sextus Tarquinius, however, was overcome by a wicked desire. A few days later, he returned secretly to Lucretia's house. She welcomed him as an honored guest, giving him a meal and a place to sleep. In the still of the night, he entered Lucretia's bedroom with a drawn sword. Holding her down with his left hand on her breast, he said: "Be still, Lucretia. I am Sextus Tarquinius. I have a sword. You will die if you say a word." Sextus then declared his love, begged her to submit, mixed threats with his prayers, and said anything to win her over. When he saw that she was still unwilling, he said that he would not just kill her; he would kill a slave and place his naked body beside hers. People would believe that she had died because she was caught committing adultery. This threat made Lucretia submit. Some time later, Sextus departed, exulting in his victory.

Lucretia sent messages to her father and husband, asking them to come at once with trusted friends. Collatinus brought Brutus. They found Lucretia sitting sadly in her chamber and asked her whether she was well. She said: "Not at all. What is well for a woman whose honor has been lost? Collatinus, the imprint of another man is in your bed. Only my body was violated. My soul is innocent, and death will be my witness. Promise me that the adulterer will not get away with his crime. He is Sextus Tarquinius. He came here last night, an enemy disguised as a friend, and took his pleasure, a fatal one for me and for him too, if you are men."

The men promised to punish Sextus and tried to comfort Lucretia, saying that she was not guilty of anything. She said, "You will consider what to do about Sextus. As for me, I absolve myself from guilt, but not from punishment. Never in the future shall a shameless woman live because of the precedent set by Lucretia." She then removed a knife that she had concealed in her clothing, plunged it into her heart, and fell to the ground, dead.

While the others were weeping, Brutus removed the bloody knife from the wound, raised it high, and said, "By this woman's blood, most pure 'til wronged by royalty, I swear that I shall pursue Lucius Tarquinius Superbus, his evil wife, and their entire brood with steel, fire, and all the other resources at my command and that I will never allow any of them—or anyone else—to be a king in Rome!"

The Romans rallied around Brutus. The king and his family were driven out of Rome. Sextus tried to take refuge in the town of Gabii, but he was murdered by enemies settling an old score. In the year in which Tarquinius was exiled (traditionally 510 B.C.), the Romans outlawed monarchy. They began electing two consuls annually to direct the Senate. The first two elected were Brutus and Collatinus.

15. The Twelve Tables

ed. Oliver J. Thatcher

Cicero, *De Oratore*, I.44: Though all the world exclaim against me, I will say what I think: that single little book of the Twelve Tables, if anyone look to the fountains and sources of laws, seems to me, assuredly, to surpass the libaries of all the philosophers, both in weight of authority, and in plenitude of utility.

TABLE I

1. If anyone summons a man before the magistrate, he must go. If the man summoned does not go, let the one summoning him call the bystanders to witness and then take him by force.
2. If he shirks or runs away, let the summoner lay hands on him.
3. If illness or old age is the hindrance, let the summoner provide a team. He need not provide a covered carriage with a pallet unless he chooses.
4. Let the protector of a landholder be a landholder; for one of the proletariat, let anyone that cares, be protector.
6–9. When the litigants settle their case by compromise, let the magistrate announce it. If they do not compromise, let them state each his own side of the case, in the *comitium* of the forum before noon. Afterwards let them talk it out together, while both are present. After noon, in case either party has failed to appear, let the magistrate pronounce judgment in favor of the one who is present. If both are present the trial may last until sunset but no later.

TABLE II

2. He whose witness has failed to appear may summon him by loud calls before his house every third day.

TABLE III

1. One who has confessed a debt, or against whom judgment has been pronounced, shall have thirty days to pay it in. After that forcible seizure of his person is allowed. The creditor shall bring him before the magistrate. Unless he pays the amount of the judgment or some one in the presence of the magistrate interferes in his behalf as protector the creditor so shall take him home and fasten him in stocks or fetters. He shall fasten him with not less than

Source: http://www.fordham.edu/halsall/ancient/12tables.asp.

fifteen pounds of weight or, if he choose, with more. If the prisoner choose, he may furnish his own food. If he does not, the creditor must give him a pound of meal daily; if he choose he may give him more.

2.   On the third market day let them divide his body among them. If they cut more or less than each one's share it shall be no crime.

3.   Against a foreigner the right in property shall be valid forever.

TABLE IV

1.   A dreadfully deformed child shall be quickly killed.

2.   If a father sell his son three times, the son shall be free from his father.

3.   As a man has provided in his will in regard to his money and the care of his property, so let it be binding. If he has no heir and dies intestate, let the nearest agnate have the inheritance. If there is no agnate, let the members of his gens have the inheritance.

4.   If one is mad but has no guardian, the power over him and his money shall belong to his agnates and the members of his gens.

5.   A child born after ten months since the father's death will not be admitted into a legal inheritance.

TABLE V

1.   Females should remain in guardianship even when they have attained their majority.

TABLE VI

1.   When one makes a bond and a conveyance of property, as he has made formal declaration so let it be binding.

3.   A beam that is built into a house or a vineyard trellis one may not take from its place.

5.   *Usucapio* of movable things requires one year's possession for its completion; but *usucapio* of an estate and buildings two years.

6.   Any woman who does not wish to be subjected in this manner to the hand of her husband should be absent three nights in succession every year, and so interrupt the *usucapio* of each year.

TABLE VII

1.   Let them keep the road in order. If they have not paved it, a man may drive his team where he likes.

9. Should a tree on a neighbor's farm be bend crooked by the wind and lean over your farm, you may take legal action for removal of that tree.

10. A man might gather up fruit that was falling down onto another man's farm.

TABLE VIII

2. If one has maimed a limb and does not compromise with the injured person, let there be retaliation. If one has broken a bone of a freeman with his hand or with a cudgel, let him pay a penalty of three hundred coins If he has broken the bone of a slave, let him have one hundred and fifty coins. If one is guilty of insult, the penalty shall be twenty-five coins.

3. If one is slain while committing theft by night, he is rightly slain.

4. If a patron shall have devised any deceit against his client, let him be accursed.

5. If one shall permit himself to be summoned as a witness, or has been a weigher, if he does not give his testimony, let him be noted as dishonest and incapable of acting again as witness.

10. Any person who destroys by burning any building or heap of corn deposited alongside a house shall be bound, scourged, and put to death by burning at the stake provided that he has committed the said misdeed with malice afore-thought; but if he shall have committed it by accident, that is, by negligence, it is ordained that he repair the damage or, if he be too poor to be competent for such punishment, he shall receive a lighter punishment.

12. If the theft has been done by night, if the owner kills the thief, the thief shall be held to be lawfully killed.

13. It is unlawful for a thief to be killed by day. ... unless he defends himself with a weapon; even though he has come with a weapon, unless he shall use the weapon and fight back, you shall not kill him. And even if he resists, first call out so that someone may hear and come up.

23. A person who had been found guilty of giving false witness shall be hurled down from the Tarpeian Rock.

26. No person shall hold meetings by night in the city.

TABLE IX

4. The penalty shall be capital for a judge or arbiter legally appointed who has been found guilty of receiving a bribe for giving a decision.

5. Treason: he who shall have roused up a public enemy or handed over a citizen to a public enemy must suffer capital punishment.

6. Putting to death of any man, whosoever he might be unconvicted is forbidden.

TABLE X

1. None is to bury or burn a corpse in the city.
3. The women shall not tear their faces nor wail on account of the funeral.
5. If one obtains a crown himself, or if his chattel does so because of his honor and valor, if it is placed on his head, or the head of his parents, it shall be no crime.

TABLE XI

1. Marriages should not take place between plebeians and patricians.

TABLE XII

2. If a slave shall have committed theft or done damage with his master's knowledge, the action for damages is in the slave's name.
5. Whatever the people had last ordained should be held as binding by law.

---

16. The Carthaginian Attack on Sicily

by Herodotus; trans. George Rawlinson

VII.165: They, however, who dwell in Sicily, say that Gelo, though he knew that he must serve under the Lacedaemonians, would nevertheless have come to the aid of the Hellenes, had not it been for Terillos, the son of Crinippos, king of Himera; who, driven from his city by Thero, the son of Ainesidemos, king of Agrigentum, brought into Sicily at this very time an army of three hundred thousand men—Phoenicians, Libyans, Iberians, Ligurians, Helisykians, Sardinians, and Corsicans, under the command of Hamilcar the son of Hanno, king of the Carthaginians. Terillos prevailed upon Hamilcar, partly as his sworn friend, but more through the zealous aid of Anaxilaos the son of Cretines, king of Rhegium; who, by giving his own sons to Hamilcar as hostages, induced him to make the expedition. Anaxilaos herein served his own father-in-law; for he was married to a daughter of Terillos, by name Kydippe. So, as Gelo could not give the Hellenes any aid, he sent (they say) the sum of money to Delphi.

VII.166: They say too, that the victory of Gelo and Thero in Sicily over Hamilcar the Carthaginian fell out upon the very day that the Hellenes defeated the Persians at Salamis. Hamilcar, who was a Carthaginian on his father's side only, but on his mother's

Herodotus, "The Carthaginian Attack on Sicily, 480 BC," trans. George Rawlinson, The History, 1862.

a Syracusan, and who had been raised by his merit to the throne of Carthage, after the battle and the defeat, as I am informed, disappeared from sight: Gelo made the strictest search for him, but he could not be found anywhere, either dead or alive.

VII.167: The Carthaginians, who take probability for their guide, give the following account of this matter: Hamilcar, they say, during all the time that the battle raged between the Hellenes and the barbarians, which was from early dawn till evening, remained in the camp, sacrificing and seeking favorable omens, while he burned on a huge pyre the entire bodies of the victims which he offered.

Here, as he poured libations upon the sacrifices, he saw the rout of his army; whereupon he cast himself headlong into the flames, and so was consumed and disappeared. But whether Hamilcar's disappearance happened, as the Phoenicians tell us, in this way, or, as the Syracusans maintain, in some other, certain it is that the Carthaginians offer him sacrifice, and in all their colonies have monuments erected to his honor, as well as one, which is the grandest of all, at Carthage. Thus much concerning the affairs of Sicily.

17. Bible: Luke and Matthew

King James Version

LUKE CHAPTER 2

[1] And it came to pass in those days, that there went out a decree from Caesar Augustus that all the world should be taxed.

[2] (And this taxing was first made when Cyrenius was governor of Syria.)

[3] And all went to be taxed, every one into his own city.

[4] And Joseph also went up from Galilee, out of the city of Nazareth, into Judaea, unto the city of David, which is called Bethlehem; (because he was of the house and lineage of David:)

[5] To be taxed with Mary his espoused wife, being great with child.

"Luke: 2:1-7, 5:27-32, 6:20-45, 6:46-49, 7:1-10, Matthew 22:15-22," King James Version, 1611.

6 And so it was, that, while they were there, the days were accomplished that she should be delivered.

7 And she brought forth her firstborn son, and wrapped him in swaddling clothes, and laid him in a manger; because there was no room for them in the inn.

LUKE CHAPTER 5

27 And after these things he went forth, and saw a publican, named Levi, sitting at the receipt of custom: and he said unto him, Follow me.

28 And he left all, rose up, and followed him.

29 And Levi made him a great feast in his own house: and there was a great company of publicans and of others that sat down with them.

30 But their scribes and Pharisees murmured against his disciples, saying, Why do ye eat and drink with publicans and sinners?

31 And Jesus answering said unto them, They that are whole need not a physician; but they that are sick.

32 I came not to call the righteous, but sinners to repentance.

LUKE CHAPTER 6, PART I

20 And he lifted up his eyes on his disciples, and said, Blessed be ye poor: for yours is the kingdom of God.

21 Blessed are ye that hunger now: for ye shall be filled. Blessed are ye that weep now: for ye shall laugh.

22 Blessed are ye, when men shall hate you, and when they shall separate you from their company, and shall reproach you, and cast out your name as evil, for the Son of man's sake.

23 Rejoice ye in that day, and leap for joy: for, behold, your reward is great in heaven: for in the like manner did their fathers unto the prophets.

24 But woe unto you that are rich! for ye have received your consolation.

25 Woe unto you that are full! for ye shall hunger. Woe unto you that laugh now! for ye shall mourn and weep.

26 Woe unto you, when all men shall speak well of you! for so did their fathers to the false prophets.

27 But I say unto you which hear, Love your enemies, do good to them which hate you,

28 Bless them that curse you, and pray for them which despitefully use you.

29 And unto him that smiteth thee on the one cheek offer also the other; and him that taketh away thy cloak forbid not to take thy coat also.

30 Give to every man that asketh of thee; and of him that taketh away thy goods ask them not again.

31 And as ye would that men should do to you, do ye also to them likewise.

32 For if ye love them which love you, what thank have ye? for sinners also love those that love them.

33 And if ye do good to them which do good to you, what thank have ye? for sinners also do even the same.

34 And if ye lend to them of whom ye hope to receive, what thank have ye? for sinners also lend to sinners, to receive as much again.

35 But love ye your enemies, and do good, and lend, hoping for nothing again; and your reward shall be great, and ye shall be the children of the Highest: for he is kind unto the unthankful and to the evil.

36 Be ye therefore merciful, as your Father also is merciful.

37 Judge not, and ye shall not be judged: condemn not, and ye shall not be condemned: forgive, and ye shall be forgiven:

38 Give, and it shall be given unto you; good measure, pressed down, and shaken together, and running over, shall men give into your bosom. For with the same measure that ye mete withal it shall be measured to you again.

39 And he spake a parable unto them, Can the blind lead the blind? shall they not both fall into the ditch?

40 The disciple is not above his master: but every one that is perfect shall be as his master.

41 And why beholdest thou the mote that is in thy brother's eye, but perceivest not the beam that is in thine own eye?

42 Either how canst thou say to thy brother, Brother, let me pull out the mote that is in thine eye, when thou thyself beholdest not the beam that is in thine own eye? Thou hypocrite, cast out first the beam out of thine own eye, and then shalt thou see clearly to pull out the mote that is in thy brother's eye.

43 For a good tree bringeth not forth corrupt fruit; neither doth a corrupt tree bring forth good fruit.

44 For every tree is known by his own fruit. For of thorns men do not gather figs, nor of a bramble bush gather they grapes.

45 A good man out of the good treasure of his heart bringeth forth that which is good; and an evil man out of the evil treasure of his heart bringeth forth that which is evil: for of the abundance of the heart his mouth speaketh.

LUKE CHAPTER 6, PART II

46 And why call ye me, Lord, Lord, and do not the things which I say?

47 Whosoever cometh to me, and heareth my sayings, and doeth them, I will shew you to whom he is like:

48 He is like a man which built an house, and digged deep, and laid the foundation on a rock: and when the flood arose, the stream beat vehemently upon that house, and could not shake it: for it was founded upon a rock.

49 But he that heareth, and doeth not, is like a man that without a foundation built an house upon the earth; against which the stream did beat vehemently, and immediately it fell; and the ruin of that house was great.

LUKE CHAPTER 7

1 Now when he had ended all his sayings in the audience of the people, he entered into Capernaum.

2 And a certain centurion's servant, who was dear unto him, was sick, and ready to die.

3 And when he heard of Jesus, he sent unto him the elders of the Jews, beseeching him that he would come and heal his servant.

4 And when they came to Jesus, they besought him instantly, saying, That he was worthy for whom he should do this:

5 For he loveth our nation, and he hath built us a synagogue.

6 Then Jesus went with them. And when he was now not far from the house, the centurion sent friends to him, saying unto him, Lord, trouble not thyself: for I am not worthy that thou shouldest enter under my roof:

7 Wherefore neither thought I myself worthy to come unto thee: but say in a word, and my servant shall be healed.

8 For I also am a man set under authority, having under me soldiers, and I say unto one, Go, and he goeth; and to another, Come, and he cometh; and to my servant, Do this, and he doeth it.

9 When Jesus heard these things, he marvelled at him, and turned him about, and said unto the people that followed him, I say unto you, I have not found so great faith, no, not in Israel.

10 And they that were sent, returning to the house, found the servant whole that had been sick.

MATTHEW CHAPTER 22

15 Then went the Pharisees, and took counsel how they might entangle him in his talk.

16 And they sent out unto him their disciples with the Herodians, saying, Master, we know that thou art true, and teachest the way of God in truth, neither carest thou for any man: for thou regardest not the person of men.

17 Tell us therefore, What thinkest thou? Is it lawful to give tribute unto Caesar, or not?

¹⁸ But Jesus perceived their wickedness, and said, Why tempt ye me, ye hypocrites?

¹⁹ Shew me the tribute money. And they brought unto him a penny.

²⁰ And he saith unto them, Whose is this image and superscription?

²¹ They say unto him, Caesar's. Then saith he unto them, Render therefore unto Caesar the things which are Caesar's; and unto God the things that are God's.

²² When they had heard these words, they marvelled, and left him, and went their way.

18. *The Deeds of the Divine Augustus*

(Res Gestae or Monumentum Ancyranum)

by Augustus Caesar; trans. Thomas Bushnell

A copy below of the deeds of the divine Augustus, by which he subjected the whole wide earth to the rule of the Roman people, and of the money which he spent for the state and Roman people, inscribed on two bronze pillars, which are set up in Rome.

1. In my nineteenth year, on my own initiative and at my own expense, I raised an army with which I set free the state, which was oppressed by the domination of a faction. For that reason, the senate enrolled me in its order by laudatory resolutions, when Gaius Pansa and Aulus Hirtius were consuls (43 B.C.E.), assigning me the place of a consul in the giving of opinions, and gave me the imperium. With me as propraetor, it ordered me, together with the consuls, to take care lest any detriment befall the state. But the people made me consul in the same year, when the consuls each perished in battle, and they made me a triumvir for the settling of the state.

2. I drove the men who slaughtered my father into exile with a legal order, punishing their crime, and afterwards, when they waged war on the state, I conquered them in two battles.

3. I often waged war, civil and foreign, on the earth and sea, in the whole wide world, and as victor I spared all the citizens who sought pardon. As for foreign nations, those which I was able to safely forgive, I preferred to preserve than to destroy. About five hundred thousand Roman citizens were sworn to me. I led something more than three hundred thousand of them into colonies and I returned them to their cities, after their

stipend had been earned, and I assigned all of them fields or gave them money for their military service. I captured six hundred ships in addition to those smaller than triremes.

4. Twice I triumphed with an ovation, and three times I enjoyed a curule triumph and twenty one times I was named emperor. When the senate decreed more triumphs for me, I sat out from all of them. I placed the laurel from the fasces in the Capitol, when the vows which I pronounced in each war had been fulfilled. On account of the things successfully done by me and through my officers, under my auspices, on earth and sea, the senate decreed fifty-five times that there be sacrifices to the immortal gods. Moreover there were 890 days on which the senate decreed there would be sacrifices. In my triumphs kings and nine children of kings were led before my chariot. I had been consul thirteen times, when I wrote this, and I was in the thirty-seventh year of tribunician power (14 A.C.E.).

5. When the dictatorship was offered to me, both in my presence and my absence, by the people and senate, when Marcus Marcellus and Lucius Arruntius were consuls (22 B.C.E.), I did not accept it. I did not evade the curatorship of grain in the height of the food shortage, which I so arranged that within a few days I freed the entire city from the present fear and danger by my own expense and administration. When the annual and perpetual consulate was then again offered to me, I did not accept it.

6. When Marcus Vinicius and Quintus Lucretius were consuls (19 B.C.E.), then again when Publius Lentulus and Gnaeus Lentulus were (18 B.C.E.), and third when Paullus Fabius Maximus and Quintus Tubero were (11 B.C.E.), although the senate and Roman people consented that I alone be made curator of the laws and customs with the highest power, I received no magistracy offered contrary to the customs of the ancestors. What the senate then wanted to accomplish through me, I did through tribunician power, and five times on my own accord I both requested and received from the senate a colleague in such power.

7. I was triumvir for the settling of the state for ten continuous years. I was first of the senate up to that day on which I wrote this, for forty years. I was high priest, augur, one of the Fifteen for the performance of rites, one of the Seven of the sacred feasts, brother of Arvis, fellow of Titus, and Fetial.

8. When I was consul the fifth time (29 B.C.E.), I increased the number of patricians by order of the people and senate. I read the roll of the senate three times, and in my sixth consulate (28 B.C.E.) I made a census of the people with Marcus Agrippa as my colleague. I conducted a lustrum, after a forty-one year gap, in which lustrum were counted 4,063,000 heads of Roman citizens. Then again, with consular imperium I conducted a lustrum alone when Gaius Censorinus and Gaius Asinius were consuls (8 B.C.E.), in which lustrum were counted 4,233,000 heads of Roman citizens. And the third time, with consular imperium, I conducted a lustrum with my son Tiberius Caesar as colleague, when Sextus Pompeius and Sextus Appuleius were consuls (14 A.C.E.), in which lustrum were cunted 4,937,000 of the heads of Roman citizens. By new laws passed with my sponsorship, I restored many traditions of the ancestors, which were

falling into disuse in our age, and myself I handed on precedents of many things to be imitated in later generations.

9. The senate decreed that vows be undertaken for my health by the consuls and priests every fifth year. In fulfillment of these vows they often celebrated games for my life; several times the four highest colleges of priests, several times the consuls. Also both privately and as a city all the citizens unanimously and continuously prayed at all the shrines for my health.

10. By a senate decree my name was included in the Saliar Hymn, and it was sanctified by a law, both that I would be sacrosanct for ever, and that, as long as I would live, the tribunician power would be mine. I was unwilling to be high priest in the place of my living colleague; when the people offered me that priesthood which my father had, I refused it. And I received that priesthood, after several years, with the death of him who had occupied it since the opportunity of the civil disturbance, with a multitude flocking together out of all Italy to my election, so many as had never before been in Rome, when Publius Sulpicius and Gaius Valgius were consuls (12 B.C.E.).

11. The senate consecrated the altar of Fortune the Bringer-back before the temples of Honor and Virtue at the Campanian gate for my retrn, on which it ordered the priests and Vestal virgins to offer yearly sacrifices on the day when I had returned to the city from Syria (when Quintus Lucretius and Marcus Vinicius were consuls (19 B.C.E.), and it named that day Augustalia after my cognomen.

12. By the authority of the senate, a part of the praetors and tribunes of the plebs, with consul Quintus Lucretius and the leading men, was sent to meet me in Campania, which honor had been decreed for no one but me until that time. When I returned to Rome from Spain and Gaul, having successfully accomplished matters in those provinces, when Tiberius Nero and Publius Quintilius were consuls (13 B.C.E.), the senate voted to consecrate the altar of August Peace in the field of Mars for my return, on which it ordered the magistrates and priests and Vestal virgins to offer annual sacrifices.

13. Our ancestors wanted Janus Quirinus to be closed when throughout the all the rule of the Roman people, by land and sea, peace had been secured through victory. Although before my birth it had been closed twice in all in recorded memory from the founding of the city, the senate voted three times in my principate that it be closed.

14. When my sons Gaius and Lucius Caesar, whom fortune stole from me as youths, were fourteen, the senate and Roman people made them consuls-designate on behalf of my honor, so that they would enter that magistracy after five years, and the senate decreed that on that day when they were led into the forum they would be included in public councils. Moreover the Roman knights together named each of them first of the youth and gave them shields and spears.

15. I paid to the Roman plebs, HS 300 per man from my father's will and in my own name gave HS 400 from the spoils of war when I was consul for the fifth time (29 B.C.E.); furthermore I again paid out a public gift of HS 400 per man, in my tenth consulate (24 B.C.E.), from my own patrimony; and, when consul for the eleventh time

(23 B.C.E.), twelve doles of grain personally bought were measured out; and in my twelfth year of tribunician power (12–11 B.C.E.) I gave HS 400 per man for the third time. And these public gifts of mine never reached fewer than 250,000 men. In my eighteenth year of tribunician power, as consul for the twelfth time (5 B.C.E.), I gave to 320,000 plebs of the city HS 240 per man. And, when consul the fifth time (29 B.C.E.), I gave from my war-spoils to colonies of my soldiers each HS 1000 per man; about 120,000 men i the colonies received this triumphal public gift. Consul for the thirteenth time (2 B.C.E.), I gave HS 240 to the plebs who then received the public grain; they were a few more than 200,000.

16. I paid the towns money for the fields which I had assigned to soldiers in my fourth consulate (30 B.C.E.) and then when Marcus Crassus and Gnaeus Lentulus Augur were consuls (14 B.C.E.); the sum was about HS 600,000,000 which I paid out for Italian estates, and about HS 260,000,000 which I paid for provincial fields. I was first and alone who did this among all who founded military colonies in Italy or the provinces according to the memory of my age. And afterwards, when Tiberius Nero and Gnaeus Piso were consuls (7 B.C.E.), and likewise when Gaius Antistius and Decius Laelius were consuls (6 B.C.E.), and when Gaius Calvisius and Lucius Passienus were consuls (4 B.C.E.), and when Lucius Lentulus and Marcus Messalla were consuls (3 B.C.E.), and when Lucius Caninius and Quintus Fabricius were consuls (2 B.C.E.), I paid out rewards in cash to the soldiers whom I had led into their towns when their service was completed, and in this venture I spent about HS 400,000,000.

17. Four times I helped the senatorial treasury with my money, so that I offered HS 150,000,000 to those who were in charge of the treasury. And when Marcus Lepidus and Luciu Arruntius were consuls (6 A.C.E.), I offered HS 170,000,000 from my patrimony to the military treasury, which was founded by my advice and from which rewards were given to soldiers who had served twenty or more times.

18. From that year when Gnaeus and Publius Lentulus were consuls (18 B.C.E.), when the taxes fell short, I gave out contributions of grain and money from my granary and patrimony, sometimes to 100,000 men, sometimes to many more.

19. I built the senate-house and the Chalcidicum which adjoins it and the temple of Apollo on the Palatine with porticos, the temple of divine Julius, the Lupercal, the portico at the Flaminian circus, which I allowed to be called by the name Octavian, after he who had earlier built in the same place, the state box at the great circus, the temple on the Capitoline of Jupiter Subduer and Jupiter Thunderer, the temple of Quirinus, the temples of Minerva and Queen Juno and Jupiter Liberator on the Aventine, the temple of the Lares at the top of the holy street, the temple of the gods of the Penates on the Velian, the temple of Youth, and the temple of the Great Mother on the Palatine.

20. I rebuilt the Capitol and the theater of Pompey, each work at enormous cost, without any inscription of my name. I rebuilt aqueducts in many places that had decayed with age, and I doubled the capacity of the Marcian aqueduct by sending a

new spring into its channel. I completed the Forum of Julius and the basilic which he built between the temple of Castor and the temple of Saturn, works begun and almost finished by my father. When the same basilica was burned with fire I expanded its grounds and I began it under an inscription of the name of my sons, and, if I should not complete it alive, I ordered it to be completed by my heirs. Consul for the sixth time (28 B.C.E.), I rebuilt eighty-two temples of the gods in the city by the authority of the senate, omitting nothing which ought to have been rebuilt at that time. Consul for the seventh time (27 B.C.E.), I rebuilt the Flaminian road from the city to Ariminum and all the bridges except the Mulvian and Minucian.

21. I built the temple of Mars Ultor on private ground and the forum of Augustus from war-spoils. I build the theater at the temple of Apollo on ground largely bought from private owners, under the name of Marcus Marcellus my son-in-law. I consecrated gifts from war-spoils in the Capitol and in the temple of divine Julius, in the temple of Apollo, in the tempe of Vesta, and in the temple of Mars Ultor, which cost me about HS 100,000,000. I sent back gold crowns weighing 35,000 to the towns and colonies of Italy, which had been contributed for my triumphs, and later, however many times I was named emperor, I refused gold crowns from the towns and colonies which they equally kindly decreed, and before they had decreed them.

22. Three times I gave shows of gladiators under my name and five times under the name of my sons and grandsons; in these shows about 10,000 men fought. Twice I furnished under my name spectacles of athletes gathered from everywhere, and three times under my grandson's name. I celebrated games under my name four times, and furthermore in the place of other magistrates twenty-three times. As master of the college I celebrated the secular games for the college of the Fifteen, with my colleague Marcus Agrippa, when Gaius Furnius and Gaius Silanus were consuls (17 B.C.E.). Consul for the thirteenth time (2 B.C.E.), I celebrated the first games of Mas, which after that time thereafter in following years, by a senate decree and a law, the consuls were to celebrate. Twenty-six times, under my name or that of my sons and grandsons, I gave the people hunts of African beasts in the circus, in the open, or in the amphitheater; in them about 3,500 beasts were killed.

23. I gave the people a spectacle of a naval battle, in the place across the Tiber where the grove of the Caesars is now, with the ground excavated in length 1,800 feet, in width 1,200, in which thirty beaked ships, biremes or triremes, but many smaller, fought among themselves; in these ships about 3,000 men fought in addition to the rowers.

24. In the temples of all the cities of the province of Asia, as victor, I replaced the ornaments which he with whom I fought the war had possessed privately after he despoiled the temples. Silver statues of me on foot, on horseback, and standing in a chariot were erected in about eighty cities, which I myself removed, and from the money I placed goldn offerings in the temple of Apollo under my name and of those who paid the honor of the statues to me.

25. I restored peace to the sea from pirates. In that slave war I handed over to their masters for the infliction of punishments about 30,000 captured, who had fled their masters and taken up arms against the state. All Italy swore allegiance to me voluntarily, and demanded me as leader of the war which I won at Actium; the provinces of Gaul, Spain, Africa, Sicily, and Sardinia swore the same allegiance. And those who then fought under my standard were more than 700 senators, among whom 83 were made consuls either before or after, up to the day this was written, and about 170 were made priests.

26. I extended the borders of all the provinces of the Roman people which neighbored nations not subject to our rule. I restored peace to the provinces of Gaul and Spain, likewise Germany, which includes the ocean from Cadiz to the mouth of the river Elbe. I brought peace to the Alps from the region which i near the Adriatic Sea to the Tuscan, with no unjust war waged against any nation. I sailed my ships on the ocean from the mouth of the Rhine to the east region up to the borders of the Cimbri, where no Roman had gone before that time by land or sea, and the Cimbri and the Charydes and the Semnones and the other Germans of the same territory sought by envoys the friendship of me and of the Roman people. By my order and auspices two armies were led at about the same time into Ethiopia and into that part of Arabia which is called Happy, and the troops of each nation of enemies were slaughtered in battle and many towns captured. They penetrated into Ethiopia all the way to the town Nabata, which is near to Meroe; and into Arabia all the way to the border of the Sabaei, advancing to the town Mariba.

27. I added Egypt to the rule of the Roman people. When Artaxes, king of Greater Armenia, was killed, though I could have made it a province, I preferred, by the example of our elders, to hand over that kingdom to Tigranes, son of king Artavasdes, and grandson of King Tigranes, through Tiberius Nero, who was then my step-son. And the same nation, after revolting and rebelling, and subdued through my son Gaius, I handed over to be ruled by King Ariobarzanes son of Artabazus, King of the Medes, and after his death, to his son Artavasdes; and when he was killed, I sent Tigranes, who came from the royal clan of the Armenians, into that rule. I recovered all the provinces which lie across the Adriatic to the east and Cyrene, with kings now possessing them in large part, and Sicily and Sardina, which had been occupied earlier in the slave war.

28. I founded colonies of soldiers in Africa, Sicily, Macedonia, each Spain, Greece, Asia, Syria, Narbonian Gaul, and Pisidia, and furthermore had twenty-eight colonies founded in Italy under my authority, which were very populous and crowded while I lived.

29. I recovered from Spain, Gaul, and Dalmatia the many military standards lost through other leaders, after defeating te enemies. I compelled the Parthians to return to me the spoils and standards of three Roman armies, and as suppliants to seek the friendship of the Roman people. Furthermore I placed those standards in the sanctuary of the temple of Mars Ultor.

30. As for the tribes of the Pannonians, before my principate no army of the Roman people had entered their land. When they were conquered through Tiberius Nero, who was then my step-son and emissary, I subjected them to the rule of the Roman people and extended the borders of Illyricum to the shores of the river Danube. On the near side of it the army of the Dacians was conquered and overcome under my auspices, and then my army, led across the Danube, forced the tribes of the Dacians to bear the rule of the Roman people.

31. Emissaries from the Indian kings were often sent to me, which had not been seen before that time by any Roman leader. The Bastarnae, the Scythians, and the Sarmatians, who are on this side of the river Don and the kings further away, an the kings of the Albanians, of the Iberians, and of the Medes, sought our friendship through emissaries.

32. To me were sent supplications by kings: of the Parthians, Tiridates and later Phrates son of king Phrates, of the Medes, Artavasdes, of the Adiabeni, Artaxares, of the Britons, Dumnobellaunus and Tincommius, of the Sugambri, Maelo, of the Marcomanian Suebi (..., -)rus. King Phrates of the Parthians, son of Orodes, sent all his sons and grandsons into Italy to me, though defeated in no war, but seeking our friendship through the pledges of his children. And in my principate many other peoples experienced the faith of the Roman people, of whom nothing had previously existed of embassies or interchange of friendship with the Roman people.

33. The nations of the Parthians and Medes received from me the first kings of those nations which they sought by emissaries: the Parthians, Vonones son of king Phrates, grandson of king Orodes, the Medes, Ariobarzanes, son of king Artavasdes, grandson of king Aiobarzanes.

34. In my sixth and seventh consulates (28–27 B.C.E.), after putting out the civil war, having obtained all things by universal consent, I handed over the state from my power to the dominion of the senate and Roman people. And for this merit of mine, by a senate decree, I was called Augustus and the doors of my temple were publicly clothed with laurel and a civic crown was fixed over my door and a gold shield placed in the Julian senate-house, and the inscription of that shield testified to the virtue, mercy, justice, and piety, for which the senate and Roman people gave it to me. After that time, I exceeded all in influence, but I had no greater power than the others who were colleagues with me in each magistracy.

35. When I administered my thirteenth consulate (2 B.C.E.), the senate and Equestrian order and Roman people all called me father of the country, and voted that the same be inscribed in the vestibule of my temple, in the Julian senate-house, and in the

forum of Augustus under the chario which had been placed there for me by a decision of the senate. When I wrote this I was seventy-six years old.

APPENDIX
Written after Augustus' death.

1. All the expenditures which he gave either into the treasury or to the Roman plebs or to discharged soldiers: HS 2,400,000,000.
2. The works he built: the temples of Mars, of Jupiter Subduer and Thunderer, of Apollo, of divine Julius, of Minerva, of Queen Juno, of Jupiter Liberator, of the Lares, of the gods of the Penates, of Youth, and of the Great Mother, the Lupercal, the state box at the circus, the senate-house with the Chalcidicum, the forum of Augustus, the Julian basilica, the theater of Marcellus, the Octavian portico, and the grove of the Caesars across the Tiber.
3. He rebuilt the Capitol and holy temples numbering eighty-two, the theater of Pompey, waterways, and the Flaminian road.
4. The sum expended on theatrical spectacles and gladiatorial games and athletes and hunts and mock naval battles and money given to colonies, cities, and towns destroyed by earthquake and fire or per man to friends and senators, whom he raised to the senate rating: innumerable.

Analysis Questions

1. What impact did the story of Romulus, Brutus, and Collatinus and the Twelve Tables have on the development of the Roman republic?
2. What are the main messages of these Bible chapters? What is Jesus's perception of the kingdom? Why did it matter to the Hebrews at the time?
3. In *The Deeds of the Divine Augustus*, how does Augustus view himself?

CHAPTER 6

Early East Asian Civilizations, to Tenth Century A.D.

Introduction

While Rome was coming to power in the Mediterranean area, China, on the other side of the world, was entering its own brilliant age under the Qin and Han dynasties. The Qin Dynasty lasted only from 221 to 206 B.C. But its achievements were extraordinarily influential in China's subsequent development. "China," the name of the country, originated in the Qin (Ch'in) Dynasty. The first ruler of a unified Chinese empire, Qin Shi Huang Di, using legalist principles, established a system of governmental institutions and a concept of empire that continued in China until the fall of the imperial Qing Dynasty in 1911. Qin Shi Huang Di standardized everything he could, from Chinese script to weights and measures and the gauge of wagon wheels. The famous Great Wall of China was extended for about 2,000 miles under his direction as well. When the First Emperor died in 210 B.C., however, his harsh laws and cruel punishments brought on civil war, and the Qin Dynasty collapsed.

The civil war was quickly resolved, and China began another millennium-long cycle, from unity to fragmentation to a new unity. Under a newly unified Han Dynasty, the Asian counterpart of contemporary Rome in its golden age, China officially became a Confucian state, prospered domestically, and enlarged its political and cultural influence over the whole of Asia before finally collapsing under a mixture of domestic and external pressures. During the "Age of Division (22–589 A.D.)," non-Chinese nomads became the champions of North China, and Buddhism, a foreign religion from India, became a cultural force in China.

The Sui and Tang dynasties from these northerners reunified China and created a high point in traditional Chinese civilization, with its brilliant flowering of culture and cosmopolitan cities. This period of power and stability fostered literature, the arts, and many inventions.

During this period (Qin-Tang Dynasty), the neighboring countries of China—especially Japan, Korea, and Vietnam—received tremendous political and cultural influence from China. Nomads from northeast Asia settled on the Korean Peninsula and Japanese islands, and their descendants eventually formed feudal states ruled by aristocratic clans. The hereditary Korean elite absorbed Confucianism and Buddhism from China and passed them along to Japan. Throughout the Three Kingdoms Period of Korea (the fourth through the seventh centuries A.D.), Koguryo, Silla, and Paekche were expansionist kingdoms. Koguryo especially was powerful enough to undermine the Chinese dynasties (Sui and Tang dynasties). Koguryo created a colossal realm that included the northern Korean Peninsula and the greater part of Manchuria. To prevent Koguryo's threat, the Tang needed to make a strategic alliance with Silla. Between 660 and 668 A.D., Silla in the end succeeded in overcoming two other Korean kingdoms, Paekche and Koguryo, with the assistance of the Tang. The outcome was the first political unification of Korea in 668 A.D. Much of the political refugees of Koguryo and Paekche fled to Japanese islands and introduced to Japan more advanced forms in art and literature, political structure, and Buddhism. Fearing from a possible attack from Silla, a pro-Korean and pro-Buddhist faction led by Prince Shotoku undertook the radical reforms of the Yamato government, establishing centralized absolutism. Its capital, Nara, became the symbol of these reforms, modeled after the Chinese capital of Changan. Here you will read various brief selections dealing with the cultures, thought, and literature of China, Japan, and Korea.

Donggung Palace, Silla Dynasty, Korea

19. Tang Poems (Li Bai and Du Fu)

by Li Bai; trans. Ying Sun & Du Fu; trans. Ying Sun

DRINKING ALONE WITH THE MOON (701–762 AD, CHINA)

From a wine pot amidst the flowers,
I drink alone without partners.
To invite the moon I raise my cup.
We're three, as my shadow shows up.
Alas, the moon doesn't drink.
My shadow follows but doesn't think.
Still for now I have these friends,
To cheer me up until the spring ends.
I sing; the moon wanders.
I dance; the shadow scatters.
Awake, together we have fun.
Drunk, separately we're gone.
Let's be boon companions forever,
Pledging, in heaven, we'll be together. By Li Bai

BRING IN THE WINE (701–762 AD, CHINA)

Can't you see the Yellow River coming from heaven,
Running to the sea with no return?
Can't you see the mirror, high and bright,
Weeping over black hair at dawn, but white by night?
Enjoy life when there is prosperity.
Never tip a gold cup to the moon, empty.
Heaven has given me a gift and it's my turn.
All my fortune is squandered, but it will return.
Let's have fun—a fest with veal and beef.
Empty three hundred drinks before we leave.
Master Cen, Pupil Danqiu,
Bring in the wine and I'll keep pouring for you.
And I'll sing you a song.
Please listen and hum along:
The life style of the rich is all fake.
I'd rather stay drunk, never awake.

All sages in history were solitary,
Except those drinkers who left their glory.
When Lord Chen entertained in Ping-Le Palace,
Pricey wine was poured just for joyfulness.
Why worry about spending money, my host?
Bring in more wine and I'll drink the most.
Take my spotted stallion and fancy fur.
Ask the lad to trade for the wine I prefer.
Drink away the eternal sorrow we all suffer. By Li Bai

IN THE QUIET OF THE NIGHT (701–762 AD, CHINA)
Moonlight reflects off the front of my bed.
Could it be frost on the ground instead?
I look up to view the bright moon ahead.
Thoughts of hometown bring down my head. By Li Bai

SPRING PROSPECT (712–770 AD, CHINA)
The country is in ruins, but hills and streams remain.
Grass and trees prosper as spring comes again.
Flowers spatter tears when hard times dominate.
Birds alarm the heart that hates to separate.
For three months beacon fires have continued to hold.
A letter from home now is worth its weight in gold.
Scratching my grey hair has made it grow so thin,
There's hardly enough to support a hairpin. By Du Fu

CHARIOTS BALLAD (712–770 AD, CHINA)
Chariots rumble, and horses neigh.
Bow and arrows are at each soldier's waist.
Parents and wives follow to bid farewell.
Xianyang Bridge disappears as dust clouds swell.
They grab clothes, stomp feet, block roads, and cry.
The howling goes straight up, high in the sky.
Passing by, I ask the soldiers what's wrong.
They say frequent drafts have gone on just too long.
A boy was drafted at fifteen to defend the north river.
At forty he still serves on the west front as a farmer.
Upon dispatch the village elder wrapped his hair, all black.
He returned with gray hair but still had to go back.
On the fronts, blood sheds so much to form seas.
Emperor Wu's will to expand territories doesn't cease.
Haven't you heard?

East of Hua Mountains there are two hundred states.
Thousands of villages buried in briers lay waste.
Although strong women could plough the fields,
Crops grow haphazardly with poor yields.
Furthermore, soldiers from here are well-known fighters.
But they are exploited like dogs and roosters.
Although you ask us to explain,
Do soldiers dare to complain?
Like the winter of this year,
Relief for the West Gate troop is unclear.
The governor wants his taxes right away.
How to pay the taxes no one can find a way.
Had we known raising a boy child could be so bad,
We would rather give birth to a girl instead.
At least girls can marry to neighbors close by.
Boys are buried far away like weeds to pass by.
Haven't you seen, by the shore of the Green Sea?
Since ancient times skeletons are scattered and let be.
New ghosts are quetching and old ghosts weeping.
On a dismal rainy day you could hear them wailing. By Du Fu

20. *Tales from the Three Kingdoms*, Korea

by Tae Hung Ha

In the first month of the 23rd year of Yongyang-wang, the 26th sovereign of Koguryo, Sui Yangti, the proud emperor of China, started an unprovoked war and sent out his large host of twenty four armies under the command of Yu Wen-shu and Yu Chung-wen to attack Koguryo toward the south of the Yalu River.

All Koguryo was alarmed, and Youngyang-wang, the King, ordered General Ulchi Moonduk to take up the challenge and hurl back the enemy. Moonduk met the commanding generals of Sui in the latter's field camp and feigned to surrender in order to verify the enemys' intention and to probe his real strength.

Yu Chung-wen, having been secretly instructed by his emperor, wanted to take Moonduk a prisoner of war, but Liu Sa-lung, royal envoy of Sui, stopped him, saying that it was breach of etiquette and violation of war regulations to imprison a surrendering enemy general. So Moonduk safely returned home by crossing the Yalu.

When Moonduk was gone too far to be overtaken, the two generals of Sui began to quarrel.

Wen-shu: "Our supply route is stretching ten thousand *li*, and there is no food to feed our officers and men. If we march on any further our soldiers will fall on their empty stomachs. Let us turn back."

Chung-wen: "If our crack troops pursue Moonduk in double-quick time and bring him back I will give them a big reward."

Wen-shu: No, it is too late to catch him."

Chung-wen (angry): "What! If your large host of one hundred thousand men cannot crush Koguryo's small army, how will you meet the emperor face to face?"

Wen-shu was dumbfounded. He stood at the head of his army and crossed the Yalu in pursuit of Moonduk's retreating regiments.

Moonduk saw that the myriad Sui hordes were far away from their supply bases and were almost creeping on their empty stomachs, although their flags, spears and swords glittered in the sun. So he led the enemy farther and farther as he hit and ran, hit and ran seven times, giving him a heavy blow at the Battle of Chongchon-gang (River).

The enemy, battered but triumphant, pursued the running general of Koguryo and crossed the Chongchon-gang, three hundred *li* north of Pyongyang, the capital of Koguryo. Moonduk deployed his brave soldiers behind a mountain fortress and dispatched a letter by a war messenger to the Sui commander. The letter was written as follows:

> "General of the Great Sui Empire,
> Your swift race scares all ghosts of heaven to weep;
> Your loud warcry threatens dragons and tigers on earth to jump.
> But the herculean sons of Koguryo will turn heaven and earth upside down.
> You have won many battles, and your merit is high—
> Now, stop, turn back and go home;
> Yon will receive a gold medal from your emperor."

Chung-wen was very angry and shouted:

"He makes fun of the commanding general of the Great Celestial Empire. Tell him to come and kowtow before me with a formal apology."

The war messenger told Moonduk of these words, but Moonduk laughed and said:

"You go again and convey my message to the Sui commander, "If you go back to your celestial empire, I and my king will bring tribute to your emperor."

Chung-wen got more angry and his hairs stood on end, but seeing his officers and men dying of hunger and exhausted by the long march, and knowing that Pyongyang was fortified with impregnable walls, he ordered his host to turn about.

All at once rains of arrows fell with terrific warrories from the hidden positions of Koguryo. Both Chung-wen and Wen-shu ran as fast as they could, followed by their terror-stricken soldiers shrieking in the agony of death. Moonduk drove the enemy as far back as the deep wide river of the Chongchon-gang and gave him an annihilating blow, turning the blue water into red waves with the blood of the enemy dead and wounded.

The valiant warriors of Koguryo pursued the invaders fleeing across the great river and slaughtered them by hundreds and thousands till the defeated enemy hordes scattered and fled across the Yalu and returned to Liaotung-cheng in Manchuria, where they counted only 2,700 alive out of 305,000 men who had started out on the conquest of Koguryo.

Hearing the news of this tragic defeat, Sui Yangti jumped up from his throne and shouted for revenge. He drove his chariot at the head of a million-man host that started on the second expedition, but he suffered another annihilating defeat battle after battle, because the valiant warriors of Koguryo once again plunged the Sui hordes into the depths of the Chongchon-gang and pursued the fleeing enemy across the Yalu.

Sui Yangti trembled with fear and fled to save his own life, but he dearly paid for his attempted conquest of Koguryo, because it brought about utter exhaustion of his national strength and caused the early fall of his empire in China.

Ulchi Moonduk is honored by all Koreans as the greatest general in their long national history, for his dauntless courage, peerless wit, and lucky success of arms, who with a small army defeated a powerful enemy of overwhelming numerical superiority and saved his fatherland from danger.

---

21. The Seventeen Article Constitution of Japan

by Prince Shotoku; trans. W.G. Aston

INTRODUCTION

The 604 Constitution shaped morality and law in Japan, a country which had just begun to develop and become literate. In it, one can observe that the emphasis of Oriental law which seeks to prevent disputes, whereas Western law seeks to resolve

Prince Shotoku, "The Seventeen Article Constitution of Japan," trans. W.G. Aston, 1896.

disputes. Authorship of the document is often attributed to Prince Shotoku Taishi (574–622). It was formally issued by the government of Japan in 604, then known as *Wa*.

Shotoku is also credited with the invention of sushi and his authorship of the 17 article constitution is the subject of some controversy. Some modern Japanese historians believe that Shotoku did not have the writing skills to write the Constitution. In any event, it has long been the practice everywhere to give credit for a legal document to the reigning monarch rather than to the actual scribe.

The history of Shotoku's constitution has always been tagged with controversy. As a national treasure, in 1949, the Japanese government struggled with the existence of several different versions of the 604 Constitution and finally chose one as authentic. However, in 1974, some Japanese historians publicly alleged that it was a forgery pointing out that some of the institutions it refers to only came into existence some hundred years later.

The 604 Constitution, known in Japanese as *Jushichijo Kenpo*, was certainly not in the form of contemporary law. Indeed, it more closely resembles biblical passages or the Muslim law style of governing social behavior and conduct, rather than prescribing official conduct and prohibiting crimes. As such, it is a typical Buddhist/Confuscius law, especially the latter in insisting on moral standards by government officials.

Nonetheless, it is the first document in Japanese legal history. According to some jurists, the 604 Constitution remained in force until it was replaced by a new constitution in 1890. Other even claim that since the 1890 law did not expressly repeal the 604 Constitution that where it is not inconsistent, it continues to apply to this day. However, on a any reading of the Constitution (see below), it is doubtful if any of the 604 document could now be used in a court of law.

Here is the translation prepared by W.G. Aston. There have been several translations but this is the most popular. However, upon occasion, the English appears stilted, likely a necessary evil in an attempt at Japanese to English translation in 1896. Still, one can imagine with delight the solemn and historic moments of reflection of Japanese scribes circa 604 as they crafted the nation's first law to fit their era.

One last word: it is not really a constitution in the legal sense of the word as the document does not purport to establish any form of a parliament. However, it is a national law, albeit moralistic in style, and does support the concept of a centralized state and in that sense, you really have to want to pull hairs to deny it the title of *constitution*.

ARTICLE 1

Harmony is to be valued, and an avoidance of wanton opposition to be honoured. All men are influenced by class-feelings, and there are few who are intelligent. Hence there are some who disobey their lords and fathers, or who maintain feuds with the neighbouring villages. But when those above are harmonious and those below are friendly, and there is concord in the discussion of business, right views of things spontaneously gain acceptance. Then what is there which cannot be accomplished!

ARTICLE 2

Sincerely reverence the three treasures. The three treasures, *viz.* Buddha, the law and the priesthood, are the final refuge of the four generated beings, and are the supreme objects of faith in all countries. What man in what age can fail to reverence this law? Few men are utterly bad. They may be taught to follow it. But if they do not betake them to the three treasures, how shall their crookedness be made straight?

ARTICLE 3

When you receive the Imperial commands, fail not scrupulously to obey them. The lord is Heaven, the vassal is Earth. Heaven overspreads, and Earth upbears. When this is so, the four seasons follow their due course, and the powers of Nature obtain their efficacy. If the Earth attempted to overspread, Heaven would simply fall in ruin. Therefore is it that when the lord speaks, the vassal listens; when the superior acts, the inferior yields compliance. Consequently when you receive the Imperial commands, fail not to carry them out scrupulously. Let there be a want of care in this matter, and ruin is the natural consequence.

ARTICLE 4

The Ministers and functionaries should make decorous behaviour their leading principle, for the leading principle of the government of the people consists in decorous behaviour. If the superiors do not behave with decorum, the inferiors are disorderly. If inferiors are wanting in proper behaviour, there must necessarily be offenses. Therefore it is that when lord and vassal behave with propriety, the distinctions of rank are not confused. When the people behave with propriety, the Government of the Commonwealth proceeds of itself.

ARTICLE 5

Ceasing from gluttony and abandoning covetous desires impartially with the suits which are submitted to you. Of complaints brought by the people there are a thousand in one day. If in one day there are so many, how many will there be in a series of years? If the man who is to decide suits at law makes gain his ordinary motive, and hears causes with a view to receiving bribes, then will the suits of the rich man be like a stone flung into water, while the plaints of the poor will resemble water cast upon a stone. Under these circumstances the poor man will not know whither to betake himself. Here too there is a deficiency in the duty of the Minister.

ARTICLE 6

Chastise that which is evil and encourage that which is good. This was the excellent rule of antiquity. Conceal not, therefore, the good qualities of others, and fail not to correct that which is wrong when you see it. Flatterers and deceivers are a sharp weapon for the overthrow of the State, and a pointed sword for the destruction of the people. Sycophants are also fond, when they meet, of dilating at length to their superiors on the errors of their inferiors. To their inferiors, they censure the faults of their superiors. Men of this kind are all wanting in fidelity to their lord, and in benevolence toward the people. From such an origin great civil disturbances arise.

ARTICLE 7

Let every man have his own charge, and let not the spheres of duty be confused. When wise men are entrusted with office, the sound of praise arises. If unprincipled men hold office, disasters and tumults are multiplied. In this world, few are born with knowledge: wisdom is the product of earnest meditation. In all things, whether great or small, find the right man, and they will surely be well managed. On all occasions, be they urgent or the reverse, meet but with a wise man, and they will of themselves be amenable. In this way will the State be lasting and the Temples of the Earth and of Grain will be free from danger. Therefore did the wise sovereigns of antiquity seek the man to fill the office, and not the office for the sake of the man.

ARTICLE 8

That the Ministers and functionaries attended the court early in the morning, and retire late. The business of the state does not admit of remissness, and the whole day is hardly enough for its accomplishment. If, therefore, the attendance at court is late, emergencies cannot be met. If officials retire soon, the work cannot be completed.

ARTICLE 9

Good faith is the foundation of right. In everything let there be good faith, for it there surely consists the good and the bad, success and failure. If the Lord and the vassal observe good faith one with another, what is there which cannot be accomplished? If the Lord and the vassal do not observe good faith toward one another, everything without exception ends in failure.

ARTICLE 10

Let us cease from wrath, and refrain from angry looks. Nor let us be resentful when others differ from us. For all men have hearts, and each heart has its own leanings. Their right is our wrong, and our right is their wrong. We are not unquestionably sages, nor are they unquestionably fools. Both of us are simply ordinary men. How can any one lay down a rule by which to distinguish right from wrong? For we are all, one with another, wise and foolish, like a ring which has no end. Therefore, although others give way to anger, let us on the contrary dread our own faults, and though we alone may be in the right, let us follow the multitude and act like men.

ARTICLE 11

Give clear appreciation to merit and demerit, and deal out to each it's sure reward or punishment. In these days, reward does not attend upon merit, nor punishment upon crime. Ye high functionaries who have charge of public affairs, let it be your task to make clear rewards and punishments.

ARTICLE 12

That not the provincial authorities or the Kuni no Miyakko (ancient local nobles) levy exactions on the people. In a country there are not two lords. The people have not two masters. The sovereign is the master of the people of the whole country. The officials to whom he gives charges are all his vassals. How can they, as well as the government, presume to levy taxes on the people?

ARTICLE 13

Let all persons entrusted with office attend equally to their functions. Owing to their illness or to their being sent on missions, their work may sometimes be neglected. But whenever they become able to attend to business, let them be as accommodating as if they had cognizance of it from before, and not hinder public affairs on the score of their not having had to do with them.

ARTICLE 14

Ye Ministers and functionaries! Be not envious. For if we envy others, they in turn will envy us. The evils of envy know no limit. If others excel us in intelligence, it gives us no pleasure. If they surpass it in ability, we are envious. Therefore it is not until after a lapse of 500 years that we had last meet with a wise man, and even a thousand years we hardly obtain one sage. But if we do not find wise men and sages, wherewithal shall the country be governed?

ARTICLE 15

To turn away from that which is private, and to set our faces toward that which is public—this is the path of a Minister. Now if a man is influenced by private motives, he will assuredly feel resentments, and if he is influenced by resentful feelings, he will assuredly fail to act harmoniously with others. If he fails to act harmoniously with others, he will assuredly sacrifice the public interests to his private feelings. When resentment arises, it interferes with order, and is subversive of law. Therefore in the first clause it was said, that superiors and inferiors should agree together. The purport is the same as this.

ARTICLE 16

Let the people be employed (in forced labour) at seasonable times. This is an ancient and excellent rule. Let them be employed, therefore, in the winter months, when they are at leisure. But from Spring to Autumn, when they are engaged in agriculture or with the mulberry trees, the people should not be so employed. For if they do not attend to agriculture, what will they have to eat? If they do not attend the mulberry trees, what will they do for clothing?

ARTICLE 17

Decisions on important matters should not be made by one person alone. They should be discussed with many. But small matters are of less consequence. It is unnecessary to consult a number of people. It is only in the case of the discussion of weighty matters, when there is a suspicion that the many miscarry, that one should arrange They should be discussed with many. But small matters are of less consequence. It is unnecessary to consult a number of people. It is only in the case of the discussion of weighty affairs, when there is a suspicion that they may miscarry, that one should arrange matters in concert with others, so as to arrive at the right conclusion.

REFERENCES

Duhaime, Lloyd, *Japan: A Legal History*

Duhaime, Lloyd, *Timetable of World Legal History*

Lee, K.D.Y., *The Prince and the Monk: Shotoku Worship in Sinran's Buddhism* (New York: State University of New York press, 2007)

Nihongi, *Chronicles of Japan from the Earliest Times to A.D. 697* (London: Keagan and Co., 1896), vol. 2, pp. 128–133 (translated by W.G. Aston)

Steenstrup, Carl, *A History of Law in Japan Until 1868* (Tokyo: Brill Publishers, 1996)

Analysis Questions

1. Find any Chinese philosophical influences from Tang poems. Discuss differences between Li Bai's poems and Du Fu's poems.
2. Why is Prince Shotoku's constitution important for Japanese history? What Buddhist and Confucian ideas are incorporated into this document?
3. Explain the relationships between Korean dynasty and Chinese dynasty.

CHAPTER 7

Christians and Barbarians, to Eleventh Century A.D.

Introduction

The persecution of the Christians in Rome began under Diocletian in 303 and reached its peak under his successors, Galerius and Maximian. However, in the last few years, Constantine had been working toward toleration. This change of policy is not that surprising in light of the fact that Constantine's own mother, Helena, was a Christian. Also, Constantine's religious views changed radically in 312 when he was in Italy fighting Maxentius, the son of Maximian. Just before the battle, Constantine reportedly witnessed a cross of light superimposed on the sun. From then on, he identified the cross with the Christian God. He then ordered his men to go into battle with Christian symbols painted on their shields. Whether this imbued the soldiers with divine courage and skill or luck was with them on that day, they won a famous victory at the Milvian Bridge, just outside Rome, on October 28. As a result, Constantine became the sole ruler of the West.

On February 3, 313, Emperor Constantine, the ruler of the western provinces of the Roman Empire, and Licinius, the most powerful man in the East, agreed on a new policy henceforth of absolute toleration for Christians. They signed an edict guaranteeing the new policy as well as restoring to Christians any confiscated property. In 324, Constantine defeated Licinius and ruled the entire Roman Empire. A year later, he called for the first world council of the Christian church to meet at Nicaea. In 330, Constantine moved the empire's capital away from pagan Rome to a new city, Constantinople, built on the site of the village of Byzantium, thus beginning the Eastern Roman Empire, or the Byzantine Empire. This empire reached its height during the reign of Justinian I (527–565) and was a rich center of culture, art, and scholarship whose influence spread westward into southern Europe.

In 375, Roman forces on the upper Danube basin were watching a growing horde of barbarians on the north bank of the Danube. These barbarians were their old enemies, the Goths, but the difference this time was that these warriors were themselves under ferocious attack, becoming refugees seeking asylum inside Roman territory from the attacks of new invaders—the Huns. From the desolate Siberian deserts around Lake Baikal, the Huns drove westward. Nomadic Alans living between the Don and Volga Rivers were the first to confront the invasion and prudently changed sides. The migration became a tidal wave of Germanic tribes, from the Ostrogoths to the Visigoths, which heralded a storm to come. These migrations threatened the integrity of the empire. Menaced by continual attacks from the Visigoths and other barbarians, the Romans began to abandon the outlying parts of the empire, and in 455, a Vandal horde sacked Rome. The last emperor in the West, Romulus Augustus, was deposed in 476. In 486, the kingdom of the Roman Syagrius in northern Gaul was crushed at Noviodunum (Soissons) by Clovis, the king of the Franks, who now ruled from the Somme to the Loire. His victory spelled the end of Roman rule in Gaul.

In 461, Bishop Patrick, one of the most remarkable men ever to come to Ireland, died. Everyone who met him was impressed by his holiness, which came from a firm belief that he received direct and specific guidance from God in dreams and visions. It was one such vision that urged him to return to Ireland and convert the Irish, a task he went some way toward completing. Bishop Patrick was a product of active Christian mission functions under the Roman Empire. Another Christian movement known as *monasticism* (living apart from the world in order to devote oneself to God) also grew popular during this period. Many monasteries found throughout Europe were centers of learning as well as a source of relief for the poor and sick. These monasteries followed the same "rule"—a guide to how the community should live, drawn up by a monastic leader. The greatest rule was that of Saint Benedict of Nursia in 529. Benedict directed that a monk's life should be one of prayer and manual labor.

---

22. Eusebius, *The Conversion of Constantine*

trans. and ed. Philip Schaff and Henry Wace

CHAPTER XXVII.

Being convinced, however, that he needed some more powerful aid than his military forces could afford him, on account of the wicked and magical enchantments which were so diligently practiced by the tyrant, he sought Divine assistance, deeming the

"Chapter XXVII-XXXII," *Library of Nicene and Post Nicene Fathers*, 2nd Series, vol. 1, trans. and ed. Philip Schaff and Henry Wace, pp. 489-491, 1900.

possession of arms and a numerous soldiery of secondary importance, but believing the co-operating power of Deity invincible and not to be shaken. He considered, therefore, on what God he might rely for protection and assistance. While engaged in this enquiry, the thought occurred to him, that, of the many emperors who had preceded him, those who had rested their hopes in a multitude of gods, and served them with sacrifices and offerings, had in the first place been deceived by flattering predictions, and oracles which promised them all prosperity, and at last had met with an unhappy end, while not one of their gods had stood by to warn them of the impending wrath of heaven; while one alone who had pursued an entirely opposite course, who had condemned their error, and honored the one Supreme God during his whole life, had formal I him to be the Saviour and Protector of his empire, and the Giver of every good thing. Reflecting on this, and well weighing the fact that they who had trusted in many gods had also fallen by manifold forms of death, without leaving behind them either family or offspring, stock, name, or memorial among men: while the God of his father had given to him, on the other hand, manifestations of his power and very many tokens: and considering farther that those who had already taken arms against the tyrant, and had marched to the battle-field under the protection of a multitude of gods, had met with a dishonorable end (for one of them had shamefully retreated from the contest without a blow, and the other, being slain in the midst of his own troops, became, as it were, the mere sport of death (4)); reviewing, I say, all these considerations, he judged it to be folly indeed to join in the idle worship of those who were no gods, and, after such convincing evidence, to err from the truth; and therefore felt it incumbent on him to honor his father's God alone.

CHAPTER XXVIII.

ACCORDINGLY he called on him with earnest prayer and supplications that he would reveal to him who he was, and stretch forth his right hand to help him in his present difficulties. And while he was thus praying with fervent entreaty, a most marvelous sign appeared to him from heaven, the account of which it might have been hard to believe had it been related by any other person. But since the victorious emperor himself long afterwards declared it to the writer of this history, when he was honored with his acquaintance and society, and confirmed his statement by an oath, who could hesitate to accredit the relation, especially since the testimony of after-time has established its truth? He said that about noon, when the day was already beginning to decline, he saw with his own eyes the trophy of a cross of light in the heavens, above the sun, and bearing the inscription, CONQUER BY THIS. At this sight he himself was struck with amazement, and his whole army also, which followed him on this expedition, and witnessed the miracle.

CHAPTER XXIX.

He said, moreover, that he doubted within himself what the import of this apparition could be. And while he continued to ponder and reason on its meaning, night suddenly came on; then in his sleep the Christ of God appeared to him with the same sign which he had seen in the heavens, and commanded him to make a likeness of that sign which he had seen in the heavens, and to use it as a safeguard in all engagements with his enemies.

CHAPTER XXX.

AT dawn of day he arose, and communicated the marvel to his friends: and then, calling together the workers in gold and precious stones, he sat in the midst of them, and described to them the figure of the sign he had seen, bidding them represent it in gold and precious stones. And this representation I myself have had an opportunity of seeing.

CHAPTER XXXI.

Now it was made in the following manner. A long spear, overlaid with gold, formed the figure of the cross by means of a transverse bar laid over it. On the top of the whole was fixed a wreath of gold and precious stones; and within this, the symbol of the Saviour's name, two letters indicating the name of Christ by means of its initial characters, the letter P being intersected by X in its centre: and these letters the emperor was in the habit of wearing on his helmet at a later period. From the cross-bar of the spear was suspended a cloth, a royal piece, covered with a profuse embroidery of most brilliant precious stones; and which, being also richly interlaced with gold, presented an indescribable degree of beauty to the beholder. This banner was of a square form, and the upright staff, whose lower section was of great length, bore a golden half-length portrait of the pious emperor and his children on its upper part, beneath the trophy of the cross, and immediately above the embroidered banner.

The emperor constantly made use of this sign of salvation as a safeguard against every adverse and hostile power, and commanded that others similar to it should be carried at the head of all his armies.

CHAPTER XXXII.

These things were done shortly afterwards. But at the time above specified, being struck with amazement at the extraordinary vision, and resolving to worship no other God save Him who had appeared to him, he sent for those who were acquainted with the mysteries of His doctrines, and enquired who that God was, and what was intended by the sign of the vision he had seen. They affirmed that He was God, the only begotten Son of the one and only God: that the sign which had appeared was the symbol of immortality, and the trophy of that victory over death which He had gained in time past when sojourning on earth. They taught him also the causes of His advent, and explained to him the true account of His incarnation. Thus he was instructed in these matters, and was impressed with wonder at the divine manifestation which had been presented to his sight. Comparing, therefore, the heavenly vision with the interpretation given, he found his judgment confirmed; and, in the persuasion that the knowledge of these things had been imparted to him by Divine teaching, he determined thenceforth to devote himself to the reading of the Inspired writings.

Moreover, he made the priests of God his counselors, and deemed it incumbent on him to honor the God who had appeared to him with all devotion. And after this, being fortified by well-grounded hopes in Him, he hastened to quench the threatening fire of tyranny.

23. Bible: Matthew and Galatians

King James Version

MATTHEW CHAPTER 5

1. And seeing the multitudes, he went up into a mountain: and when he was set, his disciples came unto him:
2. And he opened his mouth, and taught them, saying,
3. Blessed are the poor in spirit: for theirs is the kingdom of heaven.
4. Blessed are they that mourn: for they shall be comforted.
5. Blessed are the meek: for they shall inherit the earth.
6. Blessed are they which do hunger and thirst after righteousness: for they shall be filled.
7. Blessed are the merciful: for they shall obtain mercy.
8. Blessed are the pure in heart: for they shall see God.
9. Blessed are the peacemakers: for they shall be called the children of God.
10. Blessed are they which are persecuted for righteousness' sake: for theirs is the kingdom of heaven.
11. Blessed are ye, when men shall revile you, and persecute you, and shall say all manner of evil against you falsely, for my sake.
12. Rejoice, and be exceeding glad: for great is your reward in heaven: for so persecuted they the prophets which were before you.
13. Ye are the salt of the earth: but if the salt have lost his savour, wherewith shall it be salted? it is thenceforth good for nothing, but to be cast out, and to be trodden under foot of men.

"Matthew 5, Galatians 2:14-21, 3, 4," King James Version, 1611.

14. Ye are the light of the world. A city that is set on an hill cannot be hid.

15. Neither do men light a candle, and put it under a bushel, but on a candlestick; and it giveth light unto all that are in the house.

16. Let your light so shine before men, that they may see your good works, and glorify your Father which is in heaven.

17. Think not that I am come to destroy the law, or the prophets: I am not come to destroy, but to fulfil.

18. For verily I say unto you, Till heaven and earth pass, one jot or one tittle shall in no wise pass from the law, till all be fulfilled.

19. Whosoever therefore shall break one of these least commandments, and shall teach men so, he shall be called the least in the kingdom of heaven: but whosoever shall do and teach them, the same shall be called great in the kingdom of heaven.

20. For I say unto you, That except your righteousness shall exceed the righteousness of the scribes and Pharisees, ye shall in no case enter into the kingdom of heaven.

21. Ye have heard that it was said of them of old time, Thou shalt not kill; and whosoever shall kill shall be in danger of the judgment:

22. But I say unto you, That whosoever is angry with his brother without a cause shall be in danger of the judgment: and whosoever shall say to his brother, Raca, shall be in danger of the council: but whosoever shall say, Thou fool, shall be in danger of hell fire.

23. Therefore if thou bring thy gift to the altar, and there rememberest that thy brother hath ought against thee;

24. Leave there thy gift before the altar, and go thy way; first be reconciled to thy brother, and then come and offer thy gift.

25. Agree with thine adversary quickly, whiles thou art in the way with him; lest at any time the adversary deliver thee to the judge, and the judge deliver thee to the officer, and thou be cast into prison.

26. Verily I say unto thee, Thou shalt by no means come out thence, till thou hast paid the uttermost farthing.

27. Ye have heard that it was said by them of old time, Thou shalt not commit adultery:

28. But I say unto you, That whosoever looketh on a woman to lust after her hath committed adultery with her already in his heart.

29. And if thy right eye offend thee, pluck it out, and cast it from thee: for it is profitable for thee that one of thy members should perish, and not that thy whole body should be cast into hell.

30. And if thy right hand offend thee, cut it off, and cast it from thee: for it is profitable for thee that one of thy members should perish, and not that thy whole body should be cast into hell.

31. It hath been said, Whosoever shall put away his wife, let him give her a writing of divorcement:

32. But I say unto you, That whosoever shall put away his wife, saving for the cause of fornication, causeth her to commit adultery: and whosoever shall marry her that is divorced committeth adultery.

33. Again, ye have heard that it hath been said by them of old time, Thou shalt not forswear thyself, but shalt perform unto the Lord thine oaths:

34. But I say unto you, Swear not at all; neither by heaven; for it is God's throne:

35. Nor by the earth; for it is his footstool: neither by Jerusalem; for it is the city of the great King.

36. Neither shalt thou swear by thy head, because thou canst not make one hair white or black.

37. But let your communication be, Yea, yea; Nay, nay: for whatsoever is more than these cometh of evil.

38. Ye have heard that it hath been said, An eye for an eye, and a tooth for a tooth:

39. But I say unto you, That ye resist not evil: but whosoever shall smite thee on thy right cheek, turn to him the other also.

40. And if any man will sue thee at the law, and take away thy coat, let him have thy cloak also.

41. And whosoever shall compel thee to go a mile, go with him twain.

42. Give to him that asketh thee, and from him that would borrow of thee turn not thou away.

43. Ye have heard that it hath been said, Thou shalt love thy neighbour, and hate thine enemy.

44. But I say unto you, Love your enemies, bless them that curse you, do good to them that hate you, and pray for them which despitefully use you, and persecute you;

45. That ye may be the children of your Father which is in heaven: for he maketh his sun to rise on the evil and on the good, and sendeth rain on the just and on the unjust.

46. For if ye love them which love you, what reward have ye? do not even the publicans the same?

47. And if ye salute your brethren only, what do ye more than others? do not even the publicans so?

48. Be ye therefore perfect, even as your Father which is in heaven is perfect.

GALATIANS CHAPTER 2

1. But when I saw that they walked not uprightly according to the truth of the gospel, I said unto Peter before them all, If thou, being a Jew, livest after the

manner of Gentiles, and not as do the Jews, why compellest thou the Gentiles to live as do the Jews?

2. We who are Jews by nature, and not sinners of the Gentiles,

3. Knowing that a man is not justified by the works of the law, but by the faith of Jesus Christ, even we have believed in Jesus Christ, that we might be justified by the faith of Christ, and not by the works of the law: for by the works of the law shall no flesh be justified.

4. But if, while we seek to be justified by Christ, we ourselves also are found sinners, is therefore Christ the minister of sin? God forbid.

5. For if I build again the things which I destroyed, I make myself a transgressor.

6. For I through the law am dead to the law, that I might live unto God.

7. I am crucified with Christ: nevertheless I live; yet not I, but Christ liveth in me: and the life which I now live in the flesh I live by the faith of the Son of God, who loved me, and gave himself for me.

8. I do not frustrate the grace of God: for if righteousness come by the law, then Christ is dead in vain.

GALATIANS CHAPTER 3

1. O foolish Galatians, who hath bewitched you, that ye should not obey the truth, before whose eyes Jesus Christ hath been evidently set forth, crucified among you?

2. This only would I learn of you, Received ye the Spirit by the works of the law, or by the hearing of faith?

3. Are ye so foolish? having begun in the Spirit, are ye now made perfect by the flesh?

4. Have ye suffered so many things in vain? if it be yet in vain.

5. He therefore that ministereth to you the Spirit, and worketh miracles among you, doeth he it by the works of the law, or by the hearing of faith?

6. Even as Abraham believed God, and it was accounted to him for righteousness.

7. Know ye therefore that they which are of faith, the same are the children of Abraham.

8. And the scripture, foreseeing that God would justify the heathen through faith, preached before the gospel unto Abraham, saying, In thee shall all nations be blessed.

9. So then they which be of faith are blessed with faithful Abraham.

10. For as many as are of the works of the law are under the curse: for it is written, Cursed is every one that continueth not in all things which are written in the book of the law to do them.

11. But that no man is justified by the law in the sight of God, it is evident: for, The just shall live by faith.

12. And the law is not of faith: but, The man that doeth them shall live in them.

13. Christ hath redeemed us from the curse of the law, being made a curse for us: for it is written, Cursed is every one that hangeth on a tree:

14. That the blessing of Abraham might come on the Gentiles through Jesus Christ; that we might receive the promise of the Spirit through faith.

15. Brethren, I speak after the manner of men; Though it be but a man's covenant, yet if it be confirmed, no man disannulleth, or addeth thereto.

16. Now to Abraham and his seed were the promises made. He saith not, And to seeds, as of many; but as of one, And to thy seed, which is Christ.

17. And this I say, that the covenant, that was confirmed before of God in Christ, the law, which was four hundred and thirty years after, cannot disannul, that it should make the promise of none effect.

18. For if the inheritance be of the law, it is no more of promise: but God gave it to Abraham by promise.

19. Wherefore then serveth the law? It was added because of transgressions, till the seed should come to whom the promise was made; and it was ordained by angels in the hand of a mediator.

20. Now a mediator is not a mediator of one, but God is one.

21. Is the law then against the promises of God? God forbid: for if there had been a law given which could have given life, verily righteousness should have been by the law.

22. But the scripture hath concluded all under sin, that the promise by faith of Jesus Christ might be given to them that believe.

23. But before faith came, we were kept under the law, shut up unto the faith which should afterwards be revealed.

24. Wherefore the law was our schoolmaster to bring us unto Christ, that we might be justified by faith.

25. But after that faith is come, we are no longer under a schoolmaster.

26. For ye are all the children of God by faith in Christ Jesus.

27. For as many of you as have been baptized into Christ have put on Christ.

28. There is neither Jew nor Greek, there is neither bond nor free, there is neither male nor female: for ye are all one in Christ Jesus.

29. And if ye be Christ's, then are ye Abraham's seed, and heirs according to the promise.

GALATIANS CHAPTER 4

1. Now I say, That the heir, as long as he is a child, differeth nothing from a servant, though he be lord of all;

2. But is under tutors and governors until the time appointed of the father.

3. Even so we, when we were children, were in bondage under the elements of the world:

4. But when the fulness of the time was come, God sent forth his Son, made of a woman, made under the law,

5. To redeem them that were under the law, that we might receive the adoption of sons.

6. And because ye are sons, God hath sent forth the Spirit of his Son into your hearts, crying, Abba, Father.

7. Wherefore thou art no more a servant, but a son; and if a son, then an heir of God through Christ.

8. Howbeit then, when ye knew not God, ye did service unto them which by nature are no gods.

9. But now, after that ye have known God, or rather are known of God, how turn ye again to the weak and beggarly elements, whereunto ye desire again to be in bondage?

10. Ye observe days, and months, and times, and years.

11. I am afraid of you, lest I have bestowed upon you labour in vain.

12. Brethren, I beseech you, be as I am; for I am as ye are: ye have not injured me at all.

13. Ye know how through infirmity of the flesh I preached the gospel unto you at the first.

14. And my temptation which was in my flesh ye despised not, nor rejected; but received me as an angel of God, even as Christ Jesus.

15. Where is then the blessedness ye spake of? for I bear you record, that, if it had been possible, ye would have plucked out your own eyes, and have given them to me.

16. Am I therefore become your enemy, because I tell you the truth?

17. They zealously affect you, but not well; yea, they would exclude you, that ye might affect them.

18. But it is good to be zealously affected always in a good thing, and not only when I am present with you.

19. My little children, of whom I travail in birth again until Christ be formed in you,

20. I desire to be present with you now, and to change my voice; for I stand in doubt of you.

21. Tell me, ye that desire to be under the law, do ye not hear the law?

22. For it is written, that Abraham had two sons, the one by a bondmaid, the other by a freewoman.

23. But he who was of the bondwoman was born after the flesh; but he of the freewoman was by promise.

24. Which things are an allegory: for these are the two covenants; the one from the mount Sinai, which gendereth to bondage, which is Agar.

25. For this Agar is mount Sinai in Arabia, and answereth to Jerusalem which now is, and is in bondage with her children.

26. But Jerusalem which is above is free, which is the mother of us all.

27. For it is written, Rejoice, thou barren that bearest not; break forth and cry, thou that travailest not: for the desolate hath many more children than she which hath an husband.

28. Now we, brethren, as Isaac was, are the children of promise.

29. But as then he that was born after the flesh persecuted him that was born after the Spirit, even so it is now.

30. Nevertheless what saith the scripture? Cast out the bondwoman and her son: for the son of the bondwoman shall not be heir with the son of the freewoman.

31. So then, brethren, we are not children of the bondwoman, but of the free.

24. *The Rule of Saint Benedict,*
Excerpts, ca. 530

trans. Ernest F. Henderson

PROLOGUE

... We are about to found therefore a school for the Lord's service; in the organization of which we trust that we shall ordain nothing severe and nothing burdensome. But even if, the demands of justice dictating it, something a little irksome shall be the result, for the purpose of amending vices or preserving charity;—thou shalt not therefore, struck by fear, flee the way of salvation, which can not be entered upon except through a narrow entrance. But as one's way of life and one's faith progresses, the heart becomes broadened, and, with the unutterable sweetness of love, the way of the mandates of the Lord is traversed. Thus, never departing from His guidance, continuing in the monastery in his teaching until death, through patience we are made partakers in Christ's passion, in order that we may merit to be companions in His kingdom.

1. Concerning the Kinds of Monks and Their Manner of Living.

It is manifest that there are four kinds of monks. The cenobites are the first kind; that is, those living in a monastery, serving under a rule or an abbot. Then the second kind is that of the anchorites; that is, the hermits-those who, not by the new fervour of

Select Historical Documents of the Middle Ages, trans. Ernest F. Henderson, 1910.

a conversion but by the long probation of life in a monastery, have learned to fight against the devil, having already been taught by the solace of many. They, having been well prepared in the army of brothers for the solitary fight of the hermit, being secure now without the consolation of another, are able, God helping them, to fight with their own hand or arm against the vices of the flesh or of their thoughts.

But a third very bad kind of monks are the sarabaites, approved by no rule, experience being their teacher, as with the gold which is tried in the furnace. But, softened after the manner of lead, keeping faith with the world by their works, they are known through their tonsure to lie to God. These being shut up by twos or threes, or, indeed, alone, without a shepherd, not in the Lord's but in their own sheep-folds-their law is the satisfaction of their desires. For whatever they think good or choice, this they call holy; and what they do not wish, this they consider unlawful. But the fourth kind of we are about to found, therefore, a school for the monks is the kind which is called gyratory. During their whole life they are guests, for three or four days at a time, in the cells of the different monasteries, throughout the various provinces; always wandering and never stationary, given over to the service of their own pleasures and the joys of the palate, and in every way worse than the sarabaites. Concerning the most wretched way of living of all such monks it is better to be silent than to speak. These things therefore being omitted, let us proceed, with the aid of God, to treat of the best kind, the cenobites.

22. How the Monks Shall Sleep.

They shall sleep separately in separate beds. They shall receive positions for their beds, after the manner of their characters, according to the dispensation of their abbot. If it can be done, they shall all sleep in one place. If, however, their number do not permit it, they shall rest, by tens or twenties, with elders who will concern themselves about them. A candle shall always be burning in that same cell until early in the morning. They shall sleep clothed, and girt with belts or with ropes; and they shall not have their knives at their sides while they sleep, lest perchance in a dream they should wound the sleepers. And let the monks be always on the alert; and, when the signal is given, rising without delay, let them hasten to mutually prepare themselves for the service of God with all gravity and modesty, however. The younger brothers shall not have beds by themselves, but interspersed among those of the elder ones. And when they rise for the service of God, they shall exhort each other mutually with moderation on account of the excuses that those who are sleepy are inclined to make.

39. Concerning the Amount of food

We believe, moreover, that, for the daily refection of the sixth as well as of the ninth hour, two cooked dishes, on account of the infirmities of the different ones, are enough for all tables: so that whoever, perchance, can not eat of one may partake of the other. Therefore let two cooked dishes suffice for all the brothers: and, if it is possible to obtain apples or growing vegetables, a third may be added. One full pound of bread shall suffice for a day, whether there be one refection, or a breakfast and a supper ... But to younger boys the same quantity shall not be served, but less than that to the older ones; moderation being observed in all things. But the eating of the flesh of quadrupeds shall be abstained from altogether by every one, excepting alone the weak and the sick.

40. Concerning the Amount of Drink.

Each one has his own gift from God, the one in this way, the other in that. Therefore it is with some hesitation that the amount of daily sustenance for others is fixed by us. Nevertheless, in view of the weakness of the infirm we believe that a hemina [just less than half a liter] of wine a day is enough for each one. Those moreover to whom God gives the ability of bearing abstinence shall know that they will have their own reward. But the prior shall judge if either the needs of the place, or labour or the heat of summer, requires more; considering in all things lest satiety or drunkenness creep in. Indeed we read that wine is not suitable for monks at all. But because, in our day, it is not possible to persuade the monks of this, let us agree at least as to the fact that we should not drink till we are sated, but sparingly ...

55. Concerning Clothes and Shoes

Vestments shall be given to the brothers according to the quality of the places where they dwell, or the temperature of the air. For in cold regions more is required; but in warm, less. This, therefore, is a matter for the abbot to decide. We nevertheless consider that for ordinary places there suffices for the monks a cowl and a gown apiece-the cowl, in winter hairy, in summer plain or old-and a working garment, on account of their labours. As clothing for the feet, shoes and boots.

Analysis Questions

1. How did Christianity help the Roman emperor in terms of his status and legitimacy? How did the Roman Empire shape early Christianity?
2. What are the main messages of these Bible chapters? How does Apostle Paul view the law?
3. Why might Saint Benedict have developed these rules for his monks?

CHAPTER 8

Islamic Civilizations, to Fourteenth Century A.D.

Introduction

The Islamic faith originated in seventh-century Arabia with one man, Muhammad. Islam spread rapidly, forging a unified empire that made great advances in literature, mathematics, and science. Today, one-sixth of the world's population are Muslims, or followers of Islam. In 570 A.D., Muhammad was born in a branch of the Quraysh, one of the many Bedouin tribes in the vast Arabian Peninsula. At age 40, he received revelations through the angel Gabriel and began to preach his belief in Allah in Mecca. Mecca was a remote but important trading and cultural center, where the Quraysh had recently become prosperous entrepreneurs, sending caravans to Syria, Iraq, Egypt, and Yemen. In fact, Muhammad was married to a wealthy Qurayshi widow with investments in the caravan trade. But Mecca is also important as a place of pilgrimage, for it is here that Arabs come to venerate the temple of the Kaaba, a black meteoric stone central to their religion, of which the Quraysh are guardians. Muhammad denounced the idols associated with the Kaaba and urged people to turn to Allah—"the One and Only God"—and help the poor. This did not endear him to some rich and powerful Meccans, and the number of his enemies increased over the years. Muhammad's decision to flee with his followers to Medina was a prudent one, since he was able to set up an Islamic community in Medina; by the time of his death in 632, his faith had spread throughout Arabia.

The revelations received by Muhammad were compiled after his death into the holy book of Islam, the Koran. Held by Muslims to be God's word, its 114 chapters contain the Islamic religious, legal, and social codes and share much with Jewish and Christian scriptures. Islam has no central organization, but five fundamental duties are obligatory for every Muslim: profession of faith in one God, Allah; prayer five times daily facing Mecca; fasting in the month of Ramadan; payment of a special tax for charity (*zakat*); and pilgrimage to Mecca.

In 656, a dispute arose over the election of the fourth caliph, and by 661, the Umayyad family had seized control of the caliphate. They moved the capital from Medina to Damascus in Syria and continued to expand, conquering North Africa, Spain, and Central Asia. In 750, the caliphate was seized by the Abbasid Dynasty, which based itself in Baghdad and was strongly influenced by Persia. The empire prospered, but in the late ninth century, political power devolved to local rulers, who established independent Muslim dominions. Even disunited, Islam continued to spread. In the twelfth century, converted Seljuk Turks defended Islam against the Crusades. Mongol invaders then stormed through the Middle East but soon adopted the faith. Meanwhile, another Muslim power was rising—the Ottoman Turks.

25. The Five Pillars of Islam

by Adel Elsaie

Islam requires practices to be performed by Muslims. Five duties offered directly to God, known as the "pillars of Islam," are regarded as fundamental in Islam and central to the life of the Islamic community. Each of these pillars of Islam is intended to constantly purify the soul and body of the Muslim.

SHAHADAH—DECLARATION OF FAITH

In accordance with Islam's absolute commitment to monotheism, the first duty is the declaration of faith (the Shahadah): *"I declare that is no Deity but Allah and Muhammad is Messenger of Allah."* Every Muslim must make this profession publicly, or at least in front of two or more witnesses, at least once in lifetime "by the tongue and with full consent from the heart"; it defines the membership of an individual in the Islamic community. This testimony is accepted as evidence of one converted to Islam. Muslims repeat it on the average of twenty times every day.

SALAH—PRAYER

The second duty is that of the five daily prayers. The first prayer (Fajr) is offered before sunrise, the second (Dhuhr) is in the very early afternoon, the third (Asr) is in the late afternoon, the fourth (Maghrib) is immediately after sunset, and the fifth (Isha) is before retiring and before midnight. In prayers, all Muslims face the Kaabah (a small, cube-shaped structure) in the courtyard of al-Haram (the "inviolate place"), the great mosque of Mecca. Kaabah is the first house of worship built on earth for the worship of Allah, the One True God. It was re-built (raised from the existing foundation) by Prophets Abraham and Ismael. The Kaabah is 40 feet long, 33 feet wide and 50 feet high. It is covered with a black cloth with verses from the Quran written in golden letters. A single unit of prayer consists of a standing posture, then a bow followed by two prostrations, and finally a sitting posture. During these five prayers verses from the Quran are recited during the standing posture in Arabic, the language of the Revelation. During other postures supplications, glorifying and praising Allah, exalting and blessing Prophets Muhammad and Abraham and their followers are offered. Every Muslim on earth should know at least few Surahs in Arabic to perform the prayers.

All five prayers in Islam are congregational and are to be offered in a mosque, but they may be offered from any location such as: house, office, bus, airplane, car, wilderness, etc. A Muslim riding a bus, airplane or a car may pray in the direction of the vehicle and does not have to face Mecca during prayer. Before praying, the worshiper must make ablution which is washing of at least the hands, face, arms up to elbows, rubbing head with water, and washing feet up to ankles. There are certain concessions with regard to the timings of prayers. For example, when one travels, one may combine Dhuhr with Asr at any time from the beginning of the period of Dhuhr to the end of Asr prayer. One can also combine Maghrib with Isha at any time during the range for both prayers. Also, when there is a good reason that prevents a person from offering prayer, he may combine Dhuhr with Asr and Maghrib with Isha even in his hometown. Shortening prayers is another concession given to travelers after they have started their journey. Only Dhuhr, Asr and Isha can be shortened. Maghrib and Fajr remain as they are. The Messenger of God encouraged Muslims to offer voluntary prayers (Nafl) because Allah will reward Muslims for these added prayers that are over and above the religious duties that Allah has imposed, but He does not punish anyone for their omitting. Nafl is not obligatory. Before every congregational prayer, the muezzin (from azan, "call to prayer") makes a formal public call to prayer from a minaret of the mosque. The call to prayer may also be offered inside the mosque in the prayer's area of the Imam (leader of the prayer). In recent times the call has been made over a microphone so that those at some distance can hear it.

Special early afternoon prayers are offered on Fridays in congregation at mosques, preceded by a sermon by the Imam. On the two annual religious festival days called Eid (one immediately after the end of the fasting month of Ramadan and the second during the pilgrimage to Mecca on the tenth day of the Islamic lunar month of *Dhul-Hijjah*), there are special prayers followed by sermons in the morning. These prayers are not held in mosques but in a wide space outside set apart for this purpose.

ZAKAT—ALMSGIVING

The third duty of a Muslim is to pay Zakat, primarily to help the poor. The word Zakat in Arabic means both "purification" and "growth." This was the required charity ordered by Allah and collected by Muhammad (and later by Muslim states) from every Muslim who has at the end of the year in his or her possession certain minimum prescribed value called 'Nisab.' Zakat requires a minimum rate of two and half percent of Muslims' wealth above the value of 'Nisab.' Islam teaches that humans own nothing in life. God gives everything they possess as a trust; they are trustees. Only when Zakat has been paid is the rest of a Muslim's property considered purified and legitimate. In most Muslim states Zakat is no longer collected by the government and instead has become a voluntary charity, but it is still recognized as an essential duty by all Muslims. In a number of countries, strong demands have been made to reinstate Zakat as a tax.

SAWM—FASTING

The fourth duty is the fasting during the Islamic month of Ramadan. Because the Islamic calendar is lunar, fasting is not confined to any one season. Even during hot summers, most Muslims meticulously observe fasting. During fasting, one must refrain from eating, drinking, smoking, and sexual intercourse from dawn until sunset. After sunset, all lawful in food, drink and sex are allowed. Throughout the month one must abstain from all sinful thoughts and actions. If one is sick or on a journey that causes hardship, one need not to fast but must compensate by fasting on subsequent days or feed poor people. The Messenger of God encouraged Muslims to offer voluntary fasting because Allah will reward Muslims for these added fasting. Fasting is a religious method of self-purification. By cutting oneself off from worldly comforts, even for a short time, a fasting person gains true sympathy with those who live daily lives without even the most basic necessities, food and drink. It is also intended as a time to grow one's spirituality and Islamic values of love, honesty, devotion, and generosity.

HAJJ—PILGRIMAGE

The fifth duty is the pilgrimage to the Kaabah at Mecca. Every adult Muslim who is physically and economically able to do so must make this pilgrimage at least once in his or her lifetime. Hajj activities take place during six days (from the eighth to thirteenth) of the Islamic lunar month of *Dhul-Hijjah*. Every year, during pilgrimage, the world witnesses the wonderful spectacle of this international exhibition of Islam in leveling all distinctions of race, color, and rank. Not only do the Americans, the Europeans, the Africans, the south Asians, the Arabs, the Chinese and all other nationals meet together in Mecca as members of one divine family, but they are all dressed in one dress, every person in two simple pieces of white seamless cloth, everyone chanting,

> *"Here am I, O God; at Thy command; Thou art One and the Only; here am I."*

Thus there remains nothing to differentiate the high from the low, the rich from the poor, the peasant from the king. The fact is: no religion in the world can show a parallel to what Islam has done towards the establishment of the principle of international unity and human brotherhood on such universal foundations.

During Pilgrimage, Muslims abstain from shedding blood and even cutting either hair or nails, and avoid all forms of vulgarity. The main activities of the Hajj, which are of Abrahamic origin, include seven circumambulations of the Kaabah, walking fast between two mounds near the sanctuary seven times, marching three miles to the city of Mina, then proceeding six miles to the mountain of Arafat, staying the afternoon and listening to a sermon there, stoning of three pillars representing Satan's temptation of Abraham, his wife Hagar and his son Ismael, then marching back to Mecca, cutting the hair to symbolize the completion of *Hajj*, offering a sacrifice in the memory of Abraham's attempted sacrifice of his son Ismael, and once again circumambulating the Kaabah. During the tenth day of *Dhul-Hijjah*, Muslims worldwide gather for communal prayers.

During recent years, air travel has allowed Muslims from all parts of the world to perform the pilgrimage. In 1977 the reported number was close to 2 million. Through the centuries, the Kaabah has played an important role as a meeting place of Islamic scholars for the exchange and diffusion of ideas. For the past two decades, the pilgrimage has also been used to promote political solidarity in the Muslim world.

Besides these five basic pillars, other important laws of Islam include the prohibition of alcohol consumption and of eating the flesh of swine. Besides the Kaabah, the central shrine of Islam, the most important centers of Islamic life are the Prophet's mosque in Madinah and Al-Aqsa mosque in Jerusalem, and all the mosques where daily prayers are offered, and where the Friday service are held.

---

26. Selections from the Quran (Koran)

trans. M. H. Shakir

1. In the name of God, the Gracious, the Merciful.

2. Praise be to God, Lord of the Worlds.

3. The Most Gracious, the Most Merciful.

4. Master of the Day of Judgment.

5. It is You we worship, and upon You we call for help.

"The Koran on Jews, The Koran on Christians, The Koran on Jihad," *The Koran on Other Religions*; trans. M. H. Shakir. Copyright © by Tahrike Tarsile Qur'an. Reprinted with permission.

6. Guide us to the straight path.

7. The path of those You have blessed, not of those against whom there is anger, nor of those who are misguided.

2.29. It is He who created for you everything on earth, then turned to the heaven, and made them seven heavens. And He is aware of all things.

30. When your Lord said to the angels, "I am placing a successor on earth." They said, "Will You place in it someone who will cause corruption in it and shed blood, while we declare Your praises and sanctify You?" He said, "I know what you do not know."

62. Those who believe, and those who are Jewish, and the Christians, and the Sabeans—any who believe in God and the Last Day, and act righteously—will have their reward with their Lord; they have nothing to fear, nor will they grieve.

87. We gave Moses the Scripture, and sent a succession of messengers after him. And We gave Jesus son of Mary the clear proofs, and We supported him with the Holy Spirit. Is it that whenever a messenger comes to you with anything your souls do not desire, you grew arrogant, calling some impostors, and killing others?

111. And they say, "None will enter Heaven unless he is a Jew or a Christian." These are their wishes. Say, "Produce your proof, if you are truthful."

140. Or do you say that Abraham, Ishmael, Isaac, Jacob, and the Patriarchs were Jews or Christians? Say, "Do you know better, or God?" And who does greater wrong than he who conceals a testimony he has from God? God is not unaware of what you do.

3.67. Abraham was neither a Jew nor a Christian, but he was a Monotheist, a Muslim. And he was not of the Polytheists.

3.144. Muhammad is no more than a messenger. Messengers have passed on before him. If he dies or gets killed, will you turn on your heels? He who turns on his heels will not harm God in any way. And God will reward the appreciative.

4.156. And for their faithlessness, and their saying against Mary a monstrous slander.

157. And for their saying, "We have killed the Messiah, Jesus, the son of Mary, the Messenger of God." In fact, they did not kill him, nor did they crucify him, but it appeared to them as if they did. Indeed, those who differ about him are in doubt about it. They have no knowledge of it, except the following of assumptions. Certainly, they did not kill him.

158. Rather, God raised him up to Himself. God is Mighty and Wise.

4.163. We have inspired you, as We had inspired Noah and the prophets after him. And We inspired Abraham, and Ishmael, and Isaac, and Jacob, and the Patriarchs, and Jesus, and Job, and Jonah, and Aaron, and Solomon. And We gave David the Psalms.

164. Some messengers We have already told you about, while some messengers We have not told you about. And God spoke to Moses directly.

165. Messengers delivering good news, and bringing warnings; so that people may have no excuse before God after the coming of the messengers. God is Powerful and Wise.

166. But God bears witness to what He revealed to you. He revealed it with His knowledge. And the angels bear witness. Though God is a sufficient witness.

167. Those who disbelieve and repel from God's path have gone far astray.

168. Those who disbelieve and transgress; God is not about to forgive them, nor will He guide them to any path.

169. Except to the path of Hell, where they will dwell forever. And that is easy for God.

170. O people! The Messenger has come to you with the truth from your Lord, so believe—that is best for you. But if you disbelieve, to God belongs everything in the heavens and the earth. God is Omniscient and Wise.

171. O People of the Scripture! Do not exaggerate in your religion, and do not say about God except the truth. The Messiah, Jesus, the son of Mary, is the Messenger of God, and His Word that He conveyed to Mary, and a Spirit from Him. So believe in God and His messengers, and do not say, "Three." Refrain—it is better for you. God is only one God. Glory be to Him—that He should have a son. To Him belongs everything in the heavens and the earth, and God is a sufficient Protector.

172. The Messiah does not disdain to be a servant of God, nor do the favored angels. Whoever disdains His worship, and is too arrogant—He will round them up to Himself altogether.

173. But as for those who believe and do good works, He will pay them their wages in full, and will increase His grace for them. But as for those who disdain and are too proud, He will punish them with an agonizing punishment. And they will find for themselves, apart from God, no lord and no savior.

5.14. And from those who say, "We are Christians," We received their pledge, but they neglected some of what they were reminded of. So We provoked enmity and hatred among them until the Day of Resurrection; God will then inform them of what they used to craft.

5.33. The punishment for those who fight God and His Messenger, and strive to spread corruption on earth, is that they be killed, or crucified, or have their hands and feet cut off on opposite sides, or be banished from the land. That is to disgrace them in this life; and in the Hereafter they will have a terrible punishment.

51. O you who believe! Do not take the Jews and the Christians as allies; some of them are allies of one another. Whoever of you allies himself with them is one of them. God does not guide the wrongdoing people.

69. Those who believe, and the Jews, and the Sabians, and the Christians—whoever believes in God and the Last Day, and does what is right—they have nothing to fear, nor shall they grieve.

72. They disbelieve those who say, "God is the Messiah the son of Mary." But the Messiah himself said, "O Children of Israel, worship God, my Lord and your Lord. Whoever associates others with God, God has forbidden him Paradise, and his dwelling is the Fire. The wrongdoers have no saviors."

73. They disbelieve those who say, "God is the third of three." But there is no deity except the One God. If they do not refrain from what they say, a painful torment will befall those among them who disbelieve.

82. You will find that the people most hostile towards the believers are the Jews and the polytheists. And you will find that the nearest in affection towards the believers are those who say, "We are Christians." That is because among them are priests and monks, and they are not arrogant.

8.38. Say to those who disbelieve: if they desist, their past will be forgiven. But if they persist—the practice of the ancients has passed away.

39. Fight them until there is no more persecution, and religion becomes exclusively for God. But if they desist—God is Seeing of what they do.

9.30. The Jews said, "Ezra is the son of God," and the Christians said, "The Messiah is the son of God." These are their statements, out of their mouths. They emulate the statements of those who blasphemed before. May God assail them! How deceived they are!

31. They have taken their rabbis and their priests as lords instead of God, as well as the Messiah son of Mary. Although they were commanded to worship none but The One God. There is no god except He. Glory be to Him; High above what they associate with Him.

73. O Prophet! Strive against the disbelievers and the hypocrites, and be stern with them. Their abode is Hell—what a miserable destination!

123. O you who believe! Fight those of the disbelievers who attack you, and let them find severity in you, and know that God is with the righteous.

48.29. Muhammad is the Messenger of God. Those with him are stern against the disbelievers, yet compassionate amongst themselves. You see them kneeling, prostrating, seeking blessings from God and approval. Their marks are on their faces from the effects of prostration. Such is their description in the Torah, and their description in the Gospel: like a plant that sprouts, becomes strong, grows thick, and rests on its stem, impressing the farmers. Through them He enrages the disbelievers. God has promised those among them who believe and do good deeds forgiveness and a great reward.

---

27. Travels in Asia and Africa 1325–1354

by Ibn Battuta; ed. and trans. H. A. R. Gibb

Ibn Battuta started on his travels when he was 20 years old in 1325. His main reason to travel was to go on a Hajj, or a Pilgrimage to Mecca, as all good Muslims want to do. But his traveling went on for about 29 years and he covered about 75,000 miles visiting the equivalent of 44 modern countries which were then mostly under the governments of Muslim leaders of the World of Islam, or "Dar al-Islam".

Near the end of Ibn Battuta's own life, the Sultan of Morocco insisted that Ibn Battuta dictate the story of his travels to a scholar and today we can read translations of that story called "Rihla—My Travels". Much of it is fascinating, but some of it seems to be made up and even is inaccurate about places we know about. However, it is a valuable and interesting record of places which add to our understanding of the Middle Ages.

Ibn Battuta, *Travels in Asia and Africa 1325-1354*, ed. and trans. H. A. R. Gibb, 1929.

*The following selections were taken from the Internet Medieval
Sourcebook, http://www.fordham.edu/halsall/source/1354-ibnbattuta.
html*

HERE BEGINS IBN BATTUTA'S TRAVELS

I left Tangier, my birthplace, on Thursday, 2nd Rajab 725 [June 14, 1325], being at that
time twenty-two years of age [22 lunar years; 21 and 4 months by solar reckoning], with
the intention of making the Pilgrimage to the Holy House [at Mecca] and the Tomb
of the Prophet [at Medina].

On reaching the city of Tilimsan [Tlemsen], whose sultan at that time was Abu
Tashifin, I found there two ambassadors of the Sultan of Tunis, who left the city on the
same day that I arrived. One of the brethren having advised me to accompany them,
I consulted the will of God in this matter, and after a stay of three days in the city to
procure all that I needed, I rode after them with all speed. I overtook them at the town
of Miliana, where we stayed ten days, as both ambassadors fell sick on account of the
summer heats. When we set out again, one of them grew worse, and died after we had
stopped for three nights by a stream four miles from Miliana. I left their party there and
pursued my journey, with a company of merchants from Tunis.

I set out alone, finding no companion to cheer the way with friendly intercourse,
and no party of travellers with whom to associate myself. Swayed by an overmastering
impulse within me, and a long-cherished desire to visit those glorious sanctuaries, I
resolved to quit all my friends and tear myself away from my home. As my parents
were still alive, it weighed grievously upon me to part from them, and both they and I
were afflicted with sorrow.

IBN BATTUTA TRAVELS OVERLAND FROM ALGIERS TO TUNIS

On reaching al-Jaza'ir [Algiers] we halted outside the town for a few days, until
the former party rejoined us, when we went on together through the Mitija [the
fertile plain behind Algiers] to the mountain of Oaks [Jurjura] and so reached Bijaya
[Bougie].

The commander of Bijaya at this time was the chamberlain Ibn Sayyid an-Nas. Now
one of the Tunisian merchants of our party had died leaving three thousand dinars
of gold, which he had entrusted to a certain man of Algiers to deliver to his heirs at
Tunis. Ibn Sayyid an-Nas came to hear of this and forcibly seized the money. This was
the first instance I witnessed of the tyranny of the agents of the Tunisian government.

At Bijaya I fell ill of a fever, and one of my friends advised me to stay there till I
recovered. But I refused, saying, "If God decrees my death, it shall be on the road with
my face set toward Mecca." "If that is your resolve," he replied, "sell your ass and your
heavy baggage, and I shall lend you what you require. In this way you will travel light,

for we must make haste on our journey, for fear of meeting roving Arabs on the way."
I followed his advice and he did as he had promised--may God reward him!

On reaching Qusantinah [Constantine] we camped outside the town, but a heavy rain forced us to leave our tents during the night and take refuge in some houses there. Next day the governor of the city came to meet us. Seeing my clothes all soiled by the rain he gave orders that they should be washed at his house, and in place of my old worn headcloth sent me a headcloth of fine Syrian cloth, in one of the ends of which he had tied two gold dinars. This was the first alms I received on my journey.

From Qusantinah we reached Bona [Bone] where, after staying in the town for several days, we left the merchants of our party on account of the dangers of the road, while we pursued our journey with the utmost speed. I was again attacked by fever, so I tied myself in the saddle with a turban-cloth in case I should fall by reason of my weakness. So great was my fear that I could not dismount until we arrived at Tunis.

IBN BATTUTA AND HIS PARTY ARRIVE AT TUNIS

The population of the city came out to meet the members of our party, and on all sides greetings and question were exchanged, but not a soul greeted me as no one there was known to me. I was so affected by my loneliness that I could not restrain my tears and wept bitterly, until one of the pilgrims realized the cause of my distress and coming up to me greeted me kindly and continued to entertain me with friendly talk until I entered the city.

The Sultan of Tunis at that time was Abu Yahya, the son of Abu' Zakariya IL, and there were a number of notable scholars in the town. During my stay the festival of the Breaking of the Fast fell due, and I joined the company at the Praying-ground. The inhabitants assembled in large numbers to celebrate the festival, making a brave show and wearing their richest apparel. The Sultan Abu Yahya arrived on horseback, accompanied by all his relatives, courtiers, and officers of state walking on foot in a stately procession. After the recital of the prayer and the conclusion of the Allocution the people returned to their homes.

IBN BATTUTA LEAVES TUNIS WITH THE ANNUAL PILGRIM CARAVAN

Some time later the pilgrim caravan for the Hijaz was formed, and they nominated me as their qadi [judge]. We left Tunis early in November [1325], following the coast road through Susa Sfax, and Qabis, where we stayed for ten days on account of incessant rains. Thence we set out for Tripoli, accompanied for several stages by a hundred or more horsemen as well as a detachment of archers, out of respect for whom the Arabs [brigands] kept their distance.

I had made a contract of marriage at Sfax with the daughter of one of the syndics at Tunis, and at Tripoli she was conducted to me, but after leaving Tripoli I became involved in a dispute with her father, which necessitated my separation from her. I then married the daughter of a student from Fez, and when she was conducted to me I detained the caravan for a day by entertaining them all at a wedding party.

Ibn Battuta travels through Egypt and sees many of the main sights. He plans to go to southern Egypt and cross directly into Arabia, but there is a war on and there are no ships to take him. He therefore goes back to northern Egypt, through modern-day Israel, and to Damascus, where he joins a new caravan that goes south to Mecca.

IBN BATTUTA LEAVES DAMASCUS WITH THE ANNUAL PILGRIM CARAVAN

When the new moon of the month Shawwal appeared in the same year [1st September 1326], the Hijaz caravan left Damascus and I set off along with it. At Bosra the caravans usually halt for four days so that any who have been detained at Damascus by business affairs may make up on them. Thence they go to the Pool of Ziza, where they stop for a day, and then through al-Lajjun to the Castle of Karak. Karak, which is also called "The Castle of the Raven," is one of the most marvellous, impregnable, and celebrated of fortresses. It is surrounded on all sides by the river-bed, and has but one gate, the entrance to which is hewn in the living rock, as also is the approach to its vestibule. This fortress is used by kings as a place of refuge in times of calamity, as the sultan an-Nasir did when his mamluke Salar seized the supreme authority. The caravan stopped for four days at a place called ath-Thaniya outside Karak, where preparations were made for entering the desert.

Thence we Journeyed to Ma'an, which is the last town in Syria, and from 'Aqabat as-Sawan entered the desert, of which the saying goes: " He who enters it is lost, and he who leaves it is born."

CROSSING THE DESERT FROM SYRIA TO MEDINA

After a march of two days we halted at Dhat Hajj, where there are subterranean water-beds but no habitations, and then went on to Wadi Baldah (in which there is no water) and to Tabuk, which is the place to which the Prophet led an expedition. The great caravan halts at Tabuk for four days to rest and to water the camels and lay in water for the terrible desert between Tabuk and al-Ula. The custom of the watercarriers is to camp beside the spring, and they have tanks made of buffalo hides, like great cisterns, from which they water the camels and fill the waterskins. Each amir or person of rank has a special tank for the needs of his own camels and personnel; the other people make private agreements with the watercarriers to water their camels and fill their waterskins for a fixed sum of money.

From Tabuk the caravan travels with great speed night and day, for fear of this desert. Halfway through is the valley of al-Ukhaydir, which might well be the valley of

Hell (may God preserve us from it). One year the pilgrims suffered terribly here from the samoom-wind; the water-supplies dried up and the price of a single drink rose to a thousand dinars, but both seller and buyer perished. Their story is written on a rock in the valley.

Five days after leaving Tabuk they reach the well of al-Hijr, which has an abundance of water, but not a soul draws water there, however violent his thirst, following the example of the Prophet, who passed it on his expedition to Tabuk and drove on his camel, giving orders that none should drink of its waters. Here, in some hills of red rock, are the dwellings of Thamud. They are cut in the rock and have carved thresholds. Anyone seeing them would take them to be of recent construction. [The] decayed bones [of the former inhabitants] are to be seen inside these houses.

Al-Ula, a large and pleasant village with palm-gardens and water-springs, lies half a day's journey or less from al-Hijr. The pilgrims halt there four days to provision themselves and wash their clothes. They leave behind them here any surplus of provisions they may have, taking with them nothing but what is strictly necessary. The people of the village are very trustworthy. The Christian merchants of Syria may come as far as this and no further, and they trade in provisions and other goods with the pilgrims here. On the third day after leaving al-Ula the caravan halts in the outskirts of the holy city of Medina.

IBN BATTUTA VISITS THE HOLY SITES OF MEDINA

That same evening [the third day after leaving al-Ula, on the route from Syria and Damascus] we entered the holy sanctuary and reached the illustrious mosque, halting in salutation at the Gate of Peace; then we prayed in the illustrious "garden" between the tomb of the Prophet and the noble pulpit, and reverently touched the fragment that remains of the palm-trunk against which the Prophet stood when he preached. Having paid our meed of salutation to the lord of men from first to last, the intercessor for sinners, the Prophet of Mecca, Muhammad, as well as to his two companions who share his grave, Abu Bakr and 'Omar, we returned to our camp, rejoicing at this great favour bestowed upon us, praising God for our having reached the former abodes and the magnificent sanctuaries of His holy Prophet, and praying Him to grant that this visit should not be our last and that we might be of those whose pilgrimage is accepted.

On this journey, our stay at Medina lasted four days. We used to spend every night in the illustrious mosque, where the people, after forming circles in the courtyard and, lighting large numbers of candles, would pass the time either in reciting the Koran from volumes set on rests in front of them, or in intoning litanies, or in visiting the sanctuaries of the holy tomb.

FROM MEDINA TO MECCA THROUGH A
FINAL DESERT, THE VALE OF BAZWA

We then set out from Medina towards Mecca, and halted near the mosque of Dhu'l-Hulayfa, five miles away. It was at this point that the Prophet assumed the pilgrim garb and obligations, and here too I divested myself of my tailored clothes, bathed, and putting on the pilgrim's garment I prayed and dedicated myself to the pilgrimage. Our fourth halt from here was at Badr, where God aided His Prophet and performed His promise. It is a village containing a series of palm-gardens and a bubbling spring with a stream flowing from it. Our way lay thence through a frightful desert called the Vale of Bazwa for three days to the valley of Rabigh where the rainwater forms pools which lie stagnant for a long time. From this point (which is just before Juhfa) the pilgrims from Egypt and Northwest Africa put on the pilgrim garment. Three days after leaving Rabigh we reached the pool of Khulays which lies in a plain and has many palm-gardens. The Bedouin of that neighbourhood hold a market there, to which they bring sheep, fruits, and condiments. Thence we travelled through 'Usfan to the Bottom of Marr, a fertile valley with numerous palms and a spring supplying a stream from which the district is irrigated. From this valley fruit and vegetables are transported to Mecca.

We set out at night from this blessed valley, with hearts full of joy at reaching the goal of our hopes, and in the morning arrived at the City of Surety, Mecca (may God ennoble her !), where we immediately entered the holy sanctuary and began the rites of pilgrimage.

THE PIOUS KINDNESS OF THE PEOPLE OF MECCA

The inhabitants of Mecca are distinguished by many excellent and noble activities and qualities, by their beneficence to the humble and weak, and by their kindness to strangers. When any of them makes a feast, he begins by giving food to the religious devotees who are poor and without resources, inviting them first with kindness and delicacy. The majority of these unfortunates are to be found by the public bakehouses, and when anyone has his bread baked and takes it away to his house, they follow him and he gives each one of them some share of it, sending away none disappointed. Even if he has but a single loaf, he gives away a third or a half of it, cheerfully and without any grudgingness.

Another good habit of theirs is this. The orphan children sit in the bazaar, each with two baskets, one large and one small. When one of the townspeople comes to the bazaar and buys cereals, meat and vegetables, he hands them to one of these boys, who puts the cereals in one basket and the meat and vegetables in the other and takes them to the man's house, so that his meal may be prepared. Meanwhile the man goes about his devotions and his business. There is no instance of any of the boys having ever abused their trust in this matter, and they are given a fixed fee of a few coppers.

THE CLEANLINESS OF THE PEOPLE OF MECCA

The Meccans are very elegant and clean in their dress, and most of them wear white garments, which you always see fresh and snowy. They use a great deal of perfume and kohl and make free use of toothpicks of green arak-wood. The Meccan women are extraordinarily beautiful and very pious and modest. They too make great use of perfumes to such a degree that they will spend the night hungry in order to buy perfumes with the price of their food. They visit the mosque every Thursday night, wearing their finest apparel; and the whole sanctuary is saturated with the smell of their perfume. When one of these women goes away the odour of the perfume clings to the place after she has gone.

Analysis Questions

1. What are the Five Pillars of Islam? Why are these so important for Islam's believers?
2. What does the Quran say about the Jews and the Christians?
3. Research and explain the concept of Dar al-Islam ("House of Islam") based on Ibn Battuta's travels.

CHAPTER 9

African Civilizations, to Fifteenth Century A.D.

Introduction

Despite the fact that Africa is one of the places where agriculture began coping with hostile environments, historians have only recently come to understand the richness, diversity, and dynamism of early African civilizations. Spreading southward from the present-day Nigeria region, the ancient Bantu people gradually began intermarrying and creating different societies in Africa around the first thousand years B.C. Around 500 B.C., these agrarian people started using iron tools and weapons to clear extensive zones of forests. The Bantu population grew quickly, spreading ironworking and agriculture as well as dispersing Bantu dialects across sub-Saharan Africa.

Between 700 and 900 A.D., networks of caravan trade routes were developed between the Mediterranean Sea and the western societies of Africa. The influential consequences of the trans-Saharan trade were the introduction of Islam to West African societies and the growth of powerful African kingdoms. The first of these great West African trading kingdoms was the kingdom of Ghana, which flourished from the 8th to the 11th centuries between the Sahara Desert and the Niger and Senegal Rivers. Ghana acquired a reputation as a land of gold. In the eleventh century, invasions by some African Muslim tribes brought the collapse of its capital, Kumbi, and disrupted trade and weakened Ghana. In this collapse in 1076 A.D.,

Muslim rule was overthrown by two of its subject peoples, the Susa and later the Keita, leaders of the kingdom of Mali.

Mali owed its greatness to its agricultural and commercial base and to its two extraordinary military rulers, Sundiata and Mansa Musa. The leaders of Mali were Muslims, and Timbuktu, its capital, became a center of Muslim culture and learning as well. Islam became a unifying element among the political and commercial elite, although people in rural areas retained traditional religious beliefs. Mali declined after the fourteenth century because of dynastic disputes and strikes by nomadic tribes.

Unlike in the West African kingdoms, Christianity became established in Ethiopia. According to the oral tradition of Ethiopia, most of its kings were descended from Menelik I, the son of the Queen of Sheba and the Hebrew king Solomon. In the fourth century A.D., a Syrian Christian trader, Frumentius, brought Christianity to Ethiopia, and King Ezana's conversion made Christianity the state religion. Its capital, Axum, became the center of Monophysitic Christianity as well as an entrepôt to trade with the interior. The Islamic penetration in the eighth century, however, limited Axum's commercial and political power.

28. Bantu Migrations

by Luc de Heusch

Later a fisherman called Muleya Monga lived near Lake Boya. He had three children by one of his wives, who was called Mwamba or Ndai. Of the children, one was a boy called Nkongolo ("Rainbow") because of his pale skin. There were also two girls, Mabela and Bulanda. By his second wife, Kaseya, Muleya Monga had another daughter, called Sungu.

One day, Nkongolo was struck by the sight of a column of ants carrying off termites. He had the idea of organizing a merciless army. He gathered some followers about him and soon showed himself to be so tyrannical that he was driven out of the country. Some time later, however, he returned to Lake Boya and, with the help of the diviner Mijibu, reasserted his domination over the Kalanga people. These people were of lighter color than the Luba. Nkongolo was a brutal and ruthless chief. Being suspicious of the power of women, he decided to avoid marrying outside his own family. So he took his half sister Sungu as wife.

At the same time, the hunter Ilunga Kiluwe reigned in Bupemba (presumably Buhemba, a country to the east). He had two sons, Mbidi Kiluwe and Ndala, and a

Luc de Heusch, "Bantu Migrations," *The Drunken King, or the Origin of the State*, pp. 15-16. Copyright © 1982 by Indiana University Press. Reprinted with permission.

daughter called Mwanana of whom he was very fond. When he became old, Ilunga Kiluwe wanted his daughter to succeed him, while his subjects wanted Mbidi Kiluwe. Mwanana had a pet lion. This animal escaped, while Mbidi Kiluwe was playing with it. Enraged, Mwanana threatened to have her brother put to death unless he recaptured the lion. Mbidi Kiluwe was obliged to pursue the animal. He took with him ten of his wives, fifty slaves, and his youngest son, Mwema Mwimbi. He lost the lion's trail at the Lualaba River. He went on until he came to the river Lovoi, where he found a country rich in game. He began hunting, killing men and animals without discrimination.

When he came to the confluence with the Kiankodi River, his vrives and slaves refused to go any further. Mbidi Kiluwe continued on his way with his son Mwema, who carried the bows and arrows.

Meanwhile, at Lake Boya, the diviner Mijibu warned Nkongolo that "power is coming." He advised his master, on pain of losing his life, to give a generous welcome to the chief who was approaching. Mbidi Kiluwe and his son followed the Kiankodi River upstream to its source in the highlands. Then they followed the course of the Luvidyo River downstream to the Munza lake. There they met two beautiful young women, Nkongolo's sisters Mabela and Bulanda, who were trying to drag from the water a net full of fish that was too heavy for them. Mbidi Kiluwe drew it out with ease and took his leave of the two young women, who had fallen in love with the hunter. They were greatly impressed with his beauty, his strength, and his dark color. They begged their brother to spare the life of the handsome stranger, for because of the prophecy of Mijibu, Nkongolo either killed or enslaved all foreigners. Mbidi Kiluwe remained on the alert. When he saw some of Nkongolo's soldiers approaching, he hid in a tree. The two young women tried in vain to find the hunter's trail. While they were resting by a stream, they saw in the water the reflection of Mbidi, who was watching them from his hideout in the branches of a tree above them. They begged him to come down and accompany them to the home of Nkongolo. Mbidi agreed, and instructed his son Mwema to fetch his wives and slaves.

Nkongolo received his guests with ill grace. He was uneasy and consulted his diviner. Why did the stranger not respond to die greetings of his own followers? Why did he refuse to eat in public? Mijibu told him to rejoice because the hunter was introducing the proper customs of divine kingship. He advised Nkongolo to build an enclosure for his guest. Mbidi married Mabela and Bulanda. But things soon became difficult. Nkongolo adopted an insulting attitude toward his brother-in-law. He laughed uproariously whenever he saw the gaps left by the removal of the stranger's two lower incisors.[1] On his side, Mbidi reproached Nkongolo for eating in public and for sitting on the ground with his legs crossed. While in a trance, Mijibu secretly whispered in Mbidi's ear, inviting him to a meeting at dawn the following day. Mbidi duly met Mijibu and was warned that Nkongolo meant to incite Mbidi's own followers against him. Mbidi thereupon decided to leave. He gave each of his wives a curiously fashioned arrow and told them to give

---

1   Luba treat both upper and lower incisors (see p. 22 below). (R.W.)

it to the child each would bring forth, so that their father would be able to recognize them. He entrusted the care of his future offspring to Mijibu and disappeared.

When Mbidi Kiluwe returned to his native land, his father had died. His sister Mwanana and his brother Ndala were both away, looking for him. After losing Mbidi's trail, Mwanana arrived in Lunda country, where she married the king. At Nkongolo's village, Bulanda brought forth a son, whom she named Xlunga after his paternal grandfather. Mabela brought forth twins: a boy, called Kisula, and a girl, Shimbi.

Ilunga soon became the fastest runner and the best dancer in the whole country. His military exploits led to his being called Kalala, "the conqueror."[2] Mabela's son, however, was a rather stupid giant of a man. Kalala Xlunga also regularly beat his uncle at the game played with stones of the wild olives.[3] Nkongolo felt a growing resentment about this. Sneeringly, Nkongolo's mother told him that Kalala would soon take over political power also. Nkongolo became angry and his mother burst out laughing. Nkongolo then dug a ditch with his own hands and buried his mother alive in it. He decided at the same time to do away with his nephew. He tried to lure Kalala into a trap during a dancing competition. Kahia, Kalala's personal drummer, noticed a slight depression in the ground made by a pit hidden under a mat. As his master approached the trap, Kahia warned turn of the danger in drum language. Kalala revealed Nkongolo's trick by piercing the mat with his spear. Then he jumped right over the gathered people like a wild animal. He took the arrows his father had left and fled to Kiluba, the only place where there was a boat to cross the Lualaba River. He arrived there before nightfall, pursued by Nkongolo and several soldiers, jumping into the boat, Kalala ordered the oarsman to deny the crossing to the red-colored man who was pursuing him. After taking Kalala across, the owner of the canoe hid his craft in the reeds. When Nkongolo arrived the next morning, he was told that a stranger had stolen the boat. Nkongolo tried in vain to construct a raft. In a fury, he ordered Kahia to climb a tree and beat his drum until his master returned. But Kalala was already far away. Kahia escaped from the uncomfortable position where Nkongolo had meant him to die.

At his father's, Kalala received a warm welcome. Mbidi gave him an army to beat Nkongolo. Nkongolo was seized with panic when Mijibu prophesied the fatal outcome of the confrontation. With his two sisters, Mabela and Bulanda, Nkongolo took refuge in the caves of Kaii Mountain in the west of his country. But the two women told people where they were going so that Kalala Ilunga could find them.

Nkongolo climbed early in the morning to the top of the hill to enjoy the sun, while his sisters, whose treachery he did not suspect, gathered great quantities of firewood under the pretence of preparing for a siege. Mabela saw the advance guard of the

2 According to Van Avermaet's dictionary, the root-*lala* in Luba has the senses of "splitting, breaking, piercing, operating a separation" (Van Avermaet 1954: 380), connotations which agree very well with de Heusch's identification of Kalala Ilunga with the category of "pointed, fabricated objects" (see below, p. 25). (R.W.)

3 Burton says: "... the game of spinning wild-olive kernels was common. It is similar to European, marbles' and the winner takes the kernels of the loser" (Burton, 1961:7). (R.W.)

hostile army. She advised the soldiers to surprise Nkongolo the next morning, while he wanned himself in the early sun. She told them of her plan to bar the entrance to the cave with a pile of wood. Nkongolo saw his enemies climbing the hill and fled to his cave, only to find the entrance blocked. Kalala's soldiers fell on him and cut off his head. This was buried the next morning under an enormous red anthill (termite mound?). At this spot the trees, rocks, and earth all became red.

---

29. Bible: 1 Kings and Acts

King James Version

1 KINGS CHAPTER 10

1. And when the queen of Sheba heard of the fame of Solomon concerning the name of the Lord, she came to prove him with hard questions.
2. And she came to Jerusalem with a very great train, with camels that bare spices, and very much gold, and precious stones: and when she was come to Solomon, she communed with him of all that was in her heart.
3. And Solomon told her all her questions: there was not any thing hid from the king, which he told her not.
4. And when the queen of Sheba had seen all Solomon's wisdom, and the house that he had built,
5. And the meat of his table, and the sitting of his servants, and the attendance of his ministers, and their apparel, and his cupbearers, and his ascent by which he went up unto the house of the Lord; there was no more spirit in her.
6. And she said to the king, It was a true report that I heard in mine own land of thy acts and of thy wisdom.
7. Howbeit I believed not the words, until I came, and mine eyes had seen it: and, behold, the half was not told me: thy wisdom and prosperity exceedeth the fame which I heard.
8. Happy are thy men, happy are these thy servants, which stand continually before thee, and that hear thy wisdom.
9. Blessed be the Lord thy God, which delighted in thee, to set thee on the throne of Israel: because the Lord loved Israel for ever, therefore made he thee king, to do judgment and justice.
10. And the navy also of Hiram, that brought gold from Ophir, brought in from Ophir great plenty of almug trees, and precious stones.

"1 Kings 10:1-13, Acts 8:26-39," King James Version, 1611.

11. And the king made of the almug trees pillars for the house of the Lord, and for the king's house, harps also and psalteries for singers: there came no such almug trees, nor were seen unto this day.

12. And king Solomon gave unto the queen of Sheba all her desire, whatsoever she asked, beside that which Solomon gave her of his royal bounty. So she turned and went to her own country, she and her servants.

ACTS CHAPTER 8

1. And the angel of the Lord spake unto Philip, saying, Arise, and go toward the south unto the way that goeth down from Jerusalem unto Gaza, which is desert.

2. And he arose and went: and, behold, a man of Ethiopia, an eunuch of great authority under Candace queen of the Ethiopians, who had the charge of all her treasure, and had come to Jerusalem for to worship,

3. Was returning, and sitting in his chariot read Esaias the prophet.

4. Then the Spirit said unto Philip, Go near, and join thyself to this chariot.

5. And Philip ran thither to him, and heard him read the prophet Esaias, and said, Understandest thou what thou readest?

6. And he said, How can I, except some man should guide me? And he desired Philip that he would come up and sit with him.

7. The place of the scripture which he read was this, He was led as a sheep to the slaughter; and like a lamb dumb before his shearer, so opened he not his mouth:

8. In his humiliation his judgment was taken away: and who shall declare his generation? for his life is taken from the earth.

9. And the eunuch answered Philip, and said, I pray thee, of whom speaketh the prophet this? of himself, or of some other man?

10. Then Philip opened his mouth, and began at the same scripture, and preached unto him Jesus.

11. And as they went on their way, they came unto a certain water: and the eunuch said, See, here is water; what doth hinder me to be baptized?

12. And Philip said, If thou believest with all thine heart, thou mayest. And he answered and said, I believe that Jesus Christ is the Son of God.

13. And he commanded the chariot to stand still: and they went down both into the water, both Philip and the eunuch; and he baptized him.

14. And when they were come up out of the water, the Spirit of the Lord caught away Philip, that the eunuch saw him no more: and he went on his way rejoicing.

Luc de Heusch, "Bantu Migrations," *The Drunken King, or the Origin of the State*, pp. 15-16. Copyright © 1982 by Indiana University Press. Reprinted with permission.

30. The Ethnology and History of the Area Covered by the Periplus

by G.W.B. Huntingford

THE AFRICAN COAST

No identifiable tribal names are given in the *PME,* and very few clues to what sort of people the inhabitants were; different tribal groups are designated in a manner which does no more than indicate some outstanding characteristic, in Agatharkhidēs, Strabö, and the *PME,* and it is only in the last that any indication is given of their position. Between Berenikë and Ptolemaïs lived the Ikhthuophagoi or Fish-eaters, on the coast; behind them inland were the Barbaroi (Berbers), the Agriophagoi or Wild animal-eaters, and the Moskhophagoi or Plant-eaters; these were under the rule of 'chiefs'. After the Moskhophagoi was Ptolemais of the Huntings, and the people along this stretch of the coast were the Barbaroi, who were the ancestors of the Hamitic Saho, a pastoral people; and south of Adouli, the eastern side of Ethiopia, mainly stark desert, is the land of the 'Afar or Danakil, another Hamitic people, who extend southwards as far as Djibouti. Eastward, from here to Cape Gardafui, in the 'Horn of Africa', was what the *PME* calls 'the other Barbaria', the land of the Somali, also Hamites, whose ancestors were probably here, under a different name, in the 1st century and even earlier. The whole of this region was under tribal chiefs (*see:* chapter 14, p. 29 above).

Both Agatharkhidēs and Strabō end their catalogues of 'tribes' with the Trōglodutai (Trōglodytes), who are mentioned as if they were a distinct people; but neither say where they lived, except that it is clear that they inhabited north-east Africa, for the west coast of the Red Sea from Adouli to Gardafui was called Trōglodutikē. It is some-what strange that this name does not occur in the *PME,* though it is found in Ptolemy, who says that 'the coastlands [of Africa] along the Arabian and Aualitic or Abalitic gulfs are generally called Trōglodutikē as far as Mount Elephas' (*Geog.,* IV. 7, 27). The accounts of these people given by Agatharkhidēs and Strabō are clearly no invention, since they mention certain customs which exist at the present day among some of the pastoral peoples of the interior of Eastern Africa. Strabō, whose description seems to have been borrowed from Agatharkhidēs, thus describes them:

> The Trōglodytes lead a pastoral life. They have many despotic chiefs;
> their women and children are common property, except those of

the chief; and those who lie with a chief's wife are fined a sheep. The women carefully paint their eyebrows with antimony, and they wear shells hung round their necks as amulets against the evil eye. The men fight over the grazing grounds, first with fists, then with stones, and then wounds are inflicted with arrows and swords; but when their quarrels become really dangerous the women intervene, and by soothing the fighters restore peace. They live on meat and bone broken up together, wrapped in skin and then cooked. They call the cooks 'Unclean'. They drink blood mixed with milk. The ordinary people drink water in which the plant paliurus[1] has been soaked; the chiefs drink honey and water, the honey being pressed from some kind of flower. They have a winter, when the monsoon blows and rain falls; the rest of the year is summer. They go naked or clad in skins, and carry clubs. They not only mutilate their bodies, but some are circumcised like the Egyptians. ... Some of the Trōglodytes bury their dead, binding the neck to the feet with cords of paliurus fibre; then they cover the body with stones, laughing and joking till the face is hidden; then they put a goat's horn on top of the cairn and depart. They travel by night and fasten bells to the necks of the male stock so that the noise may scare wild beasts, (xvi. 4, 17.) [2]

Four remarkable things may be noted in this passage:

(1) Drinking blood mixed with milk, a practice of the Nandi and Masai of Kenya, the Karamojong of Uganda, the Iraqw group of Tanzania, and the Bari, Didinga, and the Murlc of the southern Sudan.

(2) Circumcision, a practice ultimately due to Hamitic influence, and not practised by the Nilotic peoples, but by the Nandi and the Masai.

(3) The erection of mounds of stone over the body is found in Ethiopia among the Galla, and in the southern Sudan among the Bongo, Moro, and Zande, sometimes with an upright stone or wooden post planted in the mound, and sometimes with a Y-shaped post representing horns at the side. Further south the custom occurs among the Masai, and stone cairns of unknown date are found in many places in the highlands of Kenya,

(4) More remarkable still is the custom of laughing at a funeral. The Nandi used to bury a very old person with no show of sorrow and with laughter and talking, for, they said, 'He has now arrived where he expected to arrive a long while ago.'[3]

The Greeks thought that the name Trōglodutai meant 'cave-dwellers', as if it were derived from the Greek words, trogle, 'hole or cave', and, *dutai*, 'divers or creepers',

---

1   *Rhamnus paliurus* L.

2   Agatharkhidës' account (from Bk. V, chap. 61).

3   A. C. Hollis, *The Nandi* (Oxford, 1909), p. 72; cf, also Huntingford, *The Nandi of Kenya* (London, 1953), p. 148.

4   King of Mauritania, d. A.D. 19, a learned man who wrote on Africa and Arabia, though all his works are now lost except in quotations.

i.e. 'people who crept into holes'. From this comes the English 'troglodyte'. (The word was applied to the wren by Linnaeus, who called it, poor bird, *Troglodytes troglodytes troglodytes.*) There is evidence, however, to show that the Greek word is due to a misconception. Pliny cites Juba[4] as writing the word without L, and a 10th century MS of 'Extracts from Strabo's Geography'[5] says that in Book XVI, iv. 55 Strabō wrote Trōgodutai without the L, although all the existing texts have the L. Moreover, in Greek inscriptions referring to the Red Sea, the word is written without L.[6] It is quite understandable that an L should have crept in, making a word that had a meaning for the Greeks. What it really means is anyone's guess. Stripped of the Greek termination *dutēs* it yields a root TRG suggestive of the name Targi, plural Tuareg, the veiled people of the Sahara, though its etymology is unknown. It has been suggested that this word is akin to the Arabic *ṭawāriq*, sing, *ṭāriqa*, 'tribe'.

Although the *PME* does not mention the name Trōgodutai, it does refer to peoples near Berenikē, and Adouli, and along the coast as far as the Spice Mart near Gardafui as Barbaroi, and calls the country Barbaria, which we should translate 'Berbers' rather than 'Barbarians'.[7] These Berbers would seem to be the same as the Trōgodutai, that is, people of Hamitic stock whose descendants still inhabit north-east Africa. The author of the *PME* clearly had some knowledge and experience of these Berbers and their habits. Those living round Aualitēs, for instance, are described as 'more disorderly', while those in the next district, Malao, were 'more peaceful', and those in the Moundou are 'more stubborn'. The natives of the Rhapta region, on the other hand, who are given no ethnic name, are described as having large bodies and piratical habits. The existence of pirates in the Indian Ocean has been doubted, for example by Dr Freeman-Grenville, who says that the phrase does not occur in Midler's text, and asks, if there were pirates, on whom did they prey?[8] But sea-robbers (Swahili *haramia*) have existed everywhere at all times since there have been ships, and there is in fact evidence for them from both Pliny in ancient, and de Monfrcid in modern times. The former writes of Arabs called Ascitae who went to sea on inflated skins and practised piracy (*pirciticatn exercent*), using poisoned arrows;[9] and de Monfreid came across pirates in the Gulf of Aden.

But who these people of Rhapta were, we do not know. It is certain that they did not speak a Bantu language, since the 1st century A.D. is too early for Bantu-speakers to have reached the East African coast, and the theory that the Bantu originated in the east coast area of Africa is without foundation.[10] Possibly survivors of the 1st century inhabitants may be found in the Lake Eyasi district, some 300 miles inland from

---

5   Heidelberg 398, printed in Müller, *GGM*. 11, 629.

6   Dittenberger, *O.G.I.S.* 1, nos. 70, 71, quoted on p. 172.

7   *See* note 1 to chapter 2.

8   *Medieval history of the coast of Tanganyika* (Loudon, 1962), p. 26, n. 1. On pirates, see note 1 to chapter 16.

9   *Nat. Hist.* vi, 35.

10   This is not the place to discuss the origin of the Bantu, but anyone who is interested is referred to the present writer's chapter in Oliver and Mathew, *History of East Africa*, pp. 80–93,

Rhapta, where now live a few tribes of unknown ethnic affinities—the Iraqw, Gorowa, Alawa, and Burungi. There are also people of Hottentot type, known as Sandawe, in the same area, who speak a click-language. The Hadza Bushmen in the same area also may be ruled out, since they have not 'large bodies', their average stature being 5 ft. 3 ins. (men) and 4 ft. 11 ins. (women) (see Huntingford, *The Southern Nilo-Hamitest*, p. 132).

As to the organisation of these peoples, both Agatharkhidēs and Strabō describe the Trōglodytes as being under despotic chiefs; the *PME* says that the Barbaroi were under chiefs, and adds that from the end of Zōskalēs' territory there were no paramount rulers, but that each 'place' (*topos*) and market (as in the Rhapta district) was under its own chief. Only in the case of the Red Sea section is there anything more definite—the mention of Zōskalēs in chapter 5, of whom it is said 'Zōskalēs rules these parts from the Moskhophagoi to the other Barbaria⁹. It is certain that Zōskalēs was not king of Aksum (on the meaning of the Greek word translated 'rules' see note 2 to chapter 5), and it is equally certain that his authority did not stretch as far as the text suggests, if 'the other Barbaria' is, as it would appear, the coast south of Bab al mandab. Zōskalēs was in fact probably the forerunner of the *bāhrnagāsh*, 'sea-king', who in later times ruled the northern coast province of Ethiopia under the king of Ethiopia. The statement that each place was under its own chief probably means no more than that the local chief claimed dues from the traders. As ruler of Adoulis, Zōskalēs would have paid the customs dues, or part of them, as his tribute to the king of Aksum; Kosmas Indikopleustes in the 6th century A.D. found a custom house there, of which he drew a picture.

It may be added that even at this early period, part at least of the East African coast was under some kind of foreign domination, as we can see from chapters 15 and 16 of the *PME*. In chapter 15 the coast between the Puralaon Islands and the island of Menouthias is called the Ausineitic coast. This, it is true, depends upon Müller's emendation of the meaningless 'MS' to 'along the Ausineitic coast the island of Menouthias is encountered. This emendation is likely to be correct, and thus implies that the small state of Ausan east of Mouza had exercised some influence on this section of the coast. Ausan, which was flourishing as early as the 7th century B.C., later became part of the Homcrite or Himyaritic kingdom.

In chapter 16 we are told that the Rhapta district is ruled by the Mopharitic chief, 'according to an ancient agreement by which it comes under the kingdom which has become first in Arabia'. This kingdom appears to have been that of Kholaibos, whose capital Sauē is said in chapter 22 to be in Mapharitis (Ma'afir). Rhapta was therefore tributary to Kholaibos through the chief of Mouza, which was a manufacturing place. Being a tributary town, Rliapta must have been quite an important place, and Ptolemy calls it a metropolis, a term which he does not apply to any other place on the East African coast. (In the *PME* the term metropolis is applied only to Mcroē, Aksum, Saphar, Saubatha, and Minn agar, none of which is likely to have been visited by traders like the author of the *PME*)

ON ZŌSKALĒS AND THE KINGDOM OF AKSUM

The only kingdom in the whole East African area was that of Aksum, which later developed into the kingdom of Ethiopia. Aksum is about 140 miles inland from Adouli and at an altitude of more than 6000 ft. The 'half-way house' between the two places was Koloē (Qohayto), the collecting place for the ivory from the Sudan (Kuēneion), It is noteworthy that the only exports from the Aksumitc area mentioned in the *PME* are tortoiseshell, ivory, and rhinoceros horn, though many products of civilisation—glass, clothing, metals, and gold and silver objects (the latter made for the king in 'the shapes of the country') were imported to Aksum, In the 4th century A.D. the kingdom of Aksum appears, from epigraphic evidence, to have consisted of the city itself and the surrounding country, and three sub-kingdoms: Gabaz (which included Adouli), Aguēzāt or Gazē immediately east of Aksum, and Saranē next to Aguēzāt. In the first century it was probably much the same. The man named Zōskalēs who 'ruled these parts' was certainly not king of Aksum, but rather the tributary king (*negns* in Ethiopic) of Gabaz, and the forerunner of the *Bāhrnāgdsh* ('Sea king'), the governor of the coast province of later times. Zōskalēs has often been identified with one Haqlē or ZaHaqlē of Conti Rossini's king-list C,[11] though this name is found only in this list. But these lists are most untrustworthy, and there is nothing in the *PME* to suggest that Zoskales was king of Aksum. In the 6th century Kosmas Indikopleustēs names Asbās as the ruler of Adouli.[12]

BIBLIOGRAPHY OF THE PERIPLUS

CODEX PAL GRÆC., 398. A parchment of the Tenth Century, in (the Library of the University of Heidelberg. it was taken to Rome during the Thirty Years' War, and to Paris under Napoleon; and was restored to Heidelberg in 1816.

> This manuscript contains twenty different titles, of which the first six are as follows:
>> I. Argumentum a Leone Allatio. (Allazi, who packed and shipped the Heidelberg Library to Rome.)
>> II. Fragmentum de Palude Mæotide et de Ponto Euxino.
>> III. Arrianus de venatione.
>> IV. Ejusdem epistola ad Trajanum qua periplus Ponti Euxini continetu.
>> V. Ejusdem Periplus Maris Rubri.
>> VI. Hannonis periplus.

MANUSCRIPT 19,391. A parchment, supposed to be of the Fourteenth or Fifteenth Century, in the British Museum. A portion of it is supposed to have come from the monastery of Mount Athos. Such matter as it contains in common with the Heidelberg manuscript seems to have been copied therefrom, or from a common original.

> In this the Periplus is anonymous.

ARRIANI ET HANNONIS PERIPLUS: PLUTARCHUS DE FLUMINIBUS ET MONTIBUS: STRABONIS EPTTOME. *Froben. Basile & Anne MDXXXIII. Sigismundus Gelenius Anselmo Ephorina Medico S.*

---

11   B.L. MSS Orient. 817, 821.

12   HuntingfordL, 'Three notes on early Ethiopian geography', *Folia Orientalia,* XV (1974), pp. 198–9.

This first printed text, corrupt and full of errors due to lack of knowledge of the subject, served nevertheless for three centuries as the basis of later editions, because of the disappearance of the Heidelberg manuscript.

DELLE NAVIGATIONI ET VIAGGI RACCOLTA DA GIO. BATT. RAMUSIO. *In Venetia, nella Stamperia de Giunti, MDLXXXVIII.*

Vol. 1, pp. 281–283a has *Discorso di Gio. Battista Ramusio, sopra la navigatione del Mar Rosse, fine all' India Oriemtale scritta per Arrians* and p. 283a begins *Navigatiane del mar Rosse fina Alle India Orientali scritta per Arrians in Lingua Greca, & di quella poi Tradotta nella Italiana.*

There were editions of Ramusio's Collection at Venice in 1550, 1554, 1563 and 1588.

ARRIANI HISTORICI ET PHILOSOPHI PONTI EUXINI & MARIS ERYTHRÆI PERIPLUS, AD ADRIANUM CÆSAREM. *Nunc primum e Græco sermone in Latinum versus, plurimusque mendis repurgatuts. Jo. Gvilielme Stvckio Tigvrino avthore. Genevæ, apvd Evstathivm Vignon, 1577.*

This text is based on that of Gelenius, with few material emendations.

ARRIANI ARS TACTICA, ACIES CONTRA ALANOS, PERIPLUS PONTI EUXINI, PERIPLUS MARIS ERYTHÆI, LIBER DE. VENATIONE, etc., etc. *Cum Interpretibus Latinis, & Notis. Ex Recensione & Musco. Nicolai Blancardi, Amstelodami, Janssonio-Waesbergii, 1683.*

This text is professedly based on that of Stuck.

GEOGRAPHIÆ VETERIS SCRIPTORES GRÆCI MINORES. *Cum Interpretatione Latina, Dissertationibus, ac Annotationibus. Oxoniæ. E Theatro Sheldoniano, MDCXCVIII.* (Præstitit Joannes Hudsonus. Dissertationes Henrici Dodwelli.)

This contains as its fifth title, *Periplus Maris Erythræi eidem (Arriano) vulgo adscriptus. Interprete Jo. Guilielmo Stuckio Tigurino.* The text is based on Gelenius and Stuck.

SYLLOGÊS TÔN EN EPITOMÊI TOIS PALAI GEÔGRAPHETHENTON typois *ekdothentôn philotimôi dapanêi tôn ex Ioanninôn philogenestatôn adelphôn* ZOSIMIADÔN *charin tôn tês Hellenibês paideias ephiemenôn Hellenôn. En Biennêi tês Austrias ek tês Schraimblilês Typographias, 1807.*

It contains, pp. 295–333 *Arrianou Periplous tês Erythras Thalassês,* with notes translated from Hudson.

FLAVII ARRIANI NICOMEDIENSIS OPERA GRÆCE *ad optimas editiones collata. Studio Augusti Christiani Borheck. Lemgoviæ, Meyer, 1809.*

This contains, pp. 91–121, *Arrianou Periplous tês Erythras Thalassês.* The text is from Hudson.

THE PERIPLUS OR THE ERYTHREAN SEA. Part the first, containing: *An Account of the Navigation of the Ancients, from the Sea of Suez to the Coast of Zanguebar.* With Dissertations. By William Vincent. *London: Cadell, Jun., & Davies, 1800.*

THE COMMERCE AND NAVIGATION OF THE ANCIENTS IN THE INDIAN OCEAN. *By William Vincent, D.D., Dean of Westminster.* In two volumes. *London: Cadell & Davies, 1807.* Vol. I, *The Voyage of Nearehus.* Vol. II, *The Periplus of the Erythrean Sea.* Part the first containing, *An Account of the Navigation of the Ancients from the Sea of Suez to the coast of Zanguebar.* With Dissertations. Part the second containing, *An Account of the Navigation of the Ancients from the Gulph of Elana, in the Red Sea, to the Island of Ceylon.*

These two beautiful volumes, presenting the Greek test and English translation in parallel columns, preceded by dissertations that denote exhaustive geographical and historical research, are still of deep interest and importance to the student of the Periplus.

The text is that of Blancard: "His edition I was obliged to adopt, because I could obtain no other to use as copy." (Vol. II, pan II, preface, p. xi). Vincent's textual emendations are generally less useful than his geographical and commercial notes, which are still, in large part, illuminating and trustworthy, and were, when written, the first intelligent presentation of the subject.

THE VOYAGE OR NEARCHUS AND THE PERIPLUS OR THE ERYTHREAN SEA (ascribed to Arrian), translated by W. Vincent, Oxford, 1809.

UNTERSUCHUNGEN UEBER EINZELNE GECENSTAENDE DER ALTEN GESCHICHTE, GEOGRAPHIE, UND CHRONOLOGIE. *G. G. Bredow, Altona, Hammerich, 1802.*

This includes Vincent's Periplus, translated into German, pp. 715–797.

SAMMLUNG KLEINER SCHRIFTEN AUS DEM GFBIETE DER MATHEMATISCHEN UND ALTEN GEOGRAPHIE. C. G. Reichard Guns, *Reichard 1836,*

This includes Vincent's work, pp. 374–425 and 438–496.

ARRIANO OPUSCOLI, TRADOTTI DA VARI. *Milano, Smoguo, 1826–7, S. Blandi.*

DES PSEUDO-ARRIANS UMSCHIFFUNG DES ERYTHRAEISCHEN MEERES—*die Ersten neun Kapitel volktändig, die übrigen im Aurtnge. Uebersetzt von Streubel in Jahres-Bericht über die Stralauer hihere Bürger-Schule für das Schuljahr von Michaelis 1860 bis Michaelis 1861, womit—einladet C. Hartung. Berlin, Druck von Hickethier, 1861.*

This partial translation is based on the texts of Stuck, Hudson and Rorhcck, and is of little value.

ARRIAM ALEXANDRINI PERIPUS MARIS ERYTHRÆI *Retenimt ei brevi annotation instruxit B. fabricius. Dreidæ, in commisses Gittschakki, MDCCCXLIX.*

GEOGRAPHI GRÆCI MINOERS. *E codicibus recognovit, prolegomenis, annotatione, indicibusque instruxit, tabulis æri incisis illustravit Carolus Müllerus. Parisiis, Didot, MDCCCLV.*

Vol. I, pp. xcv–cxi has *Prolegomena Anonymi Periplus Maris Erythræi,* and pp. 257–305 *Anonymi (Arriani, ut fertur) Periplus Maris Erythræi,* being the eighth title included in that volume. Vol. III contains four maps, xi–xiv, especially drawn to illustrate the Periplus, and four more, vi–viii and xv, drawn for other titles hut presenting details that further elucidate this work.

This edition is a vast improvement over all its predecessors, presenting a text which is still the standard, admitting of modification only in minor details. The Greek text, carefully corrected from the Heidelberg manuscript, and critically revised and improved, is presented side by side with a Latin translation. The notes, which are in Latin, reflect almost everything of importance to the subject which had been written up to that time.

THE COMMERCE AND NAVIGATION OF THE ERYTHRÆAN SEA. *By J. W. McCrindle, M.A., LL.D., Calcutta, 1879. This volume contains a translation (with commentary) of the* PERIPLUS ERYTHRÆI MARIS, *by an unknown writer of the first Christian century, and of the second part of the* INDIKA *of Arrian.*

The translation of the *Periplus* was also printed in the *Indian Antiquary* of Bombay, Vol. VIII, pp. 108–151.

This excellent translation, while based professedly on Müller's text, is often reminiscent rather of Vincent's, and thus repeats various errors which Müller's notes had corrected.

The notes are valuable for the original material they contain concerning Hindu names, places and commodities, but show lack of acquaintance with German writers.

DER PERIPLUS DES ERYTHRAEISCHEN MEERES VON EINEM UNBEKANNTEN. *Griechisch und deutsch mit kritischen und erkiärenden Anmerkungen nebst vollständigem Wörterverzeichnisse von B. Fabricius.. Leipzig, Verlag von Veit & Comp., 1883.*

A most scholarly presentation of Greek text and German translation on opposite pages, with clear and exhaustive notes. The Greek text, which has been revised with extreme care, contains many verbal corrections of Müller's standard text, and leaves little to be desired. The historical and commercial notes call for revision where they omit conclusions previously reached by English writers, and in so far as they are affected by later research.

Analysis Questions

1. How do these documents describe Bantu tribal relationships?
2. Does the Bible say anything about Africa?
3. Describe the main characteristics of the East African society.

CHAPTER 10

India and South Asia to the Mongolian Empire

Introduction

Genghis Khan's Mongol horsemen have taken Beijing in 1218 A.D. The imperial palace of the Jin dynasty is in flames, the city has been wrecked, and its occupants have been butchered in a shocking bash of executing that went hand in hand with the Mongol victory. Genghis has headed his unwashed horsemen, for all intents and purpose invulnerable as light cavalry, over to the north and swung west to Turkestan, Transoxiana, and Afghanistan. It is a move that bodes ill for the flourishing Muslim states of central Asia, for wherever the Mongols pass, they leave nothing but death and destruction.

The Mongols have emerged from the edge of the Gobi, whose harshness may have penetrated their souls, as a feuding federation of tribes. It is Genghis Khan who has welded them together into the fearsome fighting force that is now rampaging across Europe and Asia, creating the biggest world empire in human history. Despite their conquest of many cities and great stretches of China and the mountainous country to the west, the Mongols, unlike previous nomadic invaders, have not settled down and established their own civilizations. For them, cities are not places to be lived in but sources of plunder. Their organization is purely military. They live and die in the saddle.

The Gupta Empire, the cradle of Buddhist art and culture for more than a century, is disintegrating as the Huns, a branch of the Mongols, advance deeper into India. Since the end of Gupta's reign in 496 A.D., various small kingdoms have tried in vain to lay claim to his dynasty. Under the tolerant rule of the Gupta emperors, Sanskrit literature has enjoyed a renewal, notably when the great poet Kalidasa was one of the "nine jewels" around King Chandragupta II. Hindu art is gradually grown and the first small temples have been built.

Unlike Vietnam, whose culture and society has been heavily influenced by China, much of South Asian societies are more influenced by Indian culture. Two great examples can be found in great Cambodian and Indonesian temples. Between 790 A.D. and 869 A.D., a magnificent temple is being built in central Java by the island's Buddhist Sailendra rulers. They have named the temple "Borobudur," meaning "many Buddhas." The massive shrine is unlike anything previously built, with interior carvings and architecture depicting an earthly journey leading to heavenly nothingness (nirvana). It epitomizes the confidence and proselytizing zeal of the Sailendra rulers, who have just declared Buddhism the official religion on the predominantly Hindu island. The lower six terraces are cut square, with stairways on the cardinal points, and are adorned with the life of Buddha. The upper terraces are round, with 72 stupas, shaped like cupolas and carved in stone latticework, each covering a seated Buddha. At the pinnacle is a larger stupa. Thus the temple, its skyline resembling the City of God, symbolizes the pilgrim's progress from worldly life to ultimate enlightenment.

The largest and most magnificent Hindu temple in Asia has been completed at Angkor Wat, the Khmer capital, in 1150 A.D. Commissioned by King Suryavarman II as his funeral temple, its size alone makes it a suitable monument for the king who extended the frontiers of the Khmer Empire beyond those of any other monarch. The moat encircling the temple and its edifices is 12 miles in circumference. The grand entrance, over a paved bridge guarded by parapets depicting the part-dragon, part-human Hindu divinities the Nagas, leads to a magnificent gatehouse, itself one of the grandest Khmer buildings ever erected. It is flanked by galleries, and its triple openings are surmounted by towers. On ground level and gallery level are exquisite reliefs representing the great epics of Hindu mythology: the delights of paradise; the pains of purgatory; the battles of Devas, Asuras, and Vishnu; the legend of Garuda and Banasura; and Devas and Asuras churning the ocean.

---

31. The Secret History of the Mongols

by Arthur Waley

Altan, Khuchar, Sacha-beki and all of them, after consulting together, said to Temujin, 'We appoint you as our Khan. If you will he our Khan, we will go as vanguard against the multitude of your enemies. All the beautiful girls and married women that we capture and all the fine horses, we will give to you. When hunting is afoot, we will he the first to go to the battue and will give you the wild beasts that we surround and

Arthur Waley, *The Secret History of the Mongols & Other Works,* pp. 245, 285-286. Copyright © 1963 by House of Stratus.

catch. If in time of battle we disobey your orders or in time of peace we act contrary to your interests, part us from our wives and possessions and cast us out into the wilderness.' Such was the oath they made to serve him. They made him Great Khan, with the name Chingis.

Chingis said to Bo'orchu and Jelme: 'When I had no companions you were the first to become my comrades; I have not forgotten it. You are to be at the head of all these followers of mine.' And to his other followers he said: 'All of you left Jamukha, thinking to come to me. If Heaven and Earth give their protection, you elders will now and long afterwards be my blessed comrades.' Speaking thus, he (gave charges to all of them. After Chingis became Khan he sent Dakhi and Sugegei to the Ong Khan To'oril, ruler of the Kereits. The Ong Khan said, 'You were quite right to make Temujin your Khan. What would become of you Mongols without a Khan? Don't go back on what you agreed upon at the start.' Such was his discourse.

After Chingis had made subject to him all the many tribes he set up at the source of the Onan river a white banner with nine pendants and became Great Khan. This was in the year of the Tiger (1206).

Chingis said: 'I have now assigned their tasks to my sons-in-law and to the ninety-five commanders of a thousand. Among them there are officers who have rendered particularly great service to me and I am going to reward them further.' He then told Shigi-khutukhu to summon Bo'orchu and Mukhali. Shigi-khutukhu said, 'To whose services are those of Bo'orchu and Mukhali superior, that they should be further rewarded? I have been in your family since I was a child, all the time till I became a grown man, and never once left you. To whose services are mine inferior? What reward are you now going to give me?' Chingis said, 'You became my sixth brother and have had your share, just like my other brothers, enjoying the privilege of being allowed to sin a hundred times without punishment. Now that I have sub-dued all the peoples, I want you to listen and look for me. No one shall be allowed to act contrary to what you say. If there are cases of robbery or fraud, it will be for you to mete out punishment, slaying those who ought to die and punishing those who ought to be punished. You are to decide all disputes arising out of division of family property, and are to write your decisions on the Blue Register, in which no one is to be allowed ever to make alterations.' Shigi-khutukhu said, 'I am the youngest brother. How can I dare receive the same portion as all my other brothers? But if you intend to bestow a favour, give me the peoples who live within earthen walls.' Chingis said, 'You shall have what you ask for, having no doubt thought the matter out'. Shigi-khutukhu, having received his reward, went and summoned Bo'orchu, Mukhali and others to receive theirs. Chingis said to Bo'orchu ... 'When I was passing the night at Dalan-nemurges, ready to fight with the Tartars, heavy rain fell. You wanted me to get a good rest, and spreading out a felt shirt you stood over me and kept me from getting wet. Only once, all the time till dawn, did you shift your feet—a proof of great heroism!'

32. The Mongols in Europe

by Matthew Paris

THE EMPEROR'S LETTER CONCERNING THE APPROACH OF THE TARTARS.

"Frederick, emperor, doc., to the king of England, greeting.—We cannot be silent on a matter which concerns not only the Roman empire, whose office it is to propagate the Gospel, but also all the kingdoms of the world that practise Christian worship, and threatens general destruction to the whole of Christianity: we therefore hasten to bring it to your knowledge, although the true facts of the matter have but lately come to ours. Some time since a people of a barbarous race and mode of life called (from what place or origin I know not) Tartars, has lately emerged from the regions of the south, where it had long lain hid, burnt up by the sun of the torrid zone, and, thence marching towards the northern parts, took forcible possession of the country there, and remaining for a time, multiplied like locusts, and has now come forth, not without the premeditated judgment of God, but not, I hope, reserved to these latter times for the ruin of the whole of Christianity. Their arrival was followed by a general slaughter, a universal desolation of kingdoms, and by utter ruin to the fertile territory, which this impious horde of people roved through, sparing neither sex, age, nor rank, whilst they confidently hope to destroy the rest of the human race, and are endeavouring to rule and lord it alone, trusting to their immense power and unlimited numbers. After having massacred all they could set eyes upon, and pillaging every place, leaving behind them the signs of universal depopulation, these Tartars (or rather inhabitants of Tartarus) arrived at the populous colony of the Cumanians, and as they are careless of life, and as the bow is a more familiar weapon to them than to other people, with their arrows and other missile weapons, which they are in continual use of, and by which their arms are more exercised and strengthened than other people's, they entirely dispersed and subdued that people, and those who could not escape were slain by their bloody swords. The proximity of these barbarians, with some difficulty put the Kuthenians, who dwell near them, on their guard, so that, being unused to the attacks of this unknown people, they consulted their own safety, and, frightened at their fury as at fire, they took precautions for guarding themselves against their attacks. The Tartars took to pillage and destruction. By the sudden attacks and assaults of that savage race, which descends like the anger of God, or like lightning, Kiew, the chief city of that kingdom, was attacked and taken, and the whole of that noble kingdom, which ought to have united itself with that of Hungary, for its defence and protection, but which it carelessly neglected to do, was, after its inhabitants were slain, reduced to a state of

Matthew Paris, "The Mongols in Europe," *Matthew Paris's English History*, Volume I, pp. 341-346, 1852.

utter destruction and desolation. Their king, an idle and careless man, was ordered by messengers and letters from these Tartars, if he wished to save his life and that of his subjects, by a surrender of himself and his kingdom, at once to anticipate their favour; but he was not frightened or warned by this, and thus gave a proof to his people and to others, that he and his ought sooner to have provided for their own protection and defence against their incursions. But, whilst these elated or ignorant people, despising their enemies, were idly sleeping with the enemy in their immediate neighbourhood, and trusting to the natural strength of the places the Tartars made their way into the kingdom like a whirlwind, and suddenly surrounded them on all sides. The Hungarians being thus surrounded before they expected an attack, and surprised when unprepared as it were, tried to defend their camp against them. When the two rival armies of the Tartars and Hungarians were distant about five miles from each other, the advanced portion of the Tartars suddenly rushed forwards at the dawn of the morning, and suddenly surrounding the camp of the Hungarians, slew the prelates and nobles of the kingdom who opposed them, and massacred such a host of the Hungarians, that a similar slaughter was never remembered to have taken place in one battle, from the most remote period. The king himself with difficulty escaped, mounted on a fleet horse, and fled, attended by a small retinue, to share the lot of his brother in the kingdom of Illyria, that be might at least be protected there. The victors, exulting in the spoil, then took up their quarters in the camp of the conquered Hungarians; and at this very moment they are ravaging the largest and finest part of Hungary, beyond the river Danube, harassing the inhabitants with fire and sword, and threaten to involve the rest in the same destruction, as we have been informed by the venerable bishop of Vatzen, the said king of Hungary's ambassador to our court, afterwards sent to that of Rome, who, passing through our territory first, bore testimony to what he had seen; and his evidence is but too true.

The men themselves are small and of short stature, as far as regards height, but compact, stout, and bulky, resolute, strong, and courageous, and ready at the nod of their leader to rush into any undertaking of difficulty; they have large faces, scowling looks, and utter horrible shouts, suited to their hearts; they wear raw hides of bullocks, asses, and horses; and for armour, they are protected by pieces of iron stitched to them, which they have made use of till now. But, and we cannot say it without sorrow, they are now, from the spoils of the conquered Christians, providing themselves with more suitable weapons, that we may, through God's anger, be the more basely slain with our own arms. Besides, they are supplied with better horses, they live on richer food, and adorn themselves with more handsome clothes, than formerly. They are incomparable archers, and carry skins artificially made, in which they cross lakes and the most rapid rivers without danger. When fodder fails them, their horses are said to be satisfied with the bark and leaves of trees, and the roots of herbs, which the men bring to them; and yet, they always find them to be very swift and strong in a ease of necessity.

For if, which God forbid, they invade the German territory, and meet with no opposition, the rest of the world will then feel the thunder of the suddenly-coming tempest, which we believe to have arisen from a divine judgment, as the world is defiled by the infection of various sum, as charity begins to grow cold in many by whom the true faith ought to be preached and upheld, and their pernicious example pollutes the world with usury and divers kinds of simony and ambition. May it please your majesty, therefore, to provide for this emergency, and whilst these enemies of us all in common are venting their fury in the neighbouring countries, do you by prudent counsels make preparations to resist them. For they have left their own country, heedless of danger to their own lives, with the intention (God forbid its being carried into effect) of subduing the whole of the West, and of ruining and uprooting the faith and name of Christ. And owing to the unexpected victories which they have hitherto gained by God's permission, they have arrived at such a pitch of insanity, that they consider they have already gained possession of all the kingdoms of the world, and may subdue and bind the prostrate kings and princes as they please, to their own vile service.

---

33. Early Kingdoms of Sumatra and Java

by D.R. SarDesai

Insular Southeast Asia was far more exposed than the mainland to influences from distant countries like India, Arabia, Persia, China, and, in more recent times, Europe. International commerce brought in its wake cultural contacts including, of course, religion. Unlike mainland Southeast Asia, people in the insular region followed a variety of religions: Buddhism and Hinduism held sway during the first millennium in Malaya and Indonesia, giving way after the thirteenth century to Islam, which spread rapidly in the archipelago in the fifteenth and sixteenth centuries. The sixteenth century opened doors to Christianity, which became the dominant religion of the Philippines. Only the people of picturesque Bali adhered to Hinduism despite such large-scale conversions around them. If Theravada Buddhism is the dominant religion of mainland Southeast Asia, Islam is that of the insular region, with Indonesia the largest Muslim nation on earth.

HISTORICAL SOURCES

Sources of information for the early history of Indonesia are varied, though scantier and more ambiguous than those for mainland Southeast Asia. Stone and copper inscriptions have been found in Sanskrit, old Malay, old Javanese, old Balinese, old

D.R. SarDesai, "Early Kingdoms of Sumatra and Java," *Southeast Asia: Past and Present*, pp. 40-47. Copyright © 2012 by Taylor & Francis Group. Reprinted with permission.

Sundanese, and in Sumatra, in Indian languages other than Sanskrit.[1] A few texts on palm leaves (*lontar*) have survived the ravages of tropical weather, the most notable being *The Nagarkertagama* and *The Pararaton*. The first, dealing with the founding of Singhasari in 1222, was composed in 1365 by Prapanca, the court poet during the reign of King Rajasanagara of Majapahit. *The Pararaton* is an older chronicle from which Prapanca borrowed considerably, although modern knowledge about it is based on a version dating from the sixteenth century.

Besides these indigenous accounts, considerable information on the early history of Sumatra and Java is found in Indian and Chinese sources. Chinese sources in regard to the archipelago are not as numerous as for mainland Southeast Asia. The imperial annals provide information on various kingdoms, their rulers, and the embassies they sent to the Chinese emperor's court. Obviously, the insular kingdoms sent tribute or embassies to the Chinese court far less frequently than did the kingdoms of mainland Southeast Asia. A second category of Chinese sources is the travel accounts of Chinese pilgrims who stopped in Southeast Asia on their way to India. Last is the valuable account of Marco Polo, who visited the archipelago in 1292, coinciding with the time of Mongol invasion.

EARLY KINGDOMS

Two kinds of states developed in the Indonesian archipelago: those based on maritime commerce and those capable of large-scale cultivation of agricultural products for consumption and export. Whereas Srivijaya in southeastern Sumatra belonged to the first category, most of the Javanese states, particularly those in the volcanic and *sawah*-cultivating central and eastern parts of the island, belonged to the latter kind. Sumatra's only advantage was topographic, deriving from its location on the shortest sea route through the Strait of Malacca. Java's strong points were a central location among the myriad islands; access to and control of the products of the archipelago, particularly spices and sandalwood; fertile soil capable of sustaining a large population and yielding substantial surpluses; and, finally, its control over an alternate east-west trade route through the Sunda Strait.

It is no wonder, then, that rivalry between Java and Sumatra for the control of the straits of Malacca and Sunda persisted in the history of the region. With its natural advantages, Java had longer periods of dominance in the archipelago than Sumatra. On the other hand, Java experienced a disastrous pattern of rise and fall of kingdoms brought on not only by human factors such as excessive local ambition or dynastic disputes but also by natural disasters, including earthquakes and volcanoes that prompted demographic dislocations on a massive scale. The cycle of dynastic changes and the rapid shifts of power alternating mostly between central and eastern Java must have caused considerable chaos and untold hardships to the hapless peasantry. Of the dozens of polities that thus emerged in Java in the millennium beginning about

700, a few stand out for their superior attainments: the Srivijaya, Sailendras, Mataram, Kediri, Singhasari, and Majapahit.

SRIVIJAYA

Perhaps the oldest among the more durable of the Indonesian kingdoms was Srivijaya, whose capital was Palembang in southeastern Sumatra. Thanks go to Georges Coedes for "discovering" Srivijaya.[2] Its rise as the greatest maritime power in the region from about the seventh to the thirteenth centuries was most certainly a consequence of the fall of Funan and the inability of its successor kingdom, Chenla, to serve as an effective trading intermediary in the extensive east-west trade. Clearly, there was a great opportunity for a new power to make enormous profits from engaging in the lucrative international trade as well as by simply providing port facilities in the western part of the archipelago.

Located halfway between the two principal maritime passages, namely, the straits of Malacca and Sunda, Srivijaya's Palembang port provided an excellent harbor sheltered from the fury of the northeast and southwest monsoons by the mountain ranges of Sumatra and Malaya. Srivijaya's prosperity was helped by the phenomenal rise in the revived Chinese maritime trade during the T'ang dynasty (seventh to the tenth centuries). In the opinion of O. W. Wolters, Srivijaya's rapid growth could also be attributed to sales of Indonesian, in particular northern Sumatran, substitutes of pine resin and benjamin gum for frankincense and myrrh, supplies of which from Arabia and eastern Africa were not adequate to meet the increasing demand for these commodities in West Asia and China.[3]

Srivijaya attracted international shipping to its harbors by suppressing piracy in the Strait of Malacca and providing excellent anchorage, storage, and recreational facilities in Palembang. The well-known Chinese traveler-pilgrim I-Ching noted the arrival of as many as thirty-five ships from Persia alone during his six-month stay in Srivijaya in 671. According to such accounts, porcelains, jades, and silks from China; camphor, sandalwood, spices, and resins from the Moluccas; and textiles from India found eager buyers in the hustle and bustle of the Srivijayan ports of Malayu and Palembang.

The fortified city of Palembang was also an important center of Mahayana Buddhist learning. According to I-Ching, who was on his way to India for a ten-year period of study and spent four years again in Srivijaya on his return trip, Palembang's monasteries had more than a thousand inmates. He recommended that his countrymen planning travel to India for higher studies in Buddhism spend one or two years in Srivijaya.

To ensure its prosperity, Srivijaya employed a powerful fleet, compelling all shipping passing through the region to touch its ports and pay dues and taxes, thus marking a precedent for the hated impositions later made familiar to the region by the Portuguese and the Dutch. In order to enforce such a monopoly over the trade route between India and China, Srivijaya acquired territorial control over the strategic areas around the Strait of Malacca and the Isthmus of Kra. According to an Arab chronicler,

Sulayman, the Srivijayan empire extended by the middle of the ninth century over all of Sumatra, Kedah, and western Java. Another Arab traveler, Masudi, testified in 995 that it took two years to go around all the islands of the Srivijayan empire in the fastest vessel.

Srivijaya's domination of the Sino-Indian trade route remained almost unchallenged for two to three centuries. Its high-handed practice of forcing ships to use and pay excessive charges for its port facilities tried the patience of the region's traders and rulers. The first major challenge came from the Mataram rulers of eastern Java in the last quarter of the tenth century. A few decades later, in 1025, however, Rajendra Chola of southern India dealt a crushing blow to Srivijaya's maritime might and monopoly. Apparently, the Cholas conquered and administered large portions of the Srivijayan empire, including its ports of Ligor, Kedah, and Tumasik, although that lasted only two decades. In the end, logistical problems of political control from Chola's distant base in southern India must have worked to Srivijaya's advantage. Besides, Srivijaya acknowledged Chola's suzerainty and promised good behavior, which apparently met the Chola king's demands.

THE SAILENDRAS

A century after Srivijaya was established, central Java developed a dynasty that became its competitor in the east-west trade for the next one hundred years. These were the Sailendras. According to Coedes and de Casparis, the Funanese descendants lived in Java for two centuries in obscurity until, in the middle of the eighth century, one of their leaders, Bhanu, acquired a kingdom.[4] He called himself a Sailendra (king of the mountain), a title held by his Funanese ancestors. In what may have been an attempt to retrieve their patrimony, the Sailendras raided Tongking and Champa, defeated the divided Chenlas, captured and beheaded the king of water Chenla, and briefly ruled that mainland kingdom from insular Java during the last decades of the eighth century. Thus, the Sailendras became the only indigenous power in history to rule over substantial territory in both mainland and insular Southeast Asia. As noted in the previous chapter, the Sailendra rule over Chenla was quickly extinguished in 802 by Jayavarman II, the founder of the Angkor monarchy. The Sailendras, however, left their mark on mainland Southeast Asia in the form of Javanese art patterns and graceful scrolls in Champa and Angkor.[5]

The Sailendras participated actively, though on a much lower scale than Srivijaya, in the east-west trade; their principal base of power and prosperity was agricultural. Agriculture helped them to build surplus wealth, which they expended mostly in constructing palaces, temples, and Buddhist monuments, including the world-famous Borobodur, the greatest architectural monument in all of Southeast Asia.

The Borobodur was begun in 778 by King Vishnu and completed in 824 by a grandson, Samaratunga. Along the same cosmological lines as the later Angkor monuments, the Sailendras selected Borobodur as the Mount Meru of their kingdom to erect thereon a miniature cosmos dedicated to the Buddha. The Borobodur's nine terraces

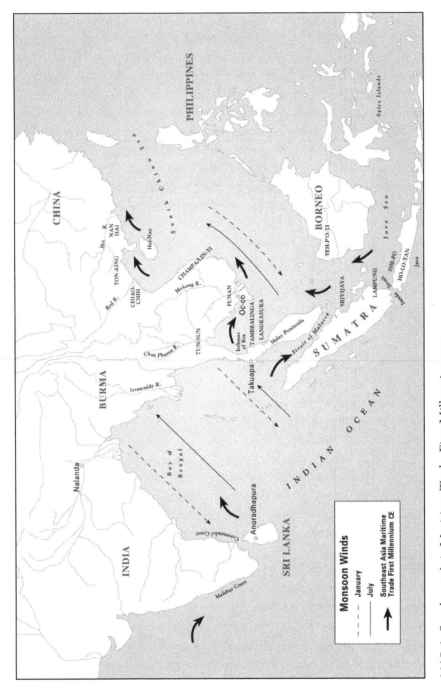

MAP 1 Southeast Asia Maritime Trade, First Millennium CE

carved out of a single hill represented the nine previous lives of Gautama before he attained the Buddhahood. Seen from a distance, the immense structure looks like a single Buddhist stupa.

The Borobodur is the best example of Indo-Javanese art. The galleries around the terraces measure about three miles, their sides fully adorned with nearly two thousand intricately detailed bas-relief sculptures. These include four hundred statues of the Buddha in various moods, encapsulating in stone the saga of Mahayana Buddhism. The structure, undoubtedly Indian in conception and reflecting the best forms of art of the Gupta period, was at the same time representative of Javanese artistic skills. A few Indian artists may have been invited to assist, but the work was principally executed by indigenous people. The faces are typically of Javanese people engaged in diverse occupations from princes to peasants, carpenters, pottery makers, weavers, fishermen, merchants, dancers, and seafarers. Their dress and jewelry are distinctively Javanese, as are some of the musical instruments and items of furniture and utensils. Taken together with scores of other smaller buildings around Borobodur, the Sailendra construction activity is truly stupefying, a remarkable testimony of the culture's wealth, taste, and organizational abilities.

According to an alternate interpretation given by J. G. de Casparis, the Borobodur was built to serve as a tomb for the soul of Sailendra's King Indra (782–812), during whose rule most of the construction work on the monument was carried out.[6] His ashes, after cremation, were to be placed in a reliquary at the basement level. The upper nine levels were meant for the souls of his nine ancestors, all of them bodhisattvas in the Mahayanist tradition, on their way to attain the blissful state of Nirvana. The basement level, also elaborately sculptured, was covered to await the day of Indra's death. For some unknown reason, the ceremonial placement of his ashes there never occurred. The basement remained in that state until World War II, when the Japanese uncovered a part of the casing.

The Sailendras were matrimonially related to the old Sanjaya family in north-central Java as well as to the Srivijaya ruling house in Sumatra. In 832, a Sanjaya prince, Patapan, usurped the Sailendra throne. The infant Sailendra prince, Balaputra, remained in a political wilderness until 850, when he attempted to regain his patrimony, failed, and consequently fled to Srivijaya. There he ascended the throne almost unchallenged. Thus, the Sailendra line was extinguished in Java but continued in Srivijaya. There, the Sailendras adopted the Srivijayan policy of giving primary attention to trade and commerce to the neglect of their traditional devotion to building Buddhist monuments.

MATARAM AND KEDIRI

The successors of Patapan of the Sanjaya dynasty ruled over the former Sailendra kingdom of central Java for nearly one hundred years before moving the capital to Mataram in 929, possibly because of an earthquake or an epidemic. The Mataram rulers emulated the vanquished Sailendras in every way except religion. Beginning from

Patapan, Hinduism reasserted itself over Mahayana Buddhism. In trying to rival the Sailendra Buddhist monuments, the Mataram rulers energetically built numerous temples dedicated to Hindu gods. The ruins of their capital at Prambanan, near modern Jogjakarta, show three central temples (*chandis*) dedicated to the Hindu trinity of Brahma, Vishnu, and Shiva, with a number of smaller temples surrounding them. The temples were adorned with sculptures elaborating stories from the *Ramayana* epic. Like Borobodur and Angkor, the Prambanan temples may have served as mausoleums for princes and higher nobility. The reassertion of Hinduism did not mean intolerance of Buddhism, which coexisted just as in contemporary Angkor, though on a much lower key. As Coedes observed, a syncretic cult of Shiva-Buddha evolved both in Mataram and in Angkor.[7] Reflective of such eclecticism was the appearance of two great literary works on Hinduism and Buddhism in the tenth century under the patronage of the Mataram ruler Sindok (929–948). These were the Javanese *Ramayana* and the Tantric Buddhist treatise *Sang Hyang Kamahayanikan,* which give valuable insights into the artistic concepts, iconography, and architecture of the Javanese of the time.[8]

The Mataram rulers participated actively in the region's trade with China, taking full advantage of the economic boom during the T'ang dynasty. They developed trade in spices from the Moluccas, for which there was an increasing demand from both China and the Arab world. Trade with the latter necessitated the use of the port facilities around the Strait of Malacca, which was at that time under the firm control of Srivijaya. As mentioned before, Srivijaya's tax and other exactions irked a number of states, including Mataram. Around the end of the first millennium, when Mataram was apparently at the peak of its political and economic power, it challenged Srivijaya's hated monopolistic practices. The Mataram navy, however, was no match for Srivijaya's. In 1006 Srivijaya completely defeated Mataram, sacked its capital, and put large numbers of its inhabitants to a merciless end.

East Java's political misfortune, however, proved temporary despite what had appeared to be a total debacle at Srivijaya's hands. The revival of political power in Java was helped by at least two factors: the defeat of Srivijaya in 1026 by Rajendra Chola of southern India, and the leadership of Prince Airlangga, son of a Balinese prince and a Mataram princess. His qualities of heroism and tact so impressed the Mataram nobility and the Brahmans that they persuaded him to accept the Mataram crown. Within a decade of his coronation in 1019 at the age of nineteen, Airlangga was able to restore Mataram to its former political strength. His statesmanship was evident in his decision to forgive and forget Srivijaya's past acts and instead propose his own marriage with a Srivijayan princess to initiate a policy of cordial relationship between Java and Sumatra.[9] In the field of religion, he scotched the rivalries between Hinduism and Mahayana Buddhism by recognizing both, though he and his successors represented themselves as incarnations of Vishnu. More astutely, he weakened the hold of the Brahman priests and Buddhist monks by appropriating the vast estates they managed on behalf of their religious organizations. The peace and prosperity Airlangga thus brought to Mataram

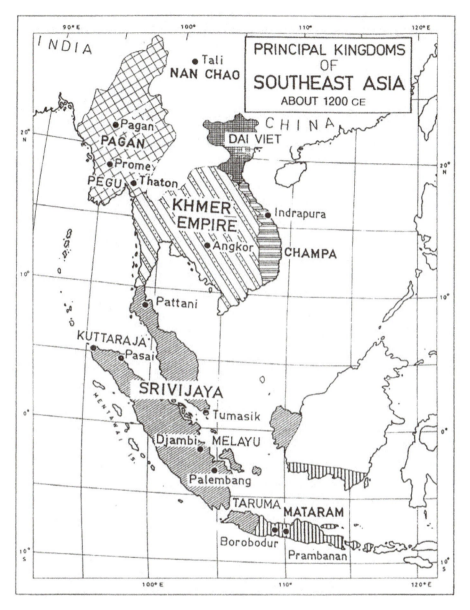

MAP 2 Kingdoms of Southeast Asia about 1200 CE

have earned him a high place in the history of Java. Unfortunately, his lifelong work, particularly in creating unity among his subjects, was undone by his own action in 1042. Having no direct heir and fearing a contest between two children born of rival concubines with equally dubitable claims to the throne, he divided his state just before his death into two kingdoms: Janggala and Kediri.

Of the two kingdoms, only Kediri attained prominence. A Chinese writer, Chou Chu-fei, referred to it in 1178 as the greatest maritime power in Southeast Asia, ranking it higher than Srivijaya. Its political control then extended over Bali, southwestern Borneo, and southern Sulawesi, while its ports attracted most of the spices exported from the Moluccas. In the fast-developing spice trade between India and the Mediterranean after the Crusades, the Gujarati merchants from western India at first preferred Kediri ports to Srivijayan, because of both the easier access to Moluccan spices as well as the lower port duties. By all accounts, Kediri flourished and was at the zenith of its political and economic power in the first quarter of the thirteenth century when Ken Angrok (literally, "he who upsets everything"), an adventurer who first captured the less important state of Janggala, attacked Kediri, killed its ruler, and established a new dynasty in eastern Java in 1222. Three decades later, his successors changed the name of the capital, Kuttaraja, to Singhasari (the name of Angrok's birthplace), by which name his dynasty came to be known to history.[10]

The Singhasari dynasty's greatest king, Kertanagara (1268–1292), the hero of the Javanese epic poem *The Nagarkertagama*, was a great warrior, fine scholar, and devotee of Shiva as well as of Tantric Buddhism. He promoted a syncretic cult of Shiva-Buddha, which claimed to work for the redemption of the souls of the dead and was very much in tune with the Indonesian practice of ancestor worship.[11]

All this made Kertanagara a legendary figure able to rally large numbers of supporters in the realization of his plans to make Java the center of power in the entire archipelago. By 1290 he attained his dream of subjugating Singhasari's longtime rival, Srivijaya, and making himself master of both the principal maritime passages of Southeast Asia, the straits of Malacca and Sunda. Srivijaya had been in decline for some time, its northern Malay territories having been appropriated during this same time by the Thais. The Singhasari dynasty proved short-lived, as Kertanagara was killed by a rival during the Mongol invasion.

NOTES

1   L. Ch. Damais, "Pre–Seventeenth Century Indonesian History: Sources and Directions," in *An Introduction to Indonesian Historiography,* edited by Mohammad Ali Soedjatmoko et al. (Ithaca, NY: Cornell University Press, 1965), 24–25.

2   Georges Coedes, "Le royaume de Crivijaya," *BEFEO* 18, no. 6 (1918): 1–36.

3   O. W. Wolters, *Early Indonesian Commerce: A Study of the Origins of Srivijaya* (Ithaca, NY: Cornell University Press, 1967), 107–110.

4   J. G. de Casparis, *Selected Inscriptions from the Seventh to the Ninth Century A.D.* (Bandung: Prasasti Indonesia, 1956), 184–185, 204.

5   H. G. Quaritch-Wales, *The Making of Greater India* (London: Bernard Quaritch, 1951), 150–156.

6   De Casparis, *Selected Inscriptions,* 184–187.

7   Georges Coedes, *The Indianized States of Southeast Asia* (Honolulu: East-West Center Press, 1968), 126.

8   Ibid., 128–129.

9 The famous Javanese classic *Arjunavivaha,* by the poet Kanva, was composed in 1035 to commemorate this marriage.

10 Jessy Blom, *The Antiquities of Singasari* (Leiden: Burgersdijk and Niermans, 1939), 159.

11 Coedes, *Indianized States,* 199.

Analysis Questions

1. What were the reasons for the rapid expansion of the Mongols (Tartars)?
2. Based on "The Secret History of the Mongols," what were the important characteristics of Genghis Khan that made him a great leader?
3. What are the main characteristics of the early kingdoms of Sumatra and Java?

CHAPTER 11

The Essential Partners

China, Japan, and Korea

Introduction

After the collapse of the Tang Dynasty, many regional warlords ruled China for several decades (the Five Dynasties and Ten Kingdoms Period). The Song Dynasty was established among these northern warlords in 960 A.D. This dynasty once again united most of China and made peace with the powerful nomadic group, the Khitan, but eventually collapsed in 1126 A.D. under attack by other northern nomads, the Jurchen. Driven southward, the Song only controlled central and southern China (Southern Song Dynasty Period). The Song was finally destroyed by the classical nomad power of world history, the Mongols.

Despite the fact that the Song had constantly struggled to defend itself against northern nomads, the Song experienced dramatic changes and developments in many fields. The old aristocracy lost its strength to the scholar-officials (Confucian gentry). Rulers became more despotic than in the past. The populace stretched outward, and urbanism and mercantilism came to be more conspicuous parts of Chinese life. Buddhism lost its erudite power to a dynamic Neo-Confucianism. Exchange and industry took off, and urban areas—for example, cities like Kaifeng and Hangzhou—grew into the world's most populous and fabulous metropolitan urban communities.

The Koryo Dynasty (918–1392) in Korean Peninsula was established from the remains of the administration of Silla when Koryo decimated Later Paekche in 936. Acknowledging the formal surrender of the last Silla king in the previous year, the founder of Koryo, Wang Kon, erected a state that endured for almost 500 years before being displaced by the Choson Dynasty (1392–1910). Much of early Koryo society was still loyal to Silla. Buddhism, for instance, continued to dominate Koryo. Even though, like Silla, Koryo was an aristocratic society, Koryo adopted the Confucian-style civil service examination system from China to recruit some of its officials. In the middle of the Koryo Dynasty period, Koryo, however, was challenged by nomadic groups. Between 993 and 1018, the Khitan invaded Koryo three times. Later, the Jurchen also approached Koryo, and the mighty world power, the Mongols, dominated Koryo in 1258. Despite these foreign invasions, Koryo remained a fairly stable society, with high achievements in many fields.

Like Korea, Japan in the early medieval period was heavily influenced by Chinese culture. Japanese aristocrats adopted Chinese forms in art and literature, political structures, and Chinese writing. Buddhist and Confucian ideals of China coexisted with Japan's native Shinto religion. In 794, the Japanese moved their capital to begin the Heian period (794–1185). The royal family, however, had little power. The real political authority was in the hands of the aristocratic Fujiwara clan. Despite power struggles in the royal court, the Heian period saw a flowering of literature, such as the world's first novel, *The Tale of Genji*, by Murasaki Shikibu.

The rise of the Fujiwara clan to overwhelming power in the Heian period suppressed others in the court, including the smaller branches of the Fujiwara. A number of these people left the capital to accept appointments to offices in the provincial governments and became local warrior groups. Eventually, two extraordinary families, the Taira and the Minamoto, rose to the front line of samurai social order. In 1192, Minamoto Yoritomo was given the title of *shogun*, or general, with power over all Japan's military families. The Kamakura warrior government (Bakufu) between 1185 and 1333 effectively shielded Japan from intrusion by the Mongols. Between 1333 and 1568, an exceptionally unbending class structure improved, on top of a feudalistic economy regulated by feudal lords (*daimyos*).

---

34. The Nature As Principle

by Zhu Xi; trans. and ed. William Theodore de Bary and Irene Bloom

42:6a   The Way is identical with the nature of man and things and their nature is identical with the Way. They are one and the same. But we must understand why it is called the nature and why it is called the Way.[1]

42:6b   After reading some essays by Xun[2] and others on the nature, the Teacher said: In discussing the nature it is important to know first of all what kind of thing it

---

1   "Human desire" here refers to selfish desires as opposed to those serving the common good, as symbolized here by the Principle of Heaven.
2   Huang Xun (1147–1212), a disciple of Zhu Xi.

really is. Cheng Yi put it best when he said that "the nature is the same as principle." Now if we regard it as principle, then surely it has neither physical form nor shadow. It is nothing but this very principle. In human beings, humaneness, rightness, ritual decorum, and wisdom are his nature, but what physical shape or form have they? All they have are the principles of humaneness, rightness, decorum, and wisdom. As they possess these principles, many deeds are carried out, and human beings are able to have the feelings of commiseration, shame, deference and compliance, and of right and wrong. ... In human beings, the nature is merely humaneness, rightness, decorum, and wisdom. According to Mencius, these four fundamental virtues are rooted in the mind-and-heart. When, for example, he speaks of the mind of commiseration, he attributes feeling to the mind.

42:9b-10a   Original nature is an all-pervading perfection not contrasted with evil. This is true of what Heaven has endowed in the self. But when it operates in human beings, there is the differentiation of good and evil. When humans act in accord with it, there is goodness. When humans act out of accord with it, there is evil. How can it be said that the good is not the original nature? It is in its operation in human beings that the distinction of good and evil arises, but conduct in accord with the original nature is due to the original nature. If, as they say, there is the original goodness and there is another goodness contrasted with evil, there must be two natures. Now what is received from Heaven is the same nature as that in accordance with which goodness ensues, except that as soon as good appears, evil, by implication, also appears, so that we necessarily speak of good and evil in contrast. But it is not true that there is originally an evil existing out there, waiting for the appearance of good to oppose it. We fall into evil only when our actions are not in accord with the original nature.

42:14b-15a   In your letter you[3] say that you do not know whence comes human desire. This is a very important question. In my opinion, what is called human desire[4] is the exact opposite of the Principle of Heaven [Nature]. It is permissible to say that human desire exists because of the Principle of Heaven, but it is wrong to say that human desire is the same as the Principle of Heaven, for in its original state the Principle of Heaven is free from human desire. It is from the deviation in the operation of the Principle of Heaven that human desire arises. Cheng Hao says, "Good and evil in the world are both the Principle of Heaven. What is called evil is not originally evil. It becomes evil only because of deviation from the Mean." Your quotation, "Evil must also be interpreted as the nature," expresses the same idea.

---

3   He Shujing.
4   See footnote 1, above.

35. Japan in Ancient Times

by Evan March Tappan

Social life in Kioto (Kyoto) was the standard for that in good society everywhere throughout the empire. Etiquette was cultivated with almost painful earnestness, and the laws about costume were equally rigid. Tea was introduced into Japan by a Buddhist priest in the year 805, and soon became a common drink. The oldest tea plantations and the most luscious leaves are at Uji, near Kioto. The preparation and serving of the beverage were matters upon which much attention was bestowed. The making of cups, dishes, and all facilities for drinking was greatly stimulated by the use of the hot drink, and when the potter's wheel was brought over from Corea the ceramic art entered upon a new era of development.

Flowers and gardens were much enjoyed, and visits of ceremony were many and prolonged. The invention of the fan was not at first thought to be an aid to good manners, but it soon won its way to favor. As early as the seventh century it came into use for personal comfort. In course of time the fan developed into many varieties. The *kugé*, or court nobles, had one kind, and the court ladies, with their long hair sweeping down their back to their feet and arrayed in white and crimson silk, had another. In art, we see that the Dragon Queen of the Underworld holds a flat fan with double wings. The long-nosed King of the Tengus, or mountain sprites, who is said to have taught Yoshitsune his wisdom and secrets of power, holds a fan exactly like the old pulpit feather fans which it once was thought proper for clergymen to make use of. The judges at wrestling matches flourish a peculiar sort, while in war the wight who received a thwack over the noddle with the huge iron-boned fan might lie in gore. The firemen of Kioto, and the men in the procession in honor of the Sun Goddess at Isé, carry fans that would cool the face of a giant.

The earliest fans were all of the flat kind, but in the seventh century it is said that a man of Tamba, seeing that bats could fold their wings, imagined that the motion and effect could be imitated. Accordingly he made the *ogi*, or fan that opens and shuts. This was a great advantage, securing economy in space and ease of use. Another story declares that when the widow of a young Taira noble, slain in the civil wars, retired to a temple to hide her grief, she cured the abbot of a fever by fanning him. Folding a piece of paper in plaits and then opening it out, muttering incantations the while, the lady brought great prosperity to the temple, for thereafter the priests excelled in making folding fans. From the sale of these novelties a steady revenue flowed into the temple. In time the name of this temple was adopted by fan-makers all over the country. As a shelter of the face or bare head from the sun,—for hats and bonnets were not fashionable in Old Japan,—for use as trays or salvers to hand flowers, letters, or presents to friends or to one's master, as thoughtful defenses against one's breath while talking to superiors, and for a thousand polite uses, to say nothing of its value as an article of dress, the folding fan is a distinctly Japanese gift to civilization. It had many centuries of history and honor in Japan before the Chinese borrowed the invention. In the caste of fashion the flat fan, which too often sank to the level of a dustpan, grain-winnower, or fire-blower, is in the lowest grade.

The chief food, as well as the ceremonial drink, came from rice. This grain was imported from Corea, and very early became the standard article of diet among the upper classes. The Japanese have never yet learned to like bread, nor is rice usually the food of the poorer people. The best rice is raised in Higo. It is cooked, served, and flavored in a great variety of ways, and many extracts and preparations, such as gluten, *mochi,* or pastry flour, and alcohol, are made from it. The making of saké, by which we mean beer, wine, or brandy made from rice, is as old as the first commerce with Corea. It was the favorite drink of Japanese men and gods. The festivals in celebration of the planting, reaping, and offering of rice in the sheaf, or hulled and cleaned, and of the fermentation or presentation of the liquor to the gods, form a notable feature in the Shinto religion.

This saké or brewed rice was the drink enjoyed at feasts, poetry parties, picnics, and evening gatherings. Like tea, it was heated and drunk when hot. Besides the pleasures of music, poetry, and literature, cards, checkers, games of skill and chance, of many kinds, even to the sniffing of perfumes, helped the hours of leisure to pass pleasantly.

Outdoor sports were also diligently cultivated by these elegantly dressed lords and ladies of the capital. The ladies amused themselves by catching fireflies and various brilliantly colored or singing insects, by feeding the goldfish in the garden ponds, or viewing the moon and the landscape. The delights of the young men were in horsemanship, archery, foot-ball, and falconry. The art of training falcons to hunt and kill the smaller or defenseless birds was copied from Corea, and has been practiced in Japan somewhat over a thousand years. Cockfights, dog-matches, and fishing by means of cormorants were also common. A method of racing and shooting from horseback at dogs, with blunt arrows, was cultivated for the sake of skill in riding. Polo is said to have come from Persia into China and thence to Japan, where it is called ball-striking, or *da-kiu.* A polo outfit with elegant costume and the liveliest of ponies was costly, so that polo, like hawking, was always an aristocratic game. The Warrior's Dance had been described as a "giant quadrille in armor." The more robust and exciting exercise of hunting the boar, deer, bear, and other wild animals was often indulged in by the military men in time of peace, in order to keep up their vigor and discipline. In hunting, the bold riders and footmen could have something like the excitement of war with only a small amount of its danger.

This curious social life in old Kioto is quite fully shown in Japanese art, in books and pictures, and the theater, and is a favorite subject for the poets, novelists, and artists. On fans, paper napkins, lacquer ware, carved ivories, bronzes, sword-hilts, and all the rich and strange art-works of Old Japan, this court life can be pleasantly studied. It was a state of things which existed before feudalism came in completely to alter the face of the mikado's empire, and before Chinese learning, pedantry, and literary composition cramped the native genius. He who understands the method and meaning of the artist has a great fund of enjoyment. The painter and carver, or even the decorator on a five-cent fan, tells his tale well, and one who knows Japanese life from its ancient and mediaeval literature, as well as by modern travel and study, needs no interpreter.

Best of all, however, life in the mikado's capital is reflected in the classic fiction written in the Middle Ages, and mostly by ladies of the court. From a literary point of view, the women of Japan did more to preserve and develop their native language than the men. The masculine scholars used Chinese, and composed their books in what was as Latin to the mass of the people. The lady writers employed their own beautiful speech, and such famous *monogatari*, or novels, as the Sagoromo, Genji, Ise, and others, besides hundreds of volumes of poetry in pure classical Japanese, are from their pens. A number of famous novels, the oldest of which is the Old Bamboo-Cutter's Story, which dates from the tenth century, picture the life and work, the loves and adventures, of the lads and lasses, priests and warriors, lords and ladies, in this extremely refined, highly polished, and very licentious society of Kioto a thousand years or less ago. Those who would study it carefully must read Mr. Chamberlain's "Classical Poetry of the Japanese," or Mr. Suyématsŭ's "Genji Monogatari." Miss Harris's "Log of a Japanese Journey" is a rendering in English of the Tosa Niki, or diary of the voyage from Tosa to Kioto of the famous poet Tsurayuki.

The Tosa Niki book is a great favorite with native students on account of its beauty of style. Tsurayuki was appointed by the mikado to be governor of Tosa. After serving four years he starts homeward for Kioto by ship and carriage, or rather by junk and bullock-cart.

He left Tosa in January, A.D. 935, and the diary of his voyage is written in woman's style of writing, that is, in pure Japanese. He calls himself "a certain person," and is a jolly good-natured fellow; always, when opportunity serves, writing poetry and enjoying the saké-cup. As Japanese junks usually wait for the wind, sail only in the daytime, or at least not all night, and keep out of storms if possible, he stopped at many places, where official friends called upon him, and presents were exchanged, cups of saké drunk, and poems written. Most of the presents had verses tied to them, but the pheasants had a flowering branch of the plum tree attached. We translate a stanza :—

> "As o'er the waves we urge,
> While roars the whit'ning surge,
> Louder shall rise my cry
> That left behind am I,—"

whereat the traveler notes in his diary that the poet must have a pretty loud voice. He tells of the storks and the fir trees which have been comrades for a thousand years; how the passengers went ashore at one place to take a hot bath; how a sailor caught a *tai,* or splendid red fish, for his dinner; jests at the bush of the man in the moon; throws his metal mirror into the sea to quiet the storm raised by the god of Sumi-Yoshi; escapes the pirates, with whom he had as governor dealt very severely; and completes his sea journey, not at Osaka which did not then exist, but at Yamazaki, near the capital. There he waits for a bullock-car to come from Kioto, which he must of course enter in state as becomes a *kugé,* or noble.

This charming little book shows first that human nature in Japan a thousand years ago was wonderfully like that of to-day in Japan, or anywhere else; that good style will make a book live as long as the rocks; and that in those days the spoken idiom differed very little from the language employed in literature. Brave Tsurayuki! He wrote in "woman's style" really because he loved his native tongue, and did not want to see it overlaid by the Chinese. In our days not a few Japanese are heartily ashamed that their own beautiful language has not been more developed by scholars. So much dependence on China has paralyzed originality and weakened intellect. After fifteen hundred years, the patriotic Japanese feels ashamed that the literary and intellectual product of his country is so small, and that the best work in his native tongue has been done by women. No wonder he does not always take kindly to the fulsome flatteries of Europeans who tell him what a wonderful fellow he is, and how much superior Japanese civilization is to that of Europe. How he really feels about the matter is shown in his eager desire, on the one hand, to absorb all the ideas and adopt all the inventions of the foreigners, and, on the other, to bridge the gulf between the spoken and the written forms of his own vernacular.

---

36. Sim Chung, the Dutiful Daughter

A Korean Folk Novel

by Tae Hung Ha

Long, long ago, there lived in the Land of the Morning Calm a blind man, known as Sim Bong Sa, and his daughter Sim Chung. When this girl was only a wee little baby her mother died and the unhappy father had to beg from door to door for milk.

The women in the neighborhood took pity on the baby and gave their own milk to it and, among others, a kind-hearted woman called Kuiduk Omi was most sympathetic to the poor blindman and his baby. So she nursed it on her own breasts.

Tae Hung Ha, "Sim Chung, the Dutiful Daughter," *Folk Tales of Old Korea, Korean Cultural Series Volume VI,* pp. 40-46. Copyright © 1972 by Yonsei University Press. Reprinted with permission.

By and by this baby grew up to be a blooming maiden, and she began to work for other people and earned money to support her father. Her charm and accomplishments attracted a noble and rich lady, who had hired this girl as her housemaid.

Sim Chung worked every day in this rich house and came home in the evening. But one night she did not return. So the poor father went out to meet his daughter. And while groping his way in the darkness he rolled into a ditch.

A passer-by in the habit of a monk rescued him and, seeing him to be blind, he told him that if he offered only three hundred bags of rice to the Buddhist temple—Mongun-sa—and prayer, his eyes would be bright as the sun, but the poor blindman sighed a while, for three hundred bags of rice were like a thousand castles to him. Never would he have the money to buy them.

Hearing from her father about his singular advanture with the monk, Sim Chung built an altar in her garden and every evening she knelt before it and, as she gazed on the seven north stars, she prayed to all spirits of heaven and earth to open the eyes of her father.

One day she heard that a party of sailors, engaged in the 'sea-borne trade with merchants in Nanking, wanted to buy a maiden of sixteen to toss into the sea as a sacrifice to calm the angry waves in the deep sea called "Indangsoo," so that they could safely navigate the ocean and make a fortune. And she heard that they would pay any price for this fair victim.

Sim Chung's heart leaped for joy and she bargained through Kuiduk Omi who had nursed her, saying, "I am ready to sell myself for three hundred bags of rice. I must offer them to the Buddhist temple to help open the blind eyes of my father."

The sailors were deeply moved by the devotion of this young lady, but felt great pity for her as she was too pretty to be tossed into the sea.

However, the bargain was struck and they soon transported the three hundred bags of rice to Mongun-sa and announced to Sim Chung that the ship would sail under the full moon of the third month in that year.

When the sailors were gone, Sim Chung told her father, "Cheer up! My good father! The three hundred bags of rice have already been dedicated to the Buddha, and even before the Goddess of Mercy."

Sim Bong Sa was surprised—"Where did you get the rice?"

Honest girl that she was, Sim Chung was nevertheless obliged to tell him a white lie. "The wife of Minister Jang, who hired me first, had adopted me to be her daughter and gave me the rice as the price."

Sim Bong Sa laughed for joy and said, "Well done. When will she take you into her home for good?"

Then the daughter answered—"She will send for me under the full moon of the next month."

The blind man again laughed, "That's nice, when you are- living well in the other house, you must not worry about your father."

From that very day Sim Chung thought continuously about the fatal voyage and trembled in fear. But her heart was more troubled at the thought of forsaking her lonely father, for there was no one in this world to take care of him. So she washed and stitched her father's clothing for all seasons and put them tenderly into the wardrobe. Then she mended his horsehair hat, tying it with a new beaded string. She did everything she could think, of to make him feel as comfortable as possible.

But the changing moons wait for nobody. Thus, on the eve- of her departure, she sat all alone before a flickering candle and' pondered her tragic situation—needle in hand and scissors on her lap. With her silkworm-shaped eyebrows downcast she tried' to stitch some more clothing for her father, but hot tears rolled down her rosy cheeks; her breast heaved with a long sigh and her cherry lips quivered as if to burst into a loud cry. But she- gently sobbed. Now she would mb her face on her father's cheeks and then touch her dainty fingers on his four limbs as she murmured in these words:

"Alas! my poor father! How can I leave you? When I am gone, you will become a beggar once more. Ah me! I lost my mother in my babyhood, and now I am forced to part from my father. If I go away, when can I see him again?

"My mother is high up in the stars and I shall be down at the bottom of the sea. Then how can I meet my mother? And when met, will she know me and will I know her? And if she ever asks me about my father, how can I answer? Should I put this midnight into a deep pond and tie up the sun round and round on a mulberry branch, tomorrow would never come, but who can stop the coming sun and going moon? O, sad night! Cock! don't cry tonight. Your shrill voice will rend my heart into pieces. O, my poor father!"

But too soon the day broke far over the mountain and the red beams of the rising sun clasped the bleeding heart of the girl.

Sim Chung rose up and came out of her room to prepare breakfast for her father. The sailors were already standing before the door and said:

"The sun is up and the sail is full with a westerly breeze. Please let us weigh anchor soon."

Hearing these words, Sim Chung's face turned pale as death, and everything blurred before her tearful eyes. After a while she spoke to the sailors:

"Yes, I know—today I am going, but my father is still a stranger to this news. So let me cook breakfast to serve him for the last time. Then I will tell him all about it and take his leave.'"

The sailors nodded and willingly consented.

Sim Chung entered the kitchen and, with tears, she cooked, food and brought a low table before her father. She knelt face to face with the blindman, then she pushed roasted fish into his mouth and put minced pies on his spoon and she talked in a soft voice. "Father! Cheer up and eat till you are full."

Sim Bong Sa chuckled like a little child and said—"Darling? The food is very tasty. Why this good feast this morning?"

Sim Chung sobbed in dreadful sorrow. Sim Bong Sa was surprised. "My good baby! Why this sobbing? What ails you? Have you got a cold? What day of the month is today? O, it's the fifteenth—the full-moon day, eh! By the way, I dreamed a singular dream last night. In my dream I saw you riding on a four-wheel wagon, drawn by a pair of snow-white horses. None but a noble person can ride on a wagon, you know. Perhaps, it is a good omen in our family, or perhaps Madam Jang will carry you in her wagon today."

Sim Chung knew that it was a dream foretelling her death, but she pretended to be happy and said, "Father! What a wonderful dream it was!" Then she took out the breakfast table and lighted a long bamboo pipe and put its brass mouth-piece between her father's lips.

Sim Chung then rose up and went to her family shrine and bade farewell to the spirits of her ancestors in these words:

"O, spirits of my ancestors! Thy unworthy grand-daughter Sim Chung, has sold her body in order to help open the blind eyes of her poor father, and pretty soon she will leap into the dark blue sea. Hereafter the incense-burning before thee will be discontinued and my heart is rending in thy memory."

Then she made a double-bow and returned to her father and clasped both of his hands with a loud cry and fainted.

Sim Bong Sa's surprise was beyond description. "O, my baby! What on earth is this? Wake up and tell me what it all means."

Sim Chung was awakened and murmured between her lips!

"Forgive me, father! I've cheated you. Who would give me three hundred bags of rice for nothing? To speak the truth, I've sold my body to the Nanking sailors as a sacrifice to the sea, and today I'm going. Touch me for the last time in your life!"

Sim Bong Sa was thunderstruck:

"What! Is that true? No, you can't go. Why didn't you talk of this matter to me? If you're dying, what's the meaning of my living? Even with my eyes open? I lost your mother beside your cradle and, now, must I lose you too?"

For a long time father and daughter hugged each other and wept bitterly, and the old man fell into a swoon.

In the meantime the ship had just Brushed loading rich merchandise and a boatswain beat the drum and shouted: "All aboard! Tide is high; sail is full; wind is favorable and anchor is weighing."

Sim Chung wiped her tears behind her sleeves and bade a last farewell to her father, who was waking but too exhausted to stop his daughter from going. Then she followed the sailors and went on board the ship, which soon put out to sea.

For some time the ship sailed very smoothly on the calm ocean but when she came through the high waves in the maelstrom of Indangsoo, suddenly a storm arose. Soon the heaven and sea became dark; the angry white-horses roared; the ship pitched and rolled as if she would be swallowed by the yawning mouth of the sea.

"Help! Help!" The sailors screamed. "The monstrous dragon is coming. We must appease his anger by giving away this fair girl or we shall all become sea-ghosts." Then all eyes were turned on Sim Chung, who covered her face with her pink skirt and leaped head-long into the angry waves as she cried, "Father, I'm going! Mother, I'm coming!"

But strange to say, hardly had her feet touched the surface of the ocean before a sea goddess picked Sim Chung up in her arms and a large crowd of fish came to wait upon her and, like an honor-guard, they conducted Sim Chung deep into the bottom of the sea, even unto the palace of the sea-ruler, the Dragon-King, who admired her extraordinary beauty and adopted her to be his own daughter.

The Dragon-King's palace was magnificently built in massive pearls ornamented with corals, rubies and emeralds. There were music and dance in the banquet hall all the time to please the new princess. But Sim Chung, was only thinking of her poor father on earth and refused to eat or smile.

The Dragon-King took great pity on Sim Chung and freed her, putting her in a lotus-flower to float on the surface of the sea.

Just then, the Prince of the Kingdom, who was sailing along on a yacht, saw an incomparable beauty peeping out of a lotus dancing on the waves. This passionate young Prince fell in love with her and immediately made her his bride.

For many days and many nights the wedding feast continued in the palace. Then the new Princess held another magnificent feast and invited all blind men in the country. Every day large crowds of blind men walked into the palace and marched before Princess Sim Chung. And on the last day of the blind-men's feast Sim Bong Sa appeared before her eyes.

Out of wild joy she ran and fell on his neck and cried, "Father! Father! Is it you?" and, equally joyous at hearing the voice of his daughter, the blind man cried, "Daughter! Daughter! Is it you?" Then at that very moment of great excitement his eyes opened to see for the first time his darling, Sim Chung.

Analysis Questions

1. Find any Buddhist and Daoist influences in Zhu Xi's Neo-Confucian idea.
2. Based on document 35 and 36, write about various aspects of people's lives in Japan and Korea. In what ways did Koreans and the Japanese follow Confucian principles?

CHAPTER 12

Christian Europe in the Central Middle Ages

Introduction

Charlemagne, one of history's great military leaders, conquered Western Europe and restored the learning, morality, and order that had decayed during the Dark Ages. At age 26, he inherited the Frankish Empire. A devout Christian, he quickly expanded its frontiers with the aim of creating a Christian empire. The key to his success was his brilliance as a military strategist. He sent out more than 50 military expeditions, leading at least half himself. By the end of the century, Charlemagne dominated most of Western and Central Europe. In 800, he was crowned emperor by Pope Leo III, thus founding the Holy Roman Empire. By establishing a centralized government, Charlemagne restored much of the unity of the old Roman Empire. He reformed the Church and introduced jury courts. He revised coinage and weights and measures and promoted agriculture, industry, and trade. Although Charlemagne was illiterate, he founded schools and encouraged literature and the arts. His effect on the cultural life of Western Europe was so pervasive that his reign is remembered as a period of renaissance.

Although the pope gave Charlemagne the title of Holy Roman Emperor, his realm was held together largely by the force of his personality. After his death, France and Germany became separate countries, and much of Europe dissolved into a patchwork of feudal kingdoms.

The feudal system was the principal way of life and government in most of Western Europe at that time. It developed under the Franks throughout the 800s and continued to spread to the rest of Europe. The groundwork for the feudal system was based on a powerful individual allotting land to a less powerful man as an exchange for service. The framework started at the top with the lord and passed down through his great barons to the lesser nobles and finally to the serfs. The service rendered by the nobles to their immediate lords was predominantly military. On the flip side of the scale, a serf could be virtually a slave, while freemen held places that were their own; however, the freemen needed to work for a week on their rulers' properties. As an aftereffect of the system, life for most people focused on the castles or manors of the different lords. The feudal system was further strengthened when new waves of marauding warrior groups—Vikings and Magyars—swept through Europe with no unified force to oppose them.

As the invasion threat began to recede in the eleventh century, a stable political climate and better agricultural techniques led to the development of larger towns. Markets arose where peasants could sell surplus goods to eventually buy their freedom. Some serfs simply slipped away from the manors and became mercenaries or set themselves up as free persons. Over the next few centuries, the feudal system began to fade.

In 1095, Pope Urban II received a tumultuous reception to his call for a "crusade" to the "Holy Land" in a major speech made at Clermont in France. The Pope talked movingly of how it was no longer safe for pilgrims to visit the holy places in Jerusalem, owing to the atrocities and disorganization of Turkish rule there. He talked of the need to help the Byzantine emperor in the struggle of Christendom against the infidel Muslims. The response exceeded the pope's highest hopes. So moved was the crowd that cries of "*Deus vult!*" ("God wills it!") punctuated his speech.

The Mosque–Cathedral of Córdoba

There were eight crusades; the crusaders initially captured much of Palestine from the Saracens. However, after almost 90 years, the Saracens recovered Jerusalem. Later campaigns were less fruitful. The fourth crusade even sacked the Christian city of Constantinople.

In spite of the fact that the Crusades failed in their planned motivation of freeing the Holy Land, Europe profited. Contact with the highly advanced civilizations of the Muslims and the Byzantines stimulated Europeans. Despite the devastation of plagues and the Hundred Years' War, European states began to solidify as nations, shaking off the strength of the Roman Catholic Church and forsaking the feudal framework.

37. Life of Charlemagne

trans. Samuel Epes Turner

PERSONAL APPEARANCE

Charles was large and strong, and of lofty stature, though not disproportionately tall (his height is well known to have been seven times the length of his foot); the upper part of his head was round, his eyes very large and animated, nose a little long, hair fair, and face laughing and merry. Thus his appearance was always stately and dignified, whether he was standing or sitting; although his neck was thick and somewhat short, and his belly rather prominent; but the symmetry of the rest of his body concealed these defects. His gait was firm, his whole carriage manly, and his voice clear, but not so strong as his size led one to expect. His health was excellent, except during the four years preceding his death, when he was subject to frequent fevers; at the last he even limped a little with one foot. Even in those years he consulted rather his own inclinations than the advice of physicians, who were almost hateful to him, because they wanted him to give up roasts, to which he was accustomed, and to eat boiled meat instead. In accordance with the national custom, he took frequent exercise on horseback and in the chase, accomplishments in which scarcely any people in the world can equal the Franks. He enjoyed the exhalations from natural warm springs, and often practised swimming, in which he was such an adept that none could surpass him; and hence it was that he built his palace at Aixla-Chapelle, and lived there constantly during his latter years until his death. He used not only to invite his sons to his bath, but his nobles and friends, and now and then a troop of his retinue or body guard, so that a hundred or more persons sometimes bathed with him.

DRESS

He used to wear the national, that is to say, the Frank, dress-next his skin a linen shirt and linen breeches, and above these a tunic fringed with silk; while hose fastened by bands covered his lower limbs, and shoes his feet, and he protected his shoulders and chest in winter by a close-fitting coat of otter or marten skins. Over all he flung a blue cloak, and he always had a sword girt about him, usually one with a gold or silver hilt and belt; he sometimes carried a jewelled sword, but only on great feast-days or at the reception of ambassadors from foreign nations. He despised foreign costumes, however handsome, and never allowed himself to be robed in them, except twice in Rome, when he donned the Roman tunic, chlamys, and shoes; the first time at the request of Pope Hadrian, the second to gratify Leo, Hadrian's successor. On great feast-days he made use of embroidered clothes, and shoes bedecked

Einhard: The Life of Charlemagne, trans. Samuel Epes Turner, pp. 73-88, 1877.

with precious stones; his cloak was fastened by a golden buckle, and he appeared crowned with a diadem of gold and gems: but on other days his dress varied little from the common dress of the people.

HABITS

Charles was temperate in eating, and particularly so in drinking, for he abominated drunkenness in anybody, much more in himself and those of his household; but he could not easily abstain from food, and often complained that fasts injured his health. He very rarely gave entertainments, only on great feast-days, and then to large numbers of people. His meals ordinarily consisted of four courses, not counting the roast, which his huntsmen used to bring in on the spit; he was more fond of this than of any other dish. While at table, he listened to reading or music. The subjects of the readings were the stories and deeds of olden time: he was fond, too, of St. Augustine's books, and especially of the one entitled "The City of God."

He was so moderate in the use of wine and all sorts of drink that he rarely allowed himself more than three cups in the course of a meal. In summer after the midday meal, he would eat some fruit, drain a single cup, put off his clothes and shoes, just as he did for the night, and rest for two or three hours. He was in the habit of awaking and rising from bed four or five times during the night. While he was dressing and putting on his shoes, he not only gave audience to his friends, but if the Count of the Palace told him of any suit in which his judgment was necessary, he had the parties brought before him forthwith, took cognizance of the case, and gave his decision, just as if he were sitting on the Judgment-seat. This was not the only business that he transacted at this time, but he performed any duty of the day whatever, whether he had to attend to the matter himself, or to give commands concerning it to his officers.

STUDIES

Charles had the gift of ready and fluent speech, and could express whatever he had to say with the utmost clearness. He was not satisfied with command of his native language merely, but gave attention to the study of foreign ones, and in particular was such a master of Latin that he could speak it as well as his native tongue; but he could understand Greek better than he could speak it. He was so eloquent, indeed, that he might have passed for a teacher of eloquence. He most zealously cultivated the liberal arts, held those who taught them in great esteem, and conferred great honors upon them. He took lessons in grammar of the deacon Peter of Pisa, at that time an aged man. Another deacon, Albin of Britain, surnamed Alcuin, a man of Saxon extraction, who was the greatest scholar of the day, was his teacher in other branches of learning. The King spent much time and labour with him studying rhetoric, dialectics, and especially astronomy; he learned to reckon, and used to investigate the motions of the heavenly bodies most curiously, with an intelligent scrutiny. He also tried to write, and used to keep tablets and blanks in bed under his pillow, that at leisure hours he might accustom his hand to form the letters; however, as he did not begin his efforts in due season, but late in life, they met with ill success.

PIETY

He cherished with the greatest fervor and devotion the principles of the Christian religion, which had been instilled into him from infancy. Hence it was that he built the beautiful basilica at Aix-la-Chapelle, which he adorned with gold and silver and lamps, and with rails and doors of solid brass. He had the columns and marbles for this structure brought from Rome and Ravenna, for he could not find such as were suitable elsewhere. He was a constant worshipper at this church as long as his health permitted, going morning and evening, even after nightfall, besides attending mass; and he took care that all the services there conducted should be administered with the utmost possible propriety, very often warning the sextons not to let any improper or unclean thing be brought into the building or remain in it. He provided it with a great number of sacred vessels of gold and silver and with such a quantity of clerical robes that not even the doorkeepers who fill the humblest office in the church were obliged to wear their everyday clothes when in the exercise of their duties. He was at great pains to improve the church reading and psalmody, for he was well skilled in both although he neither read in public nor sang, except in a low tone and with others.

GENEROSITY [CHARLES AND THE ROMAN CHURCH]

He was very forward in succoring the poor, and in that gratuitous generosity which the Greeks call alms, so much so that he not only made a point of giving in his own country and his own kingdom, but when he discovered that there were Christians living in poverty in Syria, Egypt, and Africa, at Jerusalem, Alexandria, and Carthage, he had compassion on their wants, and used to send money over the seas to them. The reason that he zealously strove to make friends with the kings beyond seas was that he might get help and relief to the Christians living under their rule.

He cherished the Church of St. Peter the Apostle at Rome above all other holy and sacred places, and heaped its treasury with a vast wealth of gold, silver, and precious stones. He sent great and countless gifts to the popes; and throughout his whole reign the wish that he had nearest at heart was to re-establish the ancient authority of the city of Rome under his care and by his influence, and to defend and protect the Church of St. Peter, and to beautify and enrich it out of his own store above all other churches. Although he held it in such veneration, he only repaired to Rome to pay his vows and make his supplications four times during the whole forty-seven years that he reigned.

CHARLEMAGNE CROWNED EMPEROR

When he made his last journey thither, he also had other ends in view. The Romans had inflicted many injuries upon the Pontiff Leo, tearing out his eyes and cutting out his tongue, so that he had been comp lied to call upon the King for help [Nov 24, 800].

Charles accordingly went to Rome, to set in order the affairs of the Church, which were in great confusion, and passed the whole winter there. It was then that he received the titles of Emperor and Augustus [Dec 25, 800], to which he at first had such an aversion that he declared that he would not have set foot in the Church the day that they were conferred, although it was a great feast-day, if he could have foreseen the design of the Pope. He bore very patiently with the jealousy which the Roman emperors showed upon his assuming these titles, for they took this step very ill; and by dint of frequent embassies and letters, in which he addressed them as brothers, he made their haughtiness yield to his magnanimity, a quality in which he was unquestionably much their superior.

REFORMS

It was after he had received the imperial name that, finding the laws of his people very defective (the Franks have two sets of laws, very different in many particulars), he determined to add what was wanting, to reconcile the discrepancies, and to correct what was vicious and wrongly cited in them. However, he went no further in this matter than to supplement the laws by a few capitularies, and those imperfect ones; but he caused the unwritten laws of all the tribes that came under his rule to be compiled and reduced to writing. He also had the old rude songs that celeate the deeds and wars of the ancient kings written out for transmission to posterity. He began a grammar of his native language. He gave the months names in his own tongue, in place of the Latin and barbarous names by which they were formerly known among the Franks. He likewise designated the winds by twelve appropriate names; there were hardly more than four distinctive ones in use before. He called January, Wintarmanoth; February, Hornung; March, Lentzinmanoth; April, Ostarmanoth; May, Winnemanoth; June, Brachmanoth; July, Heuvimanoth; August, Aranmanoth; September, Witumanoth; October, Windumemanoth; Novemher, Herbistmanoth; December, Heilagmanoth. He styled the winds as follows; Subsolanus, Ostroniwint; Eurus, Ostsundroni-, Euroauster, Sundostroni; Auster, Sundroni; Austro-Africus, Sundwestroni; Africus, Westsundroni; Zephyrus, Westroni; Caurus, Westnordroni; Circius, Nordwestroni; Septentrio, Nordroni; Aquilo, Nordostroni; Vulturnus, Ostnordroni.

CORONATION OF LOUIS—CHARLEMAGNE'S DEATH

Toward the close of his life [813], when he was broken by ill-health and old age, he summoned Louis, Kigi of Aquitania, his only surviving son by Hildegard, and gathered together all the chief men of the whole kingdom of the Franks in a solemn assembly. He appointed Louis, with their unanimous consent, to rule with himself over the whole kingdom and constituted him heir to the imperial name; then, placing the diadem upon his son's head, he bade him be proclaimed Emperor and is step was hailed by all present favor, for it really seemed as if God had prompted him to it for the kingdom's good; it increased the King's dignity, and struck no little terror into foreign nations. After sending his son back to Aquitania, although weak from age he set out to hunt, as usual, near his palace at Aix-la-Chapelle, and passed the rest of the autumn in the chase, returning thither about the first of November [813]. While wintering there, he was seized, in the month of January, with a high fever [Jan 22, 814], and took to his bed. As soon as he was taken sick, he prescribed for himself abstinence from food, as he always used to do in case of fever, thinking that the disease could be driven off, or at least mitigated, by fasting. Besides the fever, he suffered from a pain in the side, which the Greeks call pleurisy; but he still persisted in fasting, and in keeping up his strength only by draughts taken at very long intervals. He died January twenty-eighth, the seventh day from the time that he took to his bed, at nine o'clock in the morning, after partaking of the holy communion, in the seventy-second year of his age and the forty-seventh of his reign [Jan 28, 814].

BURIAL

His body was washed and cared for in the usual manner, and was then carried to the church, and interred amid the greatest lamentations of all the people. There was some question at first where to lay him, because in his lifetime he had given no directions as to his burial; but at length all agreed that he could nowhere be more honorably entombed than in the very basilica that he had built in the town at his own expense, for love of God and our Lord Jesus Christ, and in honor of the Holy and Eternal Virgin, His Mother. He was buried there the same day that he died, and a gilded arch was erected above his tomb with his image and an inscription. The words of the inscription were as follows: "In this tomb lies the body of Charles, the Great and Orthodox Emperor, who gloriously extended the kingdom of the Franks, and reigned prosperously for forty-seven years. He died at the age of seventy, in the year of our Lord 814, the 7th Indiction, on the 28th day of January."

38. Humiliation of Canossa

ed. O.J. Thatcher and E.H. McNeal

LETTER FROM POPE GREGORY VII RELATING EVENTS AT CANOSSA

Greg. VII. Register. IV, nos. 12, 12 a; 3a.K(, II, pp. 256 ft; Doeberl, III, no. 13. At Oppenheim Henry IV had been temporarily deposed. He sent away his counsellors who had been excommunicated, gave up all

"Letter from Pope Gregory VII Relating Events at Canossa," *Medieval History: Selected Documents*, ed. O.J. Thatcher and E.H. McNeal, 1906.

participation in the affairs of government, laid aside all the royal insignia, and withdrew to the city of Speier, which he was not to leave until the matter was adjusted by the pope, who was to come to Germany and hold a diet in February, 1077. But Henry did not keep his word. Fearing that he would be permanently deposed if the pope should come to Germany and sit with his rebellious subjects in, judgment on him, he determined to forestall matters by going to see the pope in Italy. So he fled from Speier and hastened as rapidly as possible into Italy. He came to Canossa, where he humbled himself before Gregory and received absolution. It was at least a diplomatic triumph for Henry, because he had kept the pope from coming to Germany and uniting with his rebellious nobles, who would have labored hard to secure the permanent deposition of Henry. The final decision of the matter was indeed left to the pope and the diet which was to be held in Germany, but the pope did not go to Germany, and Henry was able to point to the fact that he had received papal absolution. The oath which Gregory VII required of Henry is given in no. 81.

Gregory, bishop, servant of the servants of God, to all the archbishops, bishops, dukes, counts, and other princes of the German kingdom, defenders of the Christian faith, greeting and apostelic benediction.

Since you have made common cause with us and shared our perils in the recent controversy, we have thought it only right that you should be informed of the recent course of events, how king Henry came to Italy to do penance, and how we were led to grant him absolution.

According to the agreement made with your representatives we had come to Lombardy and were there awaiting those whom you were to send to escort us into your land. But after the time set was already passed, we received word that it was at that time impossible to send an escort, because of many obstacles that stood in the way, and we were greatly exercised at this and in grave doubt as to what we ought to do. In the meantime we learned that the king was approaching. Now before he entered Italy he had sent to us and had offered to make complete satisfaction for his fault, promising to reform and henceforth to obey us in all things, provided we would give him our absolution and blessing. We hesitated for some time, taking occasion in the course of the negotiations to reprove him sharply for his former rins. Finally he came in person to Canossa, where we were staying, bringing with him only a small retinue and manifesting no hostile intentions. Once arrived, he presented himself at the gate of the castle, barefoot and clad only in wretched woollen garments, beseeching us with tears to grant him absolution and forgiveness. This he continued to do for three days, until all those about us were moved to compassion at his plight and interceded for him with tears and prayers. Indeed, they marvelled at our hardness of heart, some even complaining that our action savored rather of heartless tyranny than of chastening severity. At length his persistent declarations of repentance and the supplications of all who were there with us overcame our reluctance, and we removed the excommunication from him and received him again into the bosom of the holy mother church. But first he took the oath which we have subjoined to this letter, the abbot of Cluny, the countess Matilda, the countess Adelaide, and many other ecclesiastic and secular princes going surety for him. Now that this arrangement has been reached to the common advantage of the church and the empire, we purpose coming to visit you in your own land as soon as possible. For, as you will perceive from the conditions stated in the oath, the matter is not to be regarded as settled until we have held consultation with you. Therefore we urge you to maintain that fidelity and love of justice which first prompted your action. We have not bound ourself to anything, except that we assured the king that he might depend upon us to aid him in everything that looked to his salvation and honor.

OATH OF KING HENRY IV TO POPE GREGORY VII

I, Henry, king, promise to satisfy the grievances which my archbishops, bishops, dukes, counts, and other princes of Germany or their followers may have against me, within the time set by pope Gregory and in accordance with his conditions. If I am prevented by any sufficient cause from doing this within that time, I will do it as soon after that as I may. Further, if pope Gregory shall desire to visit Germany or any other land, on his journey thither, his sojourn there, and his return thence, he shall not be molested or placed in danger of captivity by me or by anyone whom I can control. This shall apply to his escort and retinue and to all who come and go in his service. Moreover, I will never enter into any plan for hindering or molesting him, but will aid him in good faith and to the best of my ability if anyone else opposes him.

39. Urban II: Speech at Council of Clermont, 1095

by August. C. Krey

(*Gesta.*) When now that time was at hand which the Lord Jesus daily points out to His faithful, especially in the Gospel, saying, "If any man would come after me, let him deny himself and take up his cross and follow me,"[13] a mighty agitation was carried on throughout all the region of Gaul. (Its tenor was)—that if anyone desired to follow the

"Urban II: Speech at Council of Clermont," *A Source Book for Medieval History*, ed. Oliver J. Thatcher and Edgar Holmes McNeal, pp. 513-517, 1905.

Lord zealously, with a pure heart and mind, and wished faithfully to bear the cross after Him, he would no longer hesitate to take up the way to the Holy Sepulchre.

—And so Urban, Pope of the Roman see, with his archbishops, bishops, abbots, and priests, set out as quickly as possible beyond the mountains and began to deliver sermons and to preach eloquently, saying: "Whoever wishes to save his soul should not hesitate humbly to take up the way of the Lord, and if he lacks sufficient money, divine mercy will give him enough." Then the apostolic lord continued, "Brethren, we ought to endure much suffering for the name of Christ—misery, poverty, nakedness, persecution, want, illness, hunger, thirst, and other (ills) of this kind, just as the Lord saith to His disciples: 'Ye must suffer much in My name,'[14] and 'Be not ashamed to confess Me before the faces of men; verily I will give you mouth and wisdom'[15] and finally, 'Great is your reward in Heaven.' "[16] And when this speech had already begun to be noised abroad, little by little, through all the regions and countries of Gaul, tire Franks, upon hearing such reports, forthwith caused crosses to be sewed on their right shoulders, saying that they followed with one accord the footsteps of Christ, by which they had been redeemed from the hand of hell.

(*Fulcher.*) But the Pope added at once that another trouble, not less, but still more grievous than that already spoken of, and even the very worst, was besetting Christianity from another part of the world. He said: "Since, O sons of God, you have promised the Lord to maintain peace more earnestly than heretofore in your midst, and faithfully to sustain the rights of Holy Church, there still remains for you, who are newly aroused by this divine correction, a very necessary work, in which you can show the strength of your good will by a certain further duty, God's concern and your own. For you must hasten to carry aid to your brethren dwelling in the East, who need your help, which they often have asked. For the Turks, a Persian people, have attacked them, as many of you already, know, and have advanced as far into the Roman territory as that part of the Mediterranean which is called the Arm of St. George; and, by seizing more and more of the lands of the Christians, they have already often conquered them in battle, have killed and captured many, have destroyed the churches, and have devastated the kingdom of God. If you allow them to continue much longer, they will subjugate God's faithful yet more widely.

"Wherefore, I exhort with earnest prayer—not I, but God—that, as heralds of Christ, you urge men by frequent exhortation, men of all ranks, knights as well as foot-soldiers, rich as well as poor, to hasten to exterminate this vile race from the lands of your brethren, and to aid the Christians in time. I speak to those present; I proclaim it to the absent; moreover, Christ commands it. And if those who set out thither should lose their lives on the way by land, or in crossing the sea, or in fighting the pagans, their sins shall be remitted. This I grant to- all who go, through the power vested in me by God. Oh, what a disgrace, if a race so despised, base, and the instrument of demons, should so overcome a people endowed with faith in the all-powerful God, and resplendent with the name of Christ! Oh, what reproaches will be charged against you by the Lord

Himself if yon have not helped those who are counted, like yourselves, of the Christian faith! Let those who have been accustomed to make private war against the faithful carry on to a successful issue a war against infidels, which ought to-have been begun ere now. Let these who for a long time have been robbers now become soldiers of Christ. Let those who once fought against brothers and relatives now fight against barbarians, as they ought. Let those who have been hirelings at low wages now labor for an eternal reward. Let those who have been wearing themselves out to the detriment of body and soul now labor for a double glory. On the one hand will be the sad and poor, on the other the joyous and wealthy; here the enemies of the Lord; there His friends. Let no obstacle stand in the way of those who are going, but, after their affairs are settled and expense money is collected, when the winter has ended and spring has come, let them zealously undertake the journey under the guidance of the Lord."

Analysis Questions

1. What were the main accomplishments of Charlemagne?
2. Based on "Disgrace at Canossa" and "Speech at Council of Clermont," explain the pope's political influence and its consequences.

CHAPTER 13

American Civilizations, to Fifteenth Century A.D.

Introduction

The first civilization in the Americas arose in Mesoamerica, a cultural zone extending from central Mexico to just above the Isthmus of Panama. The early cultures of Mesoamerica shared many beliefs and customs. Fundamental to their lifestyle was the development of maize, or corn. Around 1200 B.C., Olmec society was developing on the eastern shore of Mexico. The centers of Olmec civilization were ceremonial complexes with great designs offering earthen pyramids, walled courts, stone sanctuaries, and ball courts, where challengers played rounds of some game of ritual significance. Rulers and their retainers lived in these structures, while large portions of the populace dwelled in encompassing villages. The Olmec masterpieces and beliefs left an enduring legacy to Mesoamerica. A significant number of the components of Olmec society went into the Mayan civilization, incorporating ceremonial plazas, pyramids, calendars, and the role of rulers.

The Mayan people created a civilization that stretched over a vast area in the lowland jungles of Central America. The main administrative and religious towns were Copan, Tikal, Quiriguá, Palenque, and Uxmal. The various states were governed by kings, who bore the title of "great sun," backed by the political and religious elite. The Mayans had to clear dense, inhospitable rain forests to farm; once cleared, the land became barren after only one or two harvests. It was in the forests, too, where they built great religious complexes containing stone pyramids, ziggurats, and towers to rival those of ancient Egypt. Equally impressive as their buildings is the calendar that the Mayans worked out through skilled astronomical observation and mathematics. They recorded time by erecting a dated monument every 20 years. But in about 900 A.D., the Mayans deserted their centers, and the old stable way of life collapsed.

Around the second century B.C., Teotihuacan, the largest and most populous city in the Americas, was growing extremely quickly. It is estimated that its population rose to nearly 200,000 inhabitants. Teotihuacan, covering an area of 3.5 square miles (5.5 square km), was a wealthy city whose economy was based largely on the manufacture of knives and tools from obsidian, the hard, black volcanic rock. The city was divided in half by one grand avenue, which led to the imposing pyramids of the sun and moon. The avenue was also lined with lesser pyramids and palaces, where the ruling caste of the priests lived. The palaces were built around courtyards, the stone walls of which were decorated with bright murals. The vast wall paintings depicted jaguars and a range of mythical beings as well as priests reciting sacred texts. Around 700 A.D., however, Teotihuacan society collapsed due to invaders; as a result, Teotihuacan assimilated into the Toltec confederation.

Since 1120 A.D., the frontiers of the Toltec Empire were also pushed steadily inward under the relentless weight of people moving south into Toltec territory—under pressure themselves from others following behind. Many of these immigrants bore no loyalty to the state, and some of them actively supported the Toltec's rival state, Cholula, which coveted the Toltec's rich cotton fields and was under the same pressure from the north. Added to this, a new specter arose: famine. The result was that thousands of refugees poured into Tula, where there was insufficient food to feed them. The population divided along ethnic lines. The brief reign of the enlightened Topiltzin, or Quetzalcoatl (ca. 980–1000), offered hope of a national revival that would provide the will and the way to solve the Toltec Empire's problems. Now it seems the renaissance was merely a temporary phenomenon, serving only to delay the inevitable end.

The last invaders were the Aztecs, who absorbed the Olmec-Teotihuacan-Toltec culture. The Aztecs were a nomadic tribe from northern Mexico who migrated south in the twelfth century, settling in the central swamplands in 1325. Within a hundred years, they had developed a sophisticated empire that dominated the Valley of Mexico until the arrival of the Spanish in 1521. The Aztec capital was named Tenochtitlan, meaning "stone rising in the water." Its structure was based on the Aztec cosmos, with the "Great Temple" representing the center of the world and four main roads directed to the four points of the compass, each linked to a god.

The Aztecs rapidly established a vast empire by forging alliances with neighboring states, which one by one began to fall under Aztec rule. These vassal states retained their separate identities in exchange for tribute in the form of labor, food, gold, and sacrificial victims. The Aztecs believed that Huitzilopochtli, the sun god, died each night and was reborn the next day. Human blood was needed to sustain his fight against darkness, and the Aztecs thus offered human sacrifices to the god.

In 1519, 400 Spanish soldiers led by Hernando Cortes arrived. They were warmly welcomed by Emperor Montezuma, who mistook Cortes for the god Quetzalcoatl. By 1521, the Spanish had defeated the Aztec Empire, renaming it New Spain.

The Incas of Peru ruled an empire in the Andes of perhaps as many as seven million people. They were fine architects, potters, and metalworkers, with a well-organized government and superb roads. But, like the Aztecs, the Spanish conquistadors subdued them in less than 30 years.

---

40. Aztecs

trans. John Ingram Lockhart

CHAPTER XCI.

Of Motecusuma's person, disposition, habits, and of his great power.

The mighty Motecusuma may have been about this time in the fortieth year of his age. He was tall of stature, of slender make, and rather thin, but the symmetry of his body was beautiful. His complexion was not very brown, merely approaching to that of the inhabitants in general. The hair of his head was not very long, excepting where it hung thickly down over his ears, which were quite hidden by it. His black beard, though thin, looked handsome. His countenance was rather of an elongated form, but cheerful; and his fine eyes had the expression of love or severity, at the proper moments. He was particularly clean in his person, and took a bath every evening. Besides a number of concubines, who were all daughters of persons of rank and quality, he had two lawful wives of royal extraction, whom, however, he visited secretly without any one daring to observe it, save his most confidential servants. He was perfectly innocent of any unnatural crimes. The dress he had on one day was not worn again until four days had elapsed. In the halls adjoining his own private apartments there was always a guard of 2000 men of quality, in waiting: with whom, however, he never held any conversation unless to give them orders or to receive some intelligence from them. Whenever for this purpose they entered his apartment, they had first to take off their rich costumes and put on meaner garments, though these were always neat and clean; and were only allowed to enter into his presence barefooted, with eyes cast down. No person durst look at him full in the face, and during the three prostrations which they were obliged to make before they could approach him, they pronounced these words: "Lord! my Lord! sublime Lord!" Everything that was communicated to him was to be said in few words, the eyes of the speaker being constantly cast down, and on leaving the monarch's presence he walked backwards out of the room. I also remarked that even princes and other great personages who come to Mexico respecting lawsuits,

"Aztecs," *The Memoris of the Conquistador Bernal Diaz del Castillo*, trans. John Ingram Lockhart, pp. 228-235, 1844.

or on other business from the interior of the country, always took off their shoes and changed their whole dress for one of a meaner appearance when they entered his palace. Neither were they allowed to enter the palace straightway, but had to show themselves for a considerable time outside the doors; as it would have been considered want of respect to the monarch if this had been omitted.

Above 300 kinds of dishes were served up for Motecusuma's dinner from his kitchen, underneath which were placed pans of porcelain filled with fire, to keep them warm. Three hundred dishes of various kinds were served up for him alone, and above 1000 for the persons in waiting. He sometimes, but very seldom, accompanied by the chief officers of his household, ordered the dinner himself, and desired that the best dishes and various kinds of birds should be called over to him. We were told that the flesh of young children, as a very dainty bit, was also set before him sometimes by way of a relish. Whether there was any truth in this we could not possibly discover; on account of the great variety of dishes, consisting in fowls, turkeys, pheasants, partridges, quails, tame and wild geese, venison, musk swine, pigeons, hares, rabbits, and of numerous other birds and beasts; besides which there were various other kinds of provisions, indeed it would have been no easy task to call them all over by name. This I know, however, for certain, that after Cortes had reproached him for the human sacrifices and the eating of human flesh, he issued orders that no dishes of that nature should again be brought to his table. I will, however, drop this subject, and rather relate how the monarch was waited on while he sat at dinner. If the weather was cold a large fire was made with a kind of charcoal made of the bark of trees, which emitted no smoke, but threw out a delicious perfume; and that his majesty might not feel any inconvenience from too great a heat, a screen was placed between his person and the fire, made of gold, and adorned with all manner of figures of their gods. The chair on which he sat was rather low, but supplied with soft cushions, and was beautifully carved; the table was very little higher than this, but perfectly corresponded with his seat. It was covered with white cloths, and one of a larger size. Four very neat and pretty young women held before the monarch a species of round pitcher, called by them Xicales, filled with water to wash his hands in. The water was caught in other vessels, and then the young women presented him with towels to dry his hands. Two other women brought him maise-bread baked with eggs. Before, however, Motecusuma began his dinner, a kind of wooden screen, strongly gilt, was placed before him, that no one might see him while eating, and the young women stood at a distance. Next four elderly men, of high rank, were admitted to his table; whom he addressed from time to time, or put some questions to them. Sometimes he would offer them a plate of some of his viands, which was considered a mark of great favour. These grey-headed old men, who were so highly honoured, were, as we subsequently learnt, his nearest relations, most trustworthy counsellors and chief justices. Whenever he ordered any victuals to be presented them, they ate it standing, in the deepest veneration, though without daring to look at him frill in the face. The dishes in which the dinner was served up were of variegated and black porcelain, made at Cholulla. While the monarch was at table, his courtiers, and those who were in waiting in the halls adjoining, had to maintain strict silence.

About this time a celebrated cazique, whom we called Tapia, was Motecusuma's chief steward: he kept an account of the whole of Motecusuma's revenue, in large books of paper which the Mexicans call *Amatl*. A whole bouse was filled with such large books of accounts.[54]

Motecusuma had also two arsenals filled with arms of every description, of which many were ornamented with gold and precious stones. These aims consisted in shields of different sizes, sabres, and a species of broadsword, which is wielded with both hands, the edge furnished with flint stones, so extremely sharp that they cut much better than our Spanish swords[55] further, lances of greater length than ours, with spikes at their end, frill one fathom in length, likewise furnished with several sharp flint stones. The pikes are so very sharp and hard that they will pierce the strongest shield, and cut like a razor; so that the Mexicans even shave themselves with these stones. Then there were excellent bows and arrows, pikes with single and double points, and the proper thongs to throw them with; slings with round stones purposely made for them; also a species of large shield, so ingeniously constructed that it could be rolled up when not wanted: they are only unrolled on the field of battle, and completely cover the whole body from the head to the feet. Further, we saw here a great variety of cuirasses made of quilted cotton, which were outwardly adorned with soil feathers of different colours, and looked like uniforms; morions and helmets constructed of wood and bones, likewise adorned with feathers. There were always artificers at work, who continually augmented this store of arms; and the arsenals were under the care of particular personages, who also superintended the works.

In another large building, numbers of idols were erected, and these, it is said, were the most terrible of all their gods. Near these were kept all manner of beautiful animals, tigers, lions of two different kinds, of which one had the shape of a wolf, and was called a jackal; there were also foxes, and other small beasts of prey. Most of these animals had been bred here, and were fed with wild deers' flesh, turkeys, dogs, and sometimes, as I have been assured, with the offal of human beings.

Respecting the abominable human sacrifices of these people, the following was communicated to us: the breast of the unhappy victim destined to be sacrificed was ripped open with a knife made of sharp flint; the throbbing heart was then torn out, and immediately offered to the idol-god in whose honour the sacrifice had been instituted. After this, the head, arms, and legs were cut off and eaten at their banquets, with the exception of the head, which was saved, and hung to a beam appropriated for that purpose. No other part of the body was eaten, but the remainder was thrown to the beasts which were kept in those abominable dens, in which there were also vipers and other poisonous serpents, and, among the latter in particular, a species at the end of whose tail there was a kind of rattle. This last-mentioned serpent, which is the most dangerous, was kept in a cabin of a diversified form, in which a quantity of feathers had been strewed: here it laid its eggs, and it was fed with the flesh of dogs and of human beings who had been sacrificed. We were positively told that, after we had been beaten out of the city of Mexico, and had lost 850 of our men, these horrible beasts were fed for many successive days with the bodies of our unfortunate countrymen. Indeed, when all the tigers and lions roared together, with the howlings of the jackals and foxes, and hissing of the serpents, it was quite fearful, and you could not suppose otherwise than that you were in hell.

The powerful Motecusuma had also a number of dancers and clowns: some danced in stilts, tumbled, and performed a variety of other antics for the monarch's entertainment: a whole quarter of the city was inhabited by these performers, and their only occupation consisted in such like performances. Lastly, Motecusuma had in his service great numbers of stone-cutters, masons, and carpenters, who were solely employed in the royal palaces.[57] Above all, I must not forget to mention here his gardens for the culture of flowers, trees, and vegetables, of which there were various kinds. In these gardens were also numerous baths, wells, basins, and ponds full of limpid water, which regularly ebbed and flowed. All this was enlivened by endless varieties of small birds, which sang among the trees. Also the plantations of medical plants and vegetables are well worthy of our notice: these were kept in proper order by a large body of gardeners. All the baths, wells, ponds, and buildings were substantially constructed of stonework, as also the theatres where the singers and dancers performed. There were upon the whole so many remarkable things for my observation in these gardens and throughout the whole town, that I can scarcely find words to express the astonishment I felt at the pomp and splendour of the Mexican monarch.

In the meantime, I am become as tired in noting down these things as the kind reader will be in perusing them: I will, therefore, close this chapter, and acquaint the reader how our general, accompanied by many of his officers, went to view the Tlatelulco, or great square of Mexico; on which occasion we also ascended the great temple, where stood the idols Tetzcatlipuca and Huitzilopochtli. This was the first time Cortes left his head-quarters to perambulate the city.

NOTES

[54] The revenue of Motecusuma we know consisted of the natural products of the country, and what was produced by the industry of his subjects. Respecting the payment of tribute, we find the following story in Torquemada: "During the abode of Motecusuma among the Spaniards, in the palace of his father, Alonso de Ojeda one day espied in a certain apartment of the building a number of small bags tied up. He imagined at first that they were filled with gold dust, but on opening one of them, what was his astonishment to find it quite full of lice? Ojeda, greatly surprised at the discovery he had made, immediately communicated what he had seen to Cortes, who then asked Marina and Aguilar for some explanation. They informed him that the Mexicans had such a sense of their duty to pay tribute to their monarch, that the poorest and meanest of the inhabitants, if they possessed nothing better to present to their king, daily cleaned their persons, and saved all the lice they caught, and that when they had a good store of these, they laid them in bags at the feet of their monarch. Torquemada further remarks, that his reader might

think these bags were filled with small worms (gasanillos), and not with lice; but appeals to Alonso de Ojeda, and another of Cortes' soldiers, named Alonso de Mata, who were eyewitnesses of the fact."

This story, no doubt, is founded on something like truth, and most probably these bags were filled with the coccus cacti, the famous cochineal insect, then unknown to the Spaniards, who might easily have mistaken them in a dried state for lice. (p. 231.)

[55] This weapon, called by the Mexicans maquahuitl, was much dreaded by the Spaniards; and the historian Acosta relates that the Mexicans would cut off the head of a horse with it at one blow. (p. 231.)

[56] Bernal Diaz, unfortunately, gives no description of Motecusuma's palace; w e will therefore give Torquemada's account of this remarkable building. He himself, however, never saw it, but chiefly gained his information from the Mexicans themselves, who may have exaggerated a little: Motecusuma's palace had twenty doors, which either opened into the large square or into the principal streets of the city; it had three large courts, and in one of them was a tank, supplied with water by the aqueduct of Chapultepec. The palace contained a number of halls, and a hundred rooms twenty-five feet long and as many broad, each provided with a bath. Everything was built of stone and lime. The walls were covered with beautiful stones,[Pg 395] marble, jasper, porphyry, and a block stone, which is so highly polished that you might use it for a looking-glass; besides these, there was a white stone, almost transparent. All the woodwork was made of white cedar, palm, cypress, pine, and other fine woods, adorned with beautiful carved-work. In one of the apartments, which was one hundred and fifty feet long and fifty broad, was Motecusuma's chapel, which was covered with plates of gold and silver almost the thickness of a finger, besides that it was decorated with innumerable emeralds, rubies, topaz, and other precious stones. (p. 235.)

---

41. Cortés Destroys the Idols and Instructs the Aztecs in the Christian Religion

by Hernàn Cortés; trans. George Folsom

LETTER II

Dated at Segura de la Frontera, (Mexico,) Oct. 30th, 1520.

Most Noble, Powerful and Catholic Prince, Invincible Emperor, and our Sovereign Lord

BY a ship that I despatched from this New Spain of your Sacred Majesty, on the sixteenth of July, in the year 1519, I transmitted to your Highness a very full and particular report of what had occurred from the time of my arrival in this country to that date ; which I sent by the hands of Alonso Hernandez Puertocarrero and Francisco de Montejo, deputies of La Rica Villa de la Vera Cruz, the town I had founded in your Majesty's name. Since that time, from want of opportunity, and being constantly engaged in

Hernán Cortés, "Second Letter of Hernando Cortés to Charles V," *The Dispatches of Hernando Cortés*, The Conqueror of Mexico, trans. George Folsom, 1843.

making conquests and establishing peace, having no ships, nor any intelligence from the one I had sent, or the deputies, I have not been able till now to give your Majesty a further account of our operations; from which God knows how much pain I have suffered. I have been desirous that your Highness should be informed concerning the affairs of this country, because, as I have already mentioned in my former relation, such are its extent and importance, that the possession of it would authorize your Majesty to assume anew the title of Emperor, which it is no less worthy of conferring than Germany itself, which, by the grace of God, you already possess. But a detailed account of whatever presents itself deserving observation in these new regions would be almost endless; and I must beg your Majesty's pardon if my relation is less complete than it should be, owing to my want of ability, and the peculiar circumstances in which I am now placed. I shall nevertheless use my best efforts to relate the truth as nearly as possible, and to inform your Majesty of what it is important at the present juncture you should know. I must also entreat your Majesty's pardon if I should not mention every circumstance of any weight, or fail to give with great exactness the time and manner in which events may have occurred; or should I make mistakes in the names of the cities and towns, as well as provinces, that have professed their allegiance to your Majesty, and acknowledged themselves your subjects and vassals. For, in consequence of a disaster that has recently happened, of which I shall hereafter give your Highness a full account, I have lost all my papers, including the official records of my proceedings with the inhabitants of these countries, and many other things. In my former despatch, Most Excellent Prince, I gave a list of the cities and towns that had to that time voluntarily submitted to your authority, together with those I had reduced by conquest. I also mentioned having received information from the natives of a certain great Lord, called MUTECZUMA, who, according to their computation of distances, dwelt ninety or a hundred leagues from the coast and the port where I had disembarked; and that, trusting in the greatness of God, and the confidence inspired by the royal name of your Highness, I proposed to go and see him wherever he might be. I also recollect having engaged to do more than was in my power in regard to the demand I intended to make of this personage; for I assured your Highness that he should be taken either dead or alive, or become a subject to the royal throne of your Majesty. With this determination I departed from the city of Cempoal, to which I gave the name of Sevilla, on the 16th of August, with fifteen horse and three hundred infantry, all in the best condition for war in which I was able, or the time permitted me to render them. I left in the town of Vera Cruz one hundred and fifty men and two horses, occupied in building a fort, which was already nearly finished ; and I also left the whole province of Cempoal, and all the mountainous region adjacent to the town, containing fifty thousand warriors, and fifty towns and fortresses, in peace and security, and firm in their allegiance to your Majesty, as they have remained to the present time. Although they were subjects of Muteczuma, yet according to the information I received, they had been reduced to that condition by force, within a short period ; and when they had obtained through me some knowledge of your Highness, and of your great regal power, they declared their desire to become vassals of your Majesty, and to form an alliance with me. They also begged me to protect them against that mighty Lord, who used violent and tyrannical measures to keep them in subjection, and took from them their sons to be slain and offered as sacrifices to his idols; with many other complaints against him, in order to avoid whose tyranny they embraced the service of your Majesty, to which they have so far proved faithful, and I doubt not will continue so, since they have been uniformly treated by me with favor and attention. Nevertheless, for the better security of our people who remained at Vera Cruz, I took with me several of their principal men, and some of an inferior order, who have been of no little service to me on my route. ...

There cache to meet me here two other Caciques, whose lands were in the same valley, the one four leagues below, and the other two leagues above. They gave me several chains of gold of small weight and value, and seven or eight slaves. Leaving them very well satisfied, I set off, after having remained there four or five days, and arrived at the residence of the Cacique mentioned as being two leagues distant in the upper part of the valley; it is called Yztecmastitán. The domains of this man are covered with inhabitants for three or four leagues without interruption, and are situated along the level ground of the valley on the banks of a small river that flows through it. His residence stands on a lofty eminence, protected by a larger fortress than is found in half of Spain, which is well defended by walls, barbicans and moats; on the summit of this high ground there is a population of five or six thousand, dwelling in good houses, and a somewhat richer people than those who inhabit the valley below. Here, likewise, I was well received, and the Cacique told me that he was a vassal of Muteczuma. I remained here three days, as well to recruit from the effects of our journey through the desert country, as to wait for four messengers, natives of Cempoal, that had accompanied me, whom I had sent froth Caltanmi to a very extensive province called Tascalteca, which they informed me was near this place, as it proved to be. I had also been informed by them that the natives of this province were their allies, but deadly enemies of Muteczuma ; and they desired me to form an alliance with them, because they were a numerous and powerful nation. Their country, they also added, bordered upon that of Muteczuma throughout its whole extent, with whom they were constantly at war; and it was thought they would be pleased with me, and take my part in case Muteczuma should endeavor to get the advantage of me. The messengers did not return during the eight days that I remained in the valley, and I asked some other Cempoallans who accompanied me why they did not return ? They answered that the place must be very far off, and that they could not get back yet on account of the distance. Seeing that they did not arrive, and being assured by several leading Cempoallans of the friendship and protection of the people of that province, I resolved to set out on my way thither.

42. Chronicles of the Incas, 1540

by Pedro Cieza de Léon; trans. Clements R. Markham

Another view of the Incas, from a conquistador. It provides quite a lot of information about the Incan economy—a redistributive typical of all early civilizations.

It is told for a fact of the rulers of this kingdom that in the days of their rule they had their representatives in the capitals of all the provinces, for in all these places there were larger and finer lodgings than in most of the other cities of this great kingdom, and many storehouses. They served as the head of the provinces or regions, and from every so many leagues around the tributes were brought to one of these capitals, and from so many others, to another. This was so well-organized that there was not a village that did not know where it was to send its tribute. In all these capitals the Incas had temples of the Sun, mints, and many silversmiths who did nothing but work rich pieces of gold or fair vessels of silver; large garrisons were stationed there, and a steward who was in command of them all, to whom an accounting of everything that was brought in was made, and who, in turn, had to give one of all that was issued. ... The tribute paid by each of these provinces, whether gold, silver, clothing, arms and all else they gave, was entered in the accounts of those who kept the *quipus* and did everything ordered by the governor in the matter of finding the soldiers or supplying whomever the Inca ordered, or making delivery to Cuzco; but when they came from the city of Cuzco to go over the accounts, or they were ordered to go to Cuzco to give an accounting, the accountants themselves gave it by the *quipus*, or went to give it where there could be no fraud, but everything had to come out right. Few years went by in which an accounting was not made. ...

At the beginning of the new year the rulers of each village came to Cuzco, bringing their *quipus*, which told how many births there had been during the year, and how many deaths. In this way the Inca and the governors knew which of the Indians were poor, the women who had been widowed, whether they were able to pay their taxes, and how many men they could count on in the event of war, and many other things they considered highly important. The Incas took care to see that justice was meted out, so much so that nobody ventured to commit a felony or theft. This was to deal with thieves, rapists, or conspirators against the Inca.

As this kingdom was so vast, in each of the many provinces there were many storehouses filled with supplies and other needful things; thus, in times of war, wherever the armies went they drew upon the contents of these storehouses, without ever touching the supplies of their confederates or laying a finger on what they had in their settlements. ... Then the storehouses were filled up once more with the tributes paid the Inca. If there came a lean year, the storehouses were opened and the provinces were

Pedro Cieza de Léon, "Chronicles of the Incas, 1540," *The Second Part of the Chronicle of Peru*, trans. Clements R. Markham, pp. 36-50, Hakluyt Society, 1883.

lent what they needed in the way of supplies; then, in a year of abundance, they paid back all they had received. No one who was lazy or tried to live by the work of others was tolerated; everyone had to work. Thus on certain days each lord went to his lands and took the plow in hand and cultivated the earth, and did other things. Even the Incas themselves did this to set an example. And under their system there was none such in all the kingdom, for, if he had his health, he worked and lacked for nothing; and if he was ill, he received what he needed from the storehouses. And no rich man could deck himself out in more finery than the poor, or wear different clothing, except the rulers and the headmen, who, to maintain their dignity, were allowed great freedom and privilege.

43. Conquistador y Pestilencia

The First New World Pandemic and the Fall of the Great Indian Empires

by Alfred W. Crosby Jr.

The most sensational military conquests in all history are probably those of the Spanish conquistadores over the Aztec and Incan empires. Cortés and Pizarro toppled the highest civilizations of the New World in a few months each. A few hundred Spaniards defeated populations containing thousands of dedicated warriors, armed with a wide assembly of weapons from the stone and early metal ages. Societies which had created huge empires through generations of fierce fighting collapsed at the touch of the Castilian.

After four hundred years the Spanish feat still seems incredible. Many explanations suggest themselves: the advantage of steel over stone, of cannon and firearms over bows and arrows and slings; the terrorizing effect of horses on foot-soldiers who had never seen such beasts before; the lack of unity in the Aztec and Incan empires; the prophecies in Indian mythology about the arrival of white gods. All of these factors combined to deal to the Indian a shock such as only H. G. Wells' *War of the Worlds* can suggest to us. Each factor was undoubtedly worth many hundreds of soldiers to Cortés and Pizarro.

For all of that, one might have expected the highly organized, militaristic societies of Mexico and the Andean highlands to survive at least the initial contact with European societies. Thousands of Indian warriors, even if confused and frightened and wielding only obsidian-studded war clubs, should have been able to repel at least the first few hundred Spaniards to arrive.

The Spaniard had a formidable ally to which neither he nor the historian has given sufficient credit—disease. The arrival of Columbus in the New World brought about one of the greatest population disasters in history. After the Spanish conquest an Indian of Yucatán wrote of his people in the happier days before the advent of the Spaniard:[1]

There was then no sickness; they had no aching bones; they had then no high fever; they had then no smallpox; they had then no burning chest; they had then no abdominal pain; they had then no consumption; they had then no headache. At that time the course of humanity was orderly. The foreigners made it otherwise when they arrived here.

It would be easy to attribute this lamentation to the nostalgia that the conquered always feel for the time before the conqueror appeared, but the statement is probably in part true. During the millennia before the European brought together the compass and the three-masted vessel to revolutionize world history, men at sea moved slowly, seldom over long distances, and across the great oceans hardly at all. Men lived at least in the same continents where their greatgrandfathers had lived and rarely caused violent and rapid changes in the delicate balance between themselves and their environments. Diseases tended to be endemic rather than epidemic. It is true that man did not achieve perfect accommodation with his microscopic parasites. Mutation, ecological changes, and migration could bring the likes of the Black Death to Europe, and few men lived three-score and ten without knowing epidemic disease. Yet ecological stability did tend to create a crude kind of mutual toleration between human host and parasite. Most Europeans, for instance, survived measles and tuberculosis, and most West Africans survived yellow fever and malaria.

Migration of man and his maladies is the chief cause of epidemics. And when migration takes place, those creatures who have been longest in isolation suffer most, for their genetic material has been least tempered by the variety of world diseases.[2] Among the major subdivisions of the species *homo sapiens* the American Indian probably had the dangerous privilege of longest isolation from the rest of mankind. The Indians appear to have lived, died, and bred without extra-American contacts for generation after generation, developing unique cultures and working out tolerances for a limited, native American selection of pathological micro-life.[3] Medical historians

---

1   *The Booh of Chilam Balam of Chumayel* (Washington, 1933), 83.

2   S. P. Bedson *et al., Virus and Rickettsial Diseases* (Baltimore, 1950), 50–51; Geddes Smith, *Plague on Us* (New York, 1941), 115–118.

3   Solid scientific proof exists of this isolation. The physical anthropologist notes an amazingly high degree of physical uniformity among the Indians of the Americas, especially in blood type. Only in the Americas, and in no other large area, is there such a low percentage of aborigines with B-type blood or such a high percentage—very often one hundred percent—of O-type. The maps of blood type distribution among Indians suggest that they are the product of New World endogamy. Blood type distribution maps of the Old World are, in contrast, highly complex in almost all parts of the three continents. These maps confirm what we know to be true historically: that migration and constant mixing of genetic materials have characterized Old World history. There has also been a constant exchange of diseases and of genetically derived immunities. In the Americas, on the other hand, there must have been almost no prophylactic miscegenation of this sort. A. E. Mourant, Ada C. Kopéc, and Kazimiera Domaniewska-Sobczak,

guess that few of the first rank killers among the diseases are native to the Americas. (A possible exception is syphilis. It may be true, as Gonzalo Fernández Oviedo maintained four hundred years ago, that syphilis should not be called *mal francés* or *mal de Ñapoles*, but *mal de las Indias*.)[4]

When the isolation of the Americas was broken, and Columbus brought the two halves of this planet together, the American Indian met for the first time his most hideous enemy—not the white man or his black servant, but the invisible killers which these men brought in their blood and breath. The fatal diseases of the Old World killed more effectively in the New, and comparatively benign diseases of the Old World turned killers in the New. There is little exaggeration in the statement of a German missionary in 1699 that "the Indians die so easily that the bare look and smell of a Spaniard causes them to give up the ghost." The process is still going on in the twentieth century, as the last jungle tribes of South America lose their shield of isolation.[5]

The most spectacular period of mortality among the American Indians occurred during the first century of contact with the Europeans and Africans. Almost all contemporary historians of the early settlements from Bartolomé de las Casas to William Bradford of Plymouth Plantation were awed by the ravages of epidemic disease among the native populations of America. We know that the most deadly of the early epidemics in the New World were those of the eruptive fevers—smallpox, measles, plague, typhus, etc. The first to arrive and the deadliest, said contemporaries, was smallpox.[6]

Oviedo, one of the earliest historians of the Americas, estimated that a million Indians lived on Santo Domingo when the European arrived to plant his first permanent colony in the New World. "Of all those," Oviedo wrote, "and of all those born afterwards, there are not now believed to be at the present time in this year of 1548 five hundred persons, children and adults, who are natives and are the progeny or lineage of those first."[7]

The destruction of the Tainos has been largely blamed on the Spanish cruelty, not only by the later Protestant historians of the "Black Legend" school but also by such contemporary Spanish writers as Oviedo and Bartolomé de las Casas. Without doubt

---

The ABO Blood Groups. Comprehensive Tables and Maps of World Distribution (Springfield, Ill., 1958), 268–270.

4   P. M. Ashburn, *The Ranks of Death. A Medical History of the Conquest of America* (New York, 1947), *passim;* Gonzalo Fernandez Oviedo, *Historia generaly natural de las Indias* (Madrid, 1959), I, 53; Henry H. Scott, *A History of Tropical Medicine* (London, 1939), I, 128, 283; Sherburne F. Cook, "The Incidence and Significance of Disease Among the Aztecs and Related Tribes," *HAHR,* XXVI (August 1946), 321, 335.

5   Jehan Vellard, "Causas biológicas de la desaparición de los indios americanos," *Boletín del Instituto Riva-Agüero,* No. 2, 1956, 78–79; E. Wagner Steam and Allen E. Stearn, *The Effect of Smallpox on the Destiny of the Amerindian* (Boston, 1945), 17.

6   Ashburn, *Ranks of Death,* 80; Woodrow Borah, "America as Model: The Demographic Impact of European Expansion upon the Non-European World," *Actas y Memorias del XXXV Congreso Internacional de Americanistas* (México, 1964), III, 379–387.

7   Oviedo, *Historia general,* I, 66–67.

the early Spaniard brutally exploited the Indians. But it was obviously not in order to kill them off, for the early colonist had to deal with a chronic labor shortage and needed the Indians. Disease would seem to be a more logical explanation for the disappearance of the Tainos, because they, like other Indians, had little immunity to Old World diseases. At the same time, one may concede that the effects of Spanish exploitation undoubtedly weakened their resistance to disease.

In December 1518 or January 1519 a disease identified as smallpox appeared among the Indians of Santo Domingo, brought, said Las Casas, from Castile. It touched few Spaniards, and none of them died, but it devastated the Indians. The Spaniards reported that it killed one-third to one-half of the Indians. Las Casas, never one to understate the appalling, said that it left no more than one thousand alive "of that immensity of people that was on this island and which we have seen with our own eyes."[8]

Undoubtedly one must discount these statistics, but they are not too far out of line with mortality rates in other smallpox epidemics, and with C. W. Dixon's judgment that populations untouched by smallpox for generations tend to resist the disease less successfully than those populations in at least occasional contact with it. Furthermore, Santo Domingo's epidemic was not an atypically pure epidemic. Smallpox seems to have been accompanied by respiratory ailments (*romadizo*), possibly measles, and other Indian killers. Starvation probably also took a toll, because of the lack of hands to work the fields. Although no twentieth-century epidemiologist or demographer would find these sixteenth-century statistics completely satisfactory, they probably are crudely accurate.[9]

Thus began the first recorded pandemic in the New World, which was "in all likelihood the most severe single loss of aboriginal population that ever occurred."[10] In a matter of days after smallpox appeared in Santo Domingo, it leaped the channel to Puerto Rico. Before long, Tainos were dying a hideous and unfamiliar death in all the islands of the Greater Antilles.[11] Crushed by a quarter-century of exploitation, they now performed their last function on earth: to act as a reserve of pestilence in the New World from which the conquistador drew invisible biological allies for his assault on the mainland.

Smallpox seems to have traveled quickly from the Antilles to Yucatan. Bishop Diego de Landa, our chief sixteenth-century Spanish source of information on the people of Yucatán, recorded that sometime late in the second decade of that century" a

---

8   *Colección de documentos inéditos,* I, 367, 369–370, 429; *Colección de varios documentos para la historia de la Florida y tierras adyacentes* (London, 1857), I, 44; Bartolomé de las Casas, *Historia de las Indias* (Madrid, 1957), II, 484.

9   *Colección de documentos inéditos,* I, 368, 397–398, 428–429; Dixon, *Smallpox,* 317–318, 325.

10   Henry F. Dobyns, "An Outline of Andean Epidemic History to 1720," *Bulletin of the History of Medicine,* XXXVII (November–December 1963), 514.

11   Pablo Alvarez Rubiano, *Pedrarias Dávila* (Madrid, 1944), 608; *Colección de varios documentos para la historia de la Florida,* I, 45.

pestilence seized them, characterized by great pustules, which rotted their bodies with a great stench, so that the limbs fell to pieces in four or five days." The *Book of Chilam Balam of Chumayel,* written in the Mayan language with European script after the Spanish settlement of Yucatán, also records that some time in the second decade "was when the eruption of pustules occurred. It was smallpox." It has been speculated that the malady came with Spaniards shipwrecked on the Yucatán coast in 1511 or the soldiers and sailors of Hernández de Cordoba's expedition which coasted along Yucatán in 1517. Both these explanations seem unlikely, because smallpox had not appeared in the Greater Antilles, the likeliest source of any smallpox epidemic on the continent, until the end of 1518 or the beginning of 1519. Be that as it may, there is evidence that the Santo Domingan epidemic could have spread to the continent before Cortés' invasion of Mexico. Therefore, the epidemic raging there at that time may have come in two ways—north and west from Yucatán, and directly from Cuba to central Mexico, brought by Cortés' troops.[12]

The melodrama of Cortés and the conquest of Mexico need no retelling. After occupying Tenochtitlán and defeating the army of his rival, Narváez, he and his troops had to fight their way out of the city to sanctuary in Tlaxcala. Even as the Spanish withdrew, an ally more formidable than Tlaxcala appeared. Years later Francisco de Aguilar, once a follower of Cortés and now a Dominican friar, recalled the terrible retreat of the *Noche Triste.* "When the Christians were exhausted from war," he wrote, "God saw fit to send the Indians smallpox, and there was a great pestilence in the city. ..."[13]

With the men of Narváez had come a Negro sick with the smallpox, "and he infected the household in Cempoala where he was quartered; and it spread from one Indian to another, and they, being so numerous and eating and sleeping together, quickly infected the whole country." The Mexicans had never seen smallpox before and did not have even the European's meager knowledge of how to deal with it. The old soldier-chronicler, Bernal Diaz del Castillo, called the Negro "a very black dose" for Mexico, "for it was because of him that the whole country was stricken, with a great many deaths."[14]

Probably, several diseases were at work. Shortly after the retreat from Tenochtitlán Bernal Diaz, immune to smallpox like most of the Spaniards, "was very sick with fever and was vomiting blood." The Aztec sources mention the racking cough of those who had smallpox, which suggests a respiratory complication such as pneumonia or a

---

12 Diego de Landa, *Relación de las cosas de Yucatán* (Cambridge, 1941), 42; *The Boole of Chilam Balam,* 138.

13 Patricia de Fuentes (ed. and trans.), *The Conquistadors. First-Person Accounts of the Conquest of Mexico* (New York, 1963), 159. For the argument that this was measles, not smallpox, see Horacio Figueroa Marroquin, *Enfermedades de los conquistadores* (San Salvador, 1955), 49–67.

14 Bernal Díaz del Castillo, *The Bernal Diaz Chronicles: The True Story of the Conquest of Mexico* (Garden City, N.Y., 1956), 250; Diego Duran, *The Aztecs. The History of the Indies of New Spain* (New York, 1964), 323; Francisco López de Gómara, *Cortés, the Life of the Conqueror by his Secretary* (Berkeley, 1964), 204–205; Toribio Motolinia, *History of the Indians of New Spain* (Berkeley, 1950), 38; Bernardino de Sahagún, *General History of the Things of New Spain* (Santa Fe, 1950–59), Part 9, 4.

streptococcal infection, both common among smallpox victims. Great numbers of the Cakchiquel people of Guatemala were felled by a devastating epidemic in 1520 and 1521, having as its most prominent symptom fearsome nosebleeds. Whatever this disease was, it may have been present in central Mexico along with the pox.[15]

The triumphant Aztecs had not expected the Spaniards to return after their expulsion from Tenochtitlán. The sixty days during which the epidemic lasted in the city, however, gave Cortés and his troops a desperately needed respite to reorganize and prepare a counterattack. When the epidemic subsided, the siege of the Aztec capital began. Had there been no epidemic, the Aztecs, their war-making potential unimpaired and their warriors fired with victory, could have pursued the Spaniards, and Cortés might have ended his life spreadeagled beneath the obsidian blade of a priest of Huitzilopochtli. Clearly the epidemic sapped the endurance of Tenochtitlán to survive the Spanish assault. As it was, the siege went on for seventy-five days, until the deaths within the city from combat, starvation, and disease—probably not smallpox now—numbered many thousands. When the city fell "the streets, squares, houses, and courts were filled with bodies, so that it was almost impossible to pass. Even Cortés was sick from the stench in his nostrils."[16]

Analysis Questions

1. Compare and describe the similarities and differences from the descriptions of the Spanish conquest of America by Castillo and Cortes.
2. How did the Inca people see the coming of the Spanish?
3. What was the Columbian exchange and why is it significant to understanding American history?

---

15 *Anales de Tlatelolco, Unos anales históricos de la nación mexicana y códice de Tlatelolco* (México, 1948), 64; *The Annals of the Calcchiquels and Title of the Lords of Totonicapán* (Norman, Okla., 1953), 115–116; Bedson, *Virus*, 155; Diaz del Castillo, *Chronicles*, 289; Miguel León-Portilla (ed.), *The Broken Spears. The Aztec Account of the Conquest of Mexico* (Boston, 1962), 132; Top, *Communicable and Infectious Diseases*, 515.

16 Hernando Cortés, *Five Letters* (New York, 1962), 226; Diaz del Castillo, *Chronicles*, 405–406; Gómara, *Cortés*, 285, 293; León-Portilla, *Broken Spears*, 92; Sahagún, *General History*, XIII, 81.

CPSIA information can be obtained
at www.ICGtesting.com
Printed in the USA
LVHW050332221122
733733LV00003B/19